MW00806096

Going Pro with Cubase® 6

Steve Pacey

Course Technology PTR
A part of Cengage Learning

COURSE TECHNOLOGY
CENGAGE Learning·

Australia • Brazil • Japan • Korea • Mexico • Singapore • Spain • United Kingdom • United States

COURSE TECHNOLOGY
CENGAGE Learning

Going Pro with Cubase® 6
Steve Pacey

Publisher and General Manager, Course Technology PTR: Stacy L. Hiquet

Associate Director of Marketing: Sarah Panella

Manager of Editorial Services: Heather Talbot

Marketing Manager: Mark Hughes

Acquisitions Editor: Orren Merton

Project/Copy Editor: Cathleen D. Small

Technical Reviewer: Matthew Loel T. Hepworth

Interior Layout Tech: MPS Limited, a Macmillan Company

Cover Designer: Mike Tanamachi

Indexer: Broccoli Information Management

Proofreader: Sandi Wilson

© 2012 Course Technology, a part of Cengage Learning.

ALL RIGHTS RESERVED. No part of this work covered by the copyright herein may be reproduced, transmitted, stored, or used in any form or by any means graphic, electronic, or mechanical, including but not limited to photocopying, recording, scanning, digitizing, taping, Web distribution, information networks, or information storage and retrieval systems, except as permitted under Section 107 or 108 of the 1976 United States Copyright Act, without the prior written permission of the publisher.

For product information and technology assistance, contact us at
Cengage Learning Customer & Sales Support, 1-800-354-9706

For permission to use material from this text or product, submit all requests online at **www.cengage.com/permissions**
Further permissions questions can be emailed to
permissionrequest@cengage.com

Nuendo, Cubase, VST and ASIO are registered trademarks of Steinberg Media Technologies GmbH. Microsoft, Windows, and Internet Explorer are either registered trademarks or trademarks of Microsoft Corporation in the United States and/or other countries. All other trademarks are the property of their respective owners.

All images © Cengage Learning unless otherwise noted.

Library of Congress Control Number: 2011924485

ISBN-13: 978-1-4354-6002-7

ISBN-10: 1-4354-6002-2

Course Technology, a part of Cengage Learning
20 Channel Center Street
Boston, MA 02210
USA

Cengage Learning is a leading provider of customized learning solutions with office locations around the globe, including Singapore, the United Kingdom, Australia, Mexico, Brazil, and Japan. Locate your local office at: **international.cengage.com/region**

Cengage Learning products are represented in Canada by Nelson Education, Ltd.

For your lifelong learning solutions, visit **courseptr.com**

Visit our corporate website at **cengage.com**

Printed in the United States of America
1 2 3 4 5 6 7 13 12 11

*To my mom and dad, who have always
given me their loving support.*

Acknowledgments

Thanks to Course Technology PTR for giving me the opportunity to write this book. Special thanks to Orren Merton, who put his trust in me once again. Special thanks to Cathleen Small for her sharp eye for details and extreme patience with a guy who's more of a Cubase dude than a professional writer. Special thanks to Matthew Loel T. Hepworth for sharing his expertise on Cubase and Macs and for making sure that my scattered thoughts translated into text that makes sense. Both of these editors' perspectives were very important to the overall development of the book, and they made my job much easier. Also, I'd like to give a shout out once again to Kim Benbow and Robert Guerin for their previous efforts on *Going Pro with Cubase 5*. Thanks to my wife, Amber, who puts up with me working late hours and never leaving my computer. Also, thanks to Matt Piper for always lending an ear and sharing his wisdom with regard to writing and technology. Thanks to the brilliant people at Steinberg for continuing to take Cubase to levels I never dreamed possible. And last but not least, thank *you* (the reader) for allowing me to share my thoughts with you on working with Cubase professionally.

About the Author

Steve Pacey is a television music producer/composer who has been a devoted Cubase user since 1990. Steve began using Cubase professionally while composing background music in EPKs from MCA/Universal films in 1994. Since then, he's written for theater, commercials, a video game, video, and various television programs, including the animated series *Head Trip* on MTV and *The Ultimate Blackjack Tour* on CBS. His most recent work is featured in *Cheech & Chong's Animated Movie*. Steve has also written two other Cubase books for Course Technology PTR: *MIDI Editing in Cubase: Skill Pack* (2007) and *Your Cubase Studio* (2008). To learn more about Steve Pacey, visit www.stevepacey.com.

Contents

Chapter 3
Taking Audio to the Limit in Cubase 6   109

Chapter 4
Mastering the Art of Mixing in Cubase 6   163

Chapter 5
Interfacing Cubase 6 with the Rest of the World   189

Introduction

What does going "pro" with Cubase mean to you? To me, it means that I feel comfortable using Cubase in a situation where the clock is ticking and my career depends on the fact that I know what I'm doing—I'm ready for any technical obstacle that might come up in the process. As a professional Cubase user, you simply can't afford to *not* know what you're doing in Cubase.

From One Pro to Another

I use Cubase professionally to produce and compose music for TV, film, and video. My first experience with a MIDI sequencer was in 1990, using an Alesis hardware sequencer. I was excited to switch to Cubase that same year, when I started on the Atari 1040ST computer. I never used the Atari computer for anything except Cubase. The Atari was my dedicated "music" computer, though I didn't own any other type of computer. I received my first paycheck using Cubase around 1994 with the same computer (along with a Roland S-330 sampler). In 1999, I stopped using tape machines and external hardware for audio and completely switched to recording digitally using Cubase. By 2000, I switched from using a hardware Akai S3000 sampler to using HALion as a virtual sampler in Cubase. Today, I have a massive sample library and tons of virtual instruments and plug-in processors, all within 4 TB of external hard drive space. In fact, the only thing that has remained the same since 1990 is that Cubase is still the heart of my studio.

It takes a lot of skill for the music professional to survive in today's demanding world. Besides knowing an instrument and the music business, if you really want a paycheck, you have to continuously relearn the technology. More than half of what I've learned regarding computers throughout my career has now become what I consider obsolete knowledge. For instance, who cares what a SCSI terminator does these days? It doesn't matter that I know what polyphonic aftertouch means! The main goal in *Going Pro with Cubase 6* is to try to cut through as much of the technical jargon as possible. I understand that as a Cubase pro user, you just want to jump into using the software. You don't need to learn things that will most likely be forgotten two years from now, when you're working in Cubase 7.0 or who knows what!

What Exactly Will This Book Cover?

If you've already worked in Cubase, you've probably realized that it's a massive program that can take you in all sorts of directions. I have written two other books (*MIDI Editing in Cubase: Skill Pack* and *Your Cubase Studio*) that I consider as covering the beginner-to-intermediate skill range. If you have absolutely conquered those books, then you are technically ready to "go pro." In *Going Pro with Cubase 6*, I'm targeting users who have already gone through my Cubase "bootcamp." This book focuses on techniques that people who have had some experience using Cubase will appreciate. Everyone's skill level is different in the professional world, and some people *are* technical geniuses. But it doesn't take a technical genius to make a living using Cubase.

The Cubase manual is massive and intimidating, and often seems as though it's missing a *lot* of basic information. Its approach breaks the program into sections and discusses certain tools in detail, but it often doesn't discuss how the different components function together in a practical scenario. As users, we can often overlook some very useful and practical aspects of the program. My goal is to be your Cubase "buddy" and break down the software for you in a way that's different from the manual. However, the manual contains a lot of valuable information, and I make some references to it throughout the book. As a matter of fact, for the first time ever, Cubase 6 now comes with a DVD video tutorial. If you haven't watched the video in its entirety yet, I highly recommend that you take the time to do so before jumping into this book, because it will give you a great head start.

In *Going Pro with Cubase 6*, I will show you how to use Cubase efficiently when you're working under pressure. I will focus on what I consider to be the "meat and potatoes" of Cubase without wasting your time with things that are not as important. I also summarize certain components in ways that the manual doesn't so that you can get a quick overview without getting lost in details. This book also steps outside the manual to discuss features from Steinberg's innovative CC121 controller and MR816 CSX audio interface. I will show you some techniques with regard to making professional-sounding mixes without even touching a fader. You'll also get step-by-step instructions on how to interface your Cubase projects with Pro Tools, Nuendo, and other DAWs available on the market. The overall goal is to get you working quickly and utilizing the newest features in Cubase 6 at a professional level without wasting your time.

Those of you who have read the previous version of this book (*Going Pro with Cubase 5*) will notice that a lot of the information is similar. That's because although Steinberg has added quite a few new features in Cubase 6, many of the same features found in Cubase 6 were also brand new in Cubase 5 (as discussed in my previous edition of the book). Because those features are still new to Cubase, I've decided to keep a lot of them for those who are still upgrading from version 4 or earlier and those who haven't read the previous book (which will be discontinued when this book is released). Many photos have been updated in this new book to match the screens of Cubase 6. Some older (less relevant) tutorials have been removed, and new, updated tutorials have been added. All in all, about 50 percent of the book has been revised or rewritten due to the new features and workings of Cubase 6.

More good news! This book is written for Cubase 6, but you can apply most of what's written in this book to Cubase Artist 6 as well. For the first time ever, you can actually open Cubase 6 and Cubase Artist 6 projects in both software versions with no compatibility issues! Also, if for some reason you decide to upgrade from Cubase Artist 6 to Cubase 6, you can do so online at any time without having to jump through any hoops. When you purchase the upgrade, the new features are now "unlocked" from the system you already own.

Here is a list of a few basic things you should understand up front that will make reading this book a more enjoyable experience:

- You should already know how to record MIDI and audio in Cubase.

- You should know how to interface your controllers and soundcards with Cubase and your computer.

- You should know the basic functions of your computer's operating system.

- You should know the basics of editing audio and MIDI within Cubase and understand how to access and use all the basic tools.

- You should have the ability to think in musical terms (such as bars and beats) and understand pitch.

Let's Go Pro!

One more thing you should know is that I am currently using a Dell Studio XPS 9100 with Windows 7. If you are using a Mac, you're probably already used to translating from PC to Mac, as most of the Cubase manual is written for PC/Mac. If, for instance, I say "press Ctrl+Z," you should automatically know that this means Command+Z on a Mac. Because I'm not working with a Mac, you will not see screenshots for Cubase with Mac in this book. Sometimes I will refer to Windows Explorer, and so on. If you're still unfamiliar with the differences between PCs and Macs, you can refer to the beginning of the Cubase manual for a brief explanation. Despite minor variations in the naming of keys on the keyboard and the way the mouse works, there really aren't that many differences between the Windows version of Cubase and the Mac version. If you still haven't figured out which computer type is more "pro," don't fret over it. Use the computer you feel comfortable with, because both platforms are considered pro. Also, make sure you have your original Cubase 6 installation disc handy, because we will be using some of the files from the disc in the walkthroughs in this book.

As a disclaimer, I'd like you to keep in mind that "going pro" with Cubase sometimes also involves getting a paycheck. I can't promise you a paycheck, but I *can* promise that if you follow along with this book, you will have an edge over half of the pros out there who are using Cubase today. Getting the gig is another book! Hopefully, you've already started building your career, and this is just another step along the way for you. So let's get going, pro!

1 Sharpening Your Cubase 6 Battle Axe

For starters, I thought I'd jump into some of the custom setup features that only advanced Cubase users can truly appreciate. Whether you are under the gun with a studio full of musicians and a producer, or you're just sitting down at your computer and getting ready to begin working, there's nothing like a well-organized playing field to save you headaches and let you focus on the sound you're capturing or to help you concentrate on the creative process rather than spending all day dealing with technical issues.

You may neglect to spend time fine-tuning your machine, but (besides getting an actual paycheck) taking the time to make these little adjustments is one thing that sets the pros apart from the amateurs.

The Pros and Cons of Running 32-Bit and 64-Bit

Cubase 6 is capable of running on 32-bit or 64-bit operating systems and can run as a 32-bit application on a 64-bit operating system as well. The big question is which is right for you. It really depends on your primary working method. Don't automatically assume that running Cubase 64-bit means that your system is more "pro." Each way of running Cubase has its pros and cons. Whichever way you choose, they all *sound* exactly the same because the quality at which they process audio is at 32-bit.

Running Cubase as a 32-bit application on a 64-bit operating system is the way to do it (if you have an option of running a 64-bit operating system). The reason to install Cubase as a 32-bit application on a 64-bit system is because you'll have more access to RAM (up to 4 GB as opposed to 2 GB when using a 32-bit operating system). The main reason to run Cubase as a 32-bit application is for compatibility.

The main reason to run Cubase as a 64-bit application, however, is for power. I opted for more power on my system. By *power*, I'm referring to the fact that you can utilize more RAM than you can probably afford. (Computers today are sold with as much as 64 GB of usable RAM.) I have 8 GB of RAM in my system. I do a lot of processing, but I rarely max out my RAM. Sample-based VST instruments are notorious RAM hogs, and I like to use a lot of VST instruments. Do the VST instruments run better on my system? Absolutely! Unfortunately, though, now I can't use my Waves plug-ins or ReWire with Cubase.

Note: There are some workarounds available. I found a software plug-in called *ReWire VST* (Google it!) that allowed me to use Reason in a way similar to using a VST instrument in Cubase. I consider this a temporary solution, as I know that eventually ReWire and my plug-ins will be able to work in Cubase while it's running as a 64-bit application.

My point is that 4 GB is still a great deal of RAM if you decide to run Cubase 32-bit on a 64-bit operating system. (Of course, make sure to have at least 4 GB of RAM in your computer.) If you're not utilizing a lot of VST instruments, and you don't mind bouncing some real-time processing once in a while, you'll have far fewer problems with compatibility issues, and you can upgrade later to Cubase 64-bit without any problems.

Working with Steinberg's CC121 Controller

There are many controllers available on the market, but I've chosen to discuss Steinberg's CC121 (for its unique abilities when using it with Cubase). Owning an external controller is common, but it's completely optional. If you're already familiar with controllers or are not interested in working with them, feel free to skip ahead to the next section in this chapter, which discusses organizing your creative media and using the MediaBay.

Even though I've used only a mouse and a computer keyboard for years, I finally decided to branch out and start using Steinberg's CC121 remote control to help me work more efficiently in the studio. Even if you've never used a controller, Steinberg's new CC121 is an easy way to jump in without any setup headaches (see Figure 1.1).

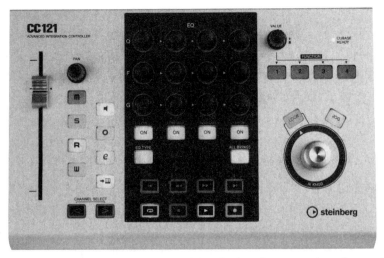

Figure 1.1 The Steinberg CC121 Advanced Integration Controller.

Don't let its simple looks fool you. The CC121 is a pro piece of gear, and although it might not appear too flashy, it shines on performance. I'm not going to go into detail on a personal review of the controller, but I think the CC121 is a very simple and well-thought-out alternative to your basic generic MIDI controller. If you're looking to get your hands on some buttons and a fader, and you want to be able to plug in and start working right away, this is the controller for you.

This controller was designed specifically for use with Cubase by Yamaha and Steinberg, and if you look at the buttons on the unit itself, you'll see that they are the same as the track buttons and Transport buttons you'll find on your computer screen in Cubase. The hands-on EQ section of the CC121 is an exact duplicate of the Cubase EQ controls.

The best part about the CC121 is that you don't have to waste time figuring out how to set up your knobs and buttons to control certain parameters in Cubase. It's a no-brainer. The manual itself is easy to follow and only a few pages long.

As with most MIDI controllers, the CC121 uses up another one of your USB ports. If you're like me, you've got hard drives and dongles filling up most of your ports. If you have to use a hub, make sure you use a powered one, because the CC121 requires a certain power load and will not work on basic hubs (such as those that are attached to computer keyboards).

The AI (*Advanced Integration*) knob is a great way to simplify your setup by utilizing your mouse. Just point to the virtual knob you would like to turn and then click to turn the AI knob to adjust your setting. That's great! I would like to point out, though, that I was led to believe that I could control any parameter in Cubase this way, but the truth of the matter is that only Steinberg's plug-ins (particularly those that are VST3) are compatible with the AI knob. This means that you still have to revert to the old "virtual" knob tweaking most of the time if you use a lot of third-party plug-ins.

The other thing I noticed is that if you have a basic mouse with a jog wheel, you can use it just as you use the AI knob on Steinberg's plug-ins—but do it with a single hand instead of using both hands. This means that as much as I like the shiny AI knob, I don't use it as often as I could, because I revert to using my good old mouse as I always have.

Again, the CC121 is set up for those who aren't into a lot of tweaking or modifying MIDI controllers, but there are some quick and easy customizable options. One of my favorites (long overdue) was the ability to create a simple volume control for the metronome. Like many, for years I've had to go to the Transport menu, select Metronome Setup, and then adjust the volume of the metronome using the virtual slider. That may not sound like very much work to you, but when you have to make adjustments constantly to the click volume, all of those actions become very redundant! I have been envying Reason's virtual Metronome Level knob for about three years, and I've been a little disappointed in Steinberg for not doing the same—until now!

The CC121 manual has a brief explanation on how to set up a Metronome Level knob, but this little feature is so nice that it deserves a dedicated walkthrough from me, too.

Getting Physical with the CC121 Metronome

Under the Devices menu, open Device Setup and select the Steinberg CC121 listing under the Remote Devices folder in the Devices panel on the left (as shown in Figure 1.2). This is the main user-definable setup page for the CC121. You can do several other customizable setups using this same dialog (such as setting zoom controls, foot-switch record buttons, control-room monitor volume controls, and so on).

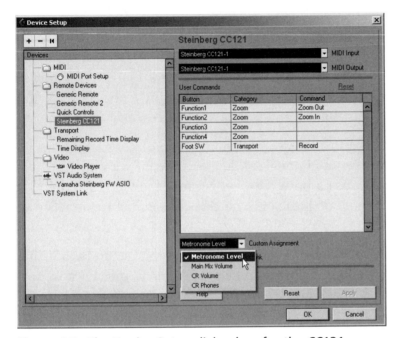

Figure 1.2 The Device Setup dialog box for the CC121.

The knob that you are setting up to become the Metronome Level knob is called the *Value knob* and is located on the top right of the actual CC121 controller (see Figure 1.3).

Figure 1.3 The Value knob.

You can assign the Value knob to adjust four different volume controls: the main mix volume, the control room (CR) volume, the control room headphone (CR Phones) volume, and (of course, my favorite) the metronome level volume. Click the Custom Assignment drop-down list in the CC121 Device Setup dialog box. You will find the four choices I have mentioned. Select Metronome Volume if it is not already selected. Afterward, click on OK. You have successfully set up your new Metronome Volume control.

If you're not sure why it's important to have control over your metronome's volume, you might not be used to recording at multiple levels. For instance, when you're recording a soft vocal track, you don't need a blaring metronome to overpower the recording. On the other hand, if you're recording a heavy-metal guitar, sometimes you have to crank that click level up just so you can hear the beat. In this case, the click itself can become deafening. Having access to that click volume control comes in really handy when you're constantly changing recording levels and you don't already have a reference beat recorded.

To utilize your new click-level control, simply push the Value knob on the CC121 to turn the click on or off; you can adjust the volume of the click by adjusting the knob. For me, if this were all the little knob on the CC121 could do, I'd still buy it! Of course, you can always change the Value knob to control the other three volumes at any time if necessary.

As you can probably see, for those who are working and don't have time to waste, the CC121 is a great addition to your Cubase studio. For more on the CC121, please refer to Chapter 4, "Mastering the Art of Mixing in Cubase 6."

Note: One thing that the CC121 manual does *not* mention is how your MIDI activity meter will continuously jump up and down in a pulsing fashion. Do not be alarmed by this. It is completely normal. If you're like me and you find this annoying, simply uncheck the MIDI Activity option from your Transport panel's setup context menu (see Figure 1.4).

Organizing Creative Media and the MediaBay

The problem of organizing media is not by any means a new one. Because I use Windows, I've been cataloging my samples using folders and Windows Explorer. Starting with Cubase 4, Steinberg decided to take on this growing issue by adding what they call the *MediaBay*. The MediaBay not only offers a place to store your sample library, but is also a place to organize every possible media tool that you can use in the music-creation process.

Note: Organizing files can seem like a headache at first, but if you plan on using the MediaBay (which I highly recommend), you can really take advantage of the MediaBay's Previewer audition features if your files are properly organized. There are more details regarding this later on in this tutorial and in the following tutorials.

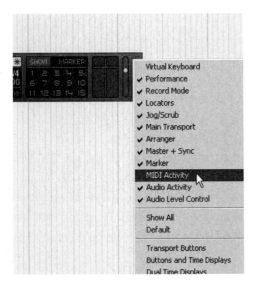

Figure 1.4 Deselecting the MIDI Activity option in the Transport menu.

Let's talk for a moment about organization. There's no single perfect solution to this ongoing issue. If you have a hard drive full of samples and already have things organized in a way that you understand, and you feel as if you can efficiently access your media as needed, using the MediaBay might appear to be a daunting, time-consuming, unnecessary task. No matter how you have organized your files, you can use the MediaBay, but to make the most of it, you might have to rethink the way you organize. This is no different than filing paperwork in a file cabinet. If it takes you hours to find something in a file cabinet that *you* organized, you might not have the best organization system. The MediaBay is the "shiny new filing cabinet," but if you don't know how to properly organize your files, using the MediaBay may not save you any time, and it could, in fact, take you longer to find what you're looking for.

Basic organization for the MediaBay doesn't have to begin in Cubase. If you already have a lot of files you're using, you should begin by using Windows Explorer (PC) or the Mac OS Finder (Mac). Using the MediaBay is like looking at the contents of your hard drive with a magnifying glass. If your hard drive is already a mess, you're only going to see a bigger mess using the MediaBay. For this reason, I recommend first reorganizing your hard drive(s) in the following manner:

- **Samples.** If you use samples (including loops, instruments, sound effects, and so on), keep them on their own hard drive—or at the very least, keep them all within one folder. Once you have them separated, break them down into categories (loops, drums, bass, guitar, sound effects, vocals). After you have put them into these basic categories, break them down even further into subcategories (rock bass, upright bass, synth bass, fretless bass, and so on). Use labeled folders within folders to make it as organized as possible. Here's what to avoid: Don't put too many different sample types in one folder and/or put too many similar types of samples in multiple folders.

For example, let's say you have 30 rock guitar samples, 1,200 acoustic guitar samples, 14 metal guitar samples, and 80 funk guitar samples. You should probably group the rock and heavy metal guitar samples together and try to break down the acoustic guitar samples into more subfolders, such as jazz acoustic, country acoustic, and rock acoustic. If you're creating loop folders, you can also include any REX files you might have, but I'd keep them separated in their own subfolders.

- **MIDI files.** If you use a lot of MIDI files, including those that accompany some sample libraries, they should all be organized in a location separate from your sample library, but using a similar organizational method as discussed with samples.

- **Video files.** If you compose or produce audio for video, then you should also have a folder (or a separate hard drive, if possible) specifically for video files. (Cubase recognizes AVI, MOV, QT, MPG, MPEG, MP4, and DV video formats.)

- **Track presets.** Track presets (whether for MIDI, audio, or Instrument tracks) should all be stored in a similar fashion as MIDI files and samples but in their own separate folder.

- **VST presets.** All of the presets that come with Cubase 6 are pre-configured in the VST Sound folder and are not modifiable. User presets must stay in the defined location. For presets, you are restricted to working from within the MediaBay, and I will explain more on how to browse VST instrument presets in the tutorial called "Auditioning VST Instruments in the MediaBay" later on in this chapter.

- **Pattern banks.** If you're creating pattern banks in Cubase 6's Beat Designer, they should be saved in their default folder and organized in groups.

The MediaBay is also capable of opening most audio files and Cubase project files. As far as projects are concerned, I like to keep all the audio and project files organized within a contact/project folder where I can easily access them without it getting too messy. I keep all my project files on a separate hard drive, which I back up regularly. If you need to look at individual audio tracks within a particular project, you can still use the MediaBay, but you can also use the Pool, which is located under the Media menu. The Pool is just as easy to use as the MediaBay when you're looking at one specific project. The MediaBay, however, can be very useful in transferring audio files from an old project into a new one. I'll demonstrate this a little later in this section. Figures 1.5 and 1.6 show some examples of how folders are organized on the creative media hard drive and the project drive.

The MediaBay can also be associated with the Sound Browser, Loop Browser, and Mini Browser. If you're new to using the MediaBay, I find that there is really no need for using either the Sound Browser or the Loop Browser, because the MediaBay handles everything in a more detailed and easily accessible manner. Both the Loop and

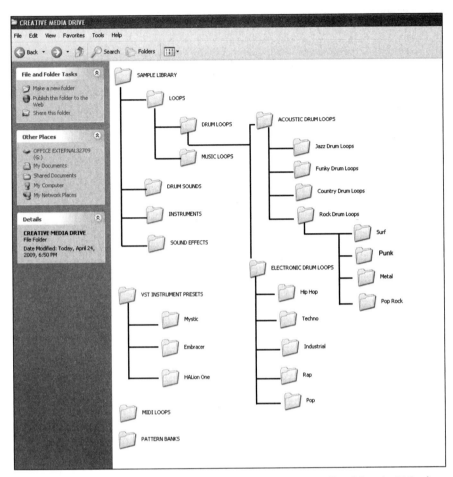

Figure 1.5 An example of organizing a creative media drive in Windows Explorer.

Sound Browsers appear to be designed as a little more clutter-free when working only with loops or sounds, and the Mini Browser is just another slimmed-down version to save you some window space. When you understand the MediaBay, you can get a grasp on these other browsers pretty quickly.

I think Steinberg's approach is that you should be able to use the MediaBay to find any type of file quickly and easily without the need for organizational skills. This might work well for people who do two or three little projects a year, but the reality is that many of you are dealing with thousands of files, and you don't have time to search through all of the files just to find a sample when you don't even know if it's going to work with your project until you *hear* it in the project itself. Also, the search features of the MediaBay are designed for the "perfect world." To get the most out of using the MediaBay, you must tag all media properly, because Cubase alone cannot tell the difference between, for instance, a sample of a drum loop and a sample of a train whistle unless *you* specify the difference by tagging the file appropriately.

The most helpful benefit to using the MediaBay is in accessing your loop library and being able to *audition* your loops all at the same tempo and then insert them into the

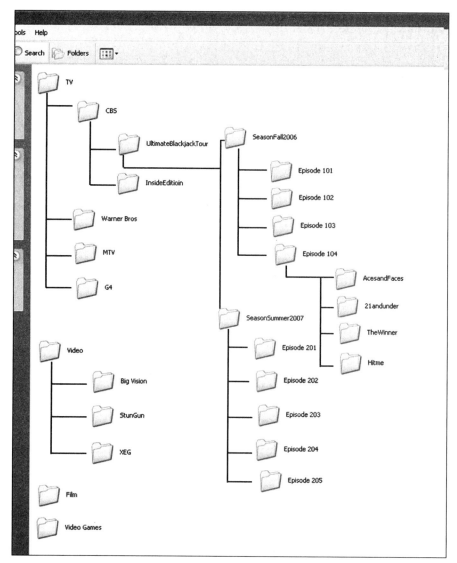

Figure 1.6 An example of organizing a project drive in Windows Explorer.

project at the correct tempo. This is a real timesaver for those who use loop libraries. It's great to have everything categorized by name and style, but auditioning and importing the audio files is the most time-consuming process when you're using Window's Explorer or Mac OS Finder. This basic function of the MediaBay is usually understated. I believe a great number of Cubase users probably skip over using the MediaBay because they simply don't want to take the time to tag their library. My point is that although tagging a library is a great way to help you organize your library, there are many other ways to benefit from using the MediaBay.

Auditioning Loops in the MediaBay

Assuming that you have your loop library organized as I described earlier, here's a simple walkthrough to get you auditioning and importing your organized loop library in no time.

Open the MediaBay, and in the Define Locations section (on the left side), locate the folder of the loops you would like to audition. Of course, the more you know what type of beat you're looking for, the easier it will be to find it. If you don't know, you can simply select the main folder so that all the loops in the main folder and subfolders are revealed in the Results (in the center of the window). In this example, I'm looking for a reggae beat on acoustic drums. I first open Loop Libraries folder, then select my Drum Loops folder, then select my Acoustic Drum Loops Folder, and finally select my Reggae Drum Loops folder so that I'm only viewing my Reggae Drum Loops in the Results display, as shown in Figure 1.7.

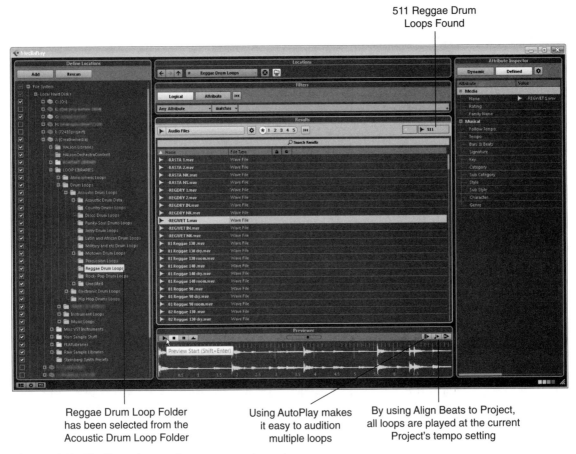

Figure 1.7 Finding the perfect reggae drum loop.

All of these drum loops have been recorded at different tempos (100 bpm, 77 bpm, 127 bpm, and so on). I've already decided that my project is at 120 bpm. Instead of having to look for and convert all my beats to 120 bpm, all I have to do is select Align Beats to Project (located on the Previewer), and every beat in the MediaBay window will automatically be time-corrected in real time to 120 bpm, regardless of its original tempo. To speed up the audition process even more, I can select Auto Play and then scroll through the list until I hear what I'm looking for.

When you find that perfect beat, there are multiple ways to get it into your project. If you're able to see your Project window and the MediaBay at the same time, dragging the file into the Project window directly from the MediaBay's Results list and onto the track where you want it is probably the easiest way to go. A little blue guideline will appear to help you position the groove where you want it on the audio track. Another easy option is to right-click on the groove you want in the Results list and then select Import into Project from the context menu. You can insert that groove at the cursor location, at the left locator position, or at the origin.

Note: Turn off the Auto Play on the Previewer in the MediaBay before you start playing around with your project again, or else you will hear that loop continuously along with your project. Also, if at any time you would like to hear your loops at their original tempos, you can always deselect Align Beats to Project on the Previewer. Keep in mind, though, that in order for Cubase to import the loop at the correct tempo, Align Beats to Project must be selected while importing the file.

That's about as easy as it gets for handling loops in Cubase. Keep in mind that your loops still need to actually *loop* correctly. If your loop has a little extra length to it, or if it's a little short, your groove will not fit like a glove into your project. That being said, if you're a Cubase master, it will be easy to tweak that groove to make it fit once you have it imported into a track.

The other thing that I would like to mention is that Cubase is using Musical Mode to get that tempo to match your project. Musical Mode will affect the quality of the recording's playback just as your standard time-stretching will. It will also put a little extra load on your computer system to continuously process that loop in real time. I go over more details on utilizing Musical Mode and alternative methods of adjusting the tempo of an audio file in Chapter 3, "Taking Audio to the Limit in Cubase 6."

I suggest that you convert that new loop into a real audio file as soon as you decide it's working for you. There are a couple of ways to do this. The easiest (and I think the best) is to select the loop and then choose Bounce Selection from the Audio menu. When you do this, your loop is automatically converted to your project's beats per minute and should sound identical to the way it sounded in Musical Mode.

Another way to change the sound is to "flatten" the Warp mode. Double-click the audio part to enter the Sample Editor, then select the Process tab from the Inspector, and then select Flatten. A pop-up window will appear, giving you a couple of different time-stretch options.

There are several other benefits to using the MediaBay. Although sounds, such as a snare drum or low E on a bass guitar, can be auditioned in the MediaBay, there is no practical use for this most of the time. Most likely, you'll need to trigger those from a sample player in order to get the most out of them. One of the best displays of how to use the MediaBay with a sample player is in using the Groove Agent ONE drum machine, which I will discuss in more detail in Chapter 2, "Maximizing MIDI in Cubase 6."

> **Note:** One of the plusses in Cubase 6 is that if you store your samples and loops on an external hard drive (as I have suggested), your hard drive has been indexed. If you take that particular hard drive to another Cubase studio, your samples and loops will be ready to use on the new system without any extra indexing. This is a real timesaver if you normally work with gigs and gigs of samples and loops and work between multiple studios.

Auditioning VST Instruments in the MediaBay

Moving away from audio loops and samples, the next benefit of using the MediaBay would be to audition VST instruments. However, there's a slight catch to auditioning VST instruments in the MediaBay. Since VST3 came around, Steinberg has grouped its factory presets in a folder called VST Sound. This includes not only the presets for the VST instruments, but also all of the presets for the effects that are included with Cubase 6.

The other catch is that the user presets aren't stored in the same location as the factory presets. To see all your presets at once in an organized manner, you are forced into using the MediaBay's filters. Furthermore, if you're using older VST2 plug-ins and presets for those VST2 instruments, the presets need to be converted to VST3 to be accessible in the Previewer. (For ways to convert FXB/FXP files, refer to "Using Presets for VSTi Configuration" in Chapter 17 of the Cubase manual.)

Assuming that you're working only with VST3 presets, you need to first select the VST Sound folder. Even though your user presets are not stored in the same location as the factory presets, as long as your factory presets are stored within the default folders (which they will be when you save a new preset), they will appear when the VST Sound folder is selected in the MediaBay. Next, to see only the presets, you need to select Plug-In Presets from the Show Media Types filter (as shown in Figure 1.8).

> **Note:** Wondering where your user preset is stored on your computer? To locate the actual preset, right-click on the file name in the MediaBay and then select Show in Explorer or Reveal in Finder, and the operating system (Windows/Mac) will reveal the location of the preset.

Now, *all* of your presets are visible. Keep in mind that this also includes the presets for all of your effects, and when you are looking for a particular trombone sound, you

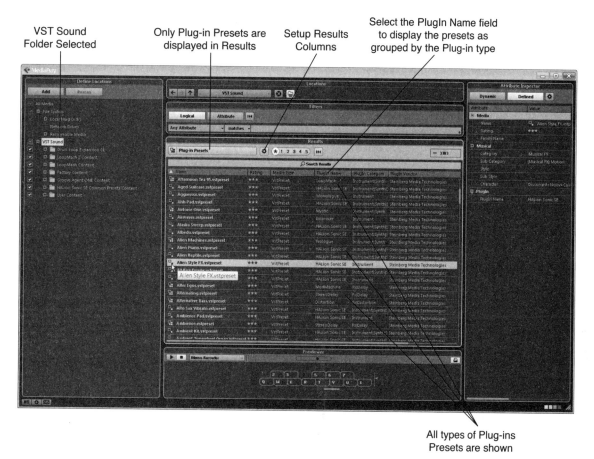

Figure 1.8 Using filters to sort out the VST instrument presets in the MediaBay.

don't need to be scrolling through your reverb patches. To work around this, you can sort the presets by clicking on the PlugIn Name field heading. (You can define column headings using the Setup Results Columns option, which looks like a button with a gear wheel on it.) Doing this will sort all of the presets into groups by their respective plug-in (HALion Sonic SE, Embracer, VST Amp Rack, and so on). This makes it a little easier to browse through the entire preset collection. If you know specifically the sound that you are looking for, *and* the sound has been tagged to fit into the predetermined categories, sorting through your trombone presets (for example) is easy. Use the Attribute filter to search the Brass category and then locate the Trombone subcategory. When Trombone is selected, all of the presets that are configured with Trombone as an attribute will appear under Results (as shown in Figure 1.9).

Now, instead of having to open each VST instrument to figure out which trombone you like best, you can use the MediaBay and audition all the trombones without even having to load a VST instrument, create a MIDI track, or scroll through individual libraries. To hear each preset, you can use your MIDI keyboard as you select different presets, you can use the mini virtual keyboard as shown in the Previewer, or you can activate the computer keyboard input and audition sound by using your QWERTY keyboard (similar to using the virtual keyboard as discussed later in Chapter 2).

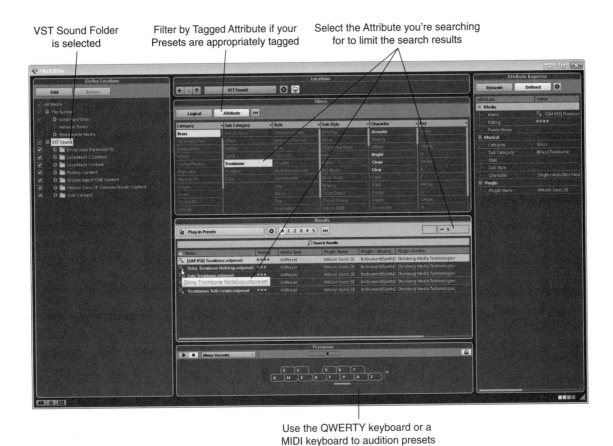

VST Sound Folder
is selected

Filter by Tagged Attribute if your
Presets are appropriately tagged

Select the Attribute you're searching
for to limit the search results

Use the QWERTY keyboard or a
MIDI keyboard to audition presets
from within the MediaBay

Figure 1.9 Using the Attribute filters to find the perfect trombone preset.

If these three methods of audition aren't enough, you can also record a mini-loop sequence using the Memo Recorder, and it will continue to loop as you scroll through the presets, making it a fast and efficient way to audition sounds. You can also load a MIDI file to loop if using the Memo Recorder is too much work for you. Keep in mind that when you're transitioning from preset to preset, there is a lot happening behind the proverbial curtain of the MediaBay, and depending on your computer's processing speed, there could be a few glitches or some lag time involved in the process of auditioning sounds.

When you have the sound you're looking for, simply double-click on the preset in the Results list. A track will appear in your project, and your sound will be ready for you to start writing some MIDI. There's no need to load the VST instrument or create a MIDI/ instrument track. Cool!

Auditioning Projects Using the MediaBay

Speaking of audition features, I would like to discuss one more feature of the Media-Bay. Let's say you work on a lot of music that is similar. Maybe you've produced a track that features a guitar part that you'd like to use in another project. There have been ways to do this in the past, but nothing as easy as it is with the MediaBay. While working in your new project, just open the MediaBay and select your old project (from your project drive) from the Browser. Once you've selected your project, browse for audio files in the Results list just as you would browse for a loop. Remember that you can audition and import the file at your current project's tempo.

If you're looking for MIDI files, you might need to actually go back into your old project, which is a little more complicated. Select the project from the MediaBay, and when it asks whether you would like to activate (so that you can hear) the project, select No. Then minimize your old project's window so that you can see the old and new projects together. Lastly, select the MIDI track you're looking for from the old project and drag it into the new project on a free MIDI track.

Note: In case you didn't know, Cubase asks if you would like to activate the project because it can only have one project "active" (where you can *hear* it) at one time. You can always activate the old project when you open it; you'll just need to reactivate your new project when you go back into it.

Creating Templates for a Speedy Startup

The last thing I want to see when I start up Cubase is an uninspiring blank "canvas." The good news is that you don't have to start from scratch if you use a preset template. It can help you get the creative juices flowing a lot faster.

To some, the idea of working with a template sounds like working within boundaries or limits. It's not like this at all when it comes to working in Cubase. Using templates can actually get you right into the creative process and skip all the boring setup procedures that usually come with preparing for a day in the studio. Whether you're regularly recording a 72-piece MIDI or live orchestra, a 12-piece ska ensemble, a 6-piece rock group, a jazz duo, or a solo harmonica, using a customized template can take your startup time from 45 minutes to 45 seconds.

First, let's go to the very beginning. Restart Cubase. On startup (assuming you're using the default startup), the Project Assistant window should open, giving you multiple options. You can open a recent project from the Recent list or use any of the preset templates located under the Recording, Scoring, Production, Mastering, or More categories listed at the top of the Project Assistant window (see Figure 1.10). If you want, you can just select one of the preset choices and start working on a project. But I'm going to show you how to create your own preset templates and store them in the appropriate location, and also how to get rid of all those extra presets you never use.

Before you get too wrapped up in this, I'll let you know that a template is pretty much identical to any project file. Many people choose to start with preexisting projects and then erase parts and save as a new project name. That practice is fine, but working with a template can save you several steps and could also prevent you from creating a "messy" work area.

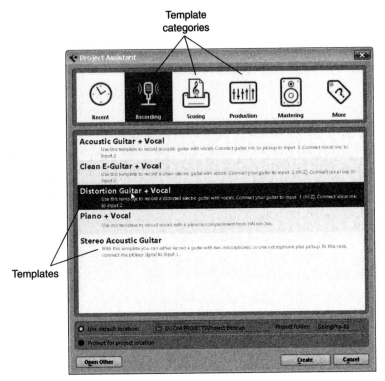

Figure 1.10 Use the New Project dialog box to select a template.

Create a new project from scratch (by selecting Empty under the More category) or by using any one of the preexisting templates, just as you would at the start of any project. Start by adding and naming all your tracks (whether they are MIDI, audio, or something else). Take the time to color-code and size your tracks the way you like them. Next, if you use VST instruments, load them up and get your presets set the way you like them. This is a must for composers like me. For example, if I need a big-band arrangement, I can call up a big-band template and save a ton of time going through and finding all the instruments and samples I would need to create a big-band piece. Before the invention of VST instruments, this alone could take a composer 45 minutes to an hour to load and set up.

> **Note:** As much as I love them, some VST instruments create a major load on your system's processor and can sometimes crash or stall a system when it's booting up. As a test, I recommend saving these types of templates at different stages (in other words, fewer VST instruments, more VST instruments, most VST instruments) and under different template names so that if you have problems with the "heavy load" VST instrument template, you can always revert to a lighter-load template instead.

Don't forget to set up your processors and EQ on your audio tracks. If there is a tempo at which you generally record, go ahead and set that to the correct tempo and time signature. Set your left and right locators where you would like them. Often, I like to set my left locator where the start of the song would be and the right where I *think* the end might be.

You no doubt have your own preferences when it comes to the way you need your workspace to look. Maybe you like to see the VST Mixer at all times. Maybe you need to see a video screen on one monitor. Anything you can do in advance to save yourself from taking those extra little steps toward getting the music into the computer should be set up and saved as a template.

Also, just because you're calling this a template, that doesn't mean you can't include audio tracks or MIDI tracks. Let's say, for instance, you like a certain groove, and even though you might not use it in the final mix, you like to use it as a guide for your other tracks. You can save that groove with the template, whether it's a MIDI or an audio track, and it will be there at startup when you open the template. Some people actually like to have a recorded click track to play with, as opposed to using the Cubase metronome. (This is especially good for clicks that need to stop and start throughout a performance.) These click tracks are great to save with a template.

But let's not forget the basics. Before you save your template, go ahead and designate the settings in the Project Setup by selecting it from Cubase's Project menu (located on the menu bar). Here you can set the sample rate, bit depth, file type, and pan law, and you're good to go.

Once you're finished making all your settings so that everything looks the way you want it to when you start working on a new project in Cubase, then you are ready to save it as a template. To do so, just select Save as Template from the File menu. This is not the normal Save As option but its own specific option. The Save as Template dialog box will appear, as shown in Figure 1.11.

Make sure the attributes are displayed by selecting the display option located in the bottom-left corner of the dialog box. Ignore the Content Summary attribute because it is not modifiable. From the Template Category attribute, click on the empty Value field and select the category where you would like your template to appear in the Project Assistant.

Under New Preset, create a new name for your preset. When creating a name, choose one that pertains to this particular setup (such as Big Band Setup or Steve's Piano Setup) and enter the name in the field. Then click OK. Close the original project and then select New Project from the File menu. This time, when the New Project dialog appears, you'll find your new template right there waiting for you in the list in the category you specified. Select it and reload what you've just created.

Now that you've created one template, you can create multiple templates. You'll see the new templates located in the categories you've specified and also listed in the Save as

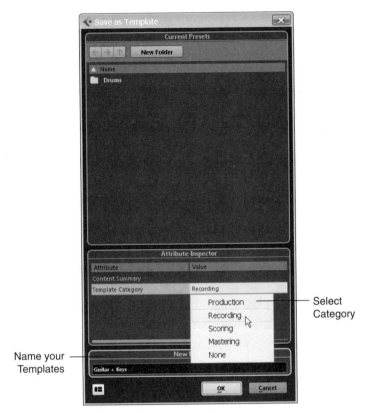

Figure 1.11 The Save as Template window.

Template window. Because I might go from working on a heavy-metal piece of music to an orchestral piece and then over to a hip-hop piece, it's nice to have a variety of templates in my arsenal. Even if you have little changes, such as more audio/MIDI tracks, saving the template with a new template name will just give you another possible option when making your selection at startup.

Diving In and Taking Control of Your Templates

To take template creation one step further, let's say you'd like to bypass the template menu option and go straight into your new template as soon as you start up Cubase. You can do this only with one template at a time, but if you always want the same thing at startup, why not skip those few extra clicks when launching Cubase and get straight into your project?

Here's how it works. First, load the template that you would like to boot up into Cubase by creating a new project and selecting that template from the Project Assistant. Once your template is up and Cubase appears the way you want it to, go back to the File menu and click Save as Template once more. This time, however, name your template Default. After you have done this, close the project, go back to the File menu, and select Preferences. When you're in the Preferences window, select General on the left side and click the On Startup drop-down list (located in the middle of the window).

Select Open 'Default' Template, as shown in Figure 1.12. When you're finished, click Apply at the bottom of the window and then click OK. When the Preferences window closes, close Cubase and restart. On boot-up, Cubase will open your new template!

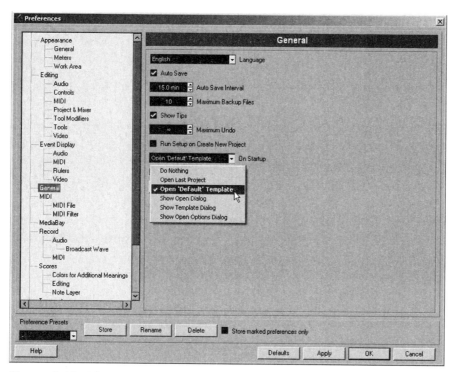

Figure 1.12 The On Startup drop-down list in the Preferences window.

Now that *you* are the one deciding what a template should be, and you know how to skip a few steps to get right into your work on startup, there's one more thing I would like to show you—how to get rid of the useless templates that you may never use.

Steinberg stores its factory-made preset templates in a folder within the Steinberg Cubase 6 program folder. The folder is called Templates (simple enough). If you've had multiple versions of Cubase installed on your system, you might have other Cubase folders that will also contain a Templates folder. When you find that folder on your system, you can move any templates you find to be useless to another folder outside of the Templates folder. You can also delete the files, but simply moving the files outside of the original folder will remove them from the Project Assistant. The files have the same name as what appeared in the Project Assistant. If there are particular presets that you'd like to keep in the Templates list, just keep their related project files in the Templates folder.

In looking at that folder, you may have realized that your templates were not in the same folder along with the presets. That's because Steinberg stores user template presets in an entirely different location. The easy way to discover the location of any of the existing templates (including yours) is to simply right-click on the template name from within the Project Assistant and select Show in Explorer/Reveal in Finder. Once you have found the folder that contains all of your custom templates, you can easily modify them by deleting, removing, renaming, or creating folders to contain a collection of templates.

Note: Storing templates in folders is purely for organizing. Although folders can also be viewed and edited from within the Save as Template window, they cannot be viewed within the Project Assistant.

Now that you know where both locations for templates are on your system, you can actually move all the files so that they are located in one folder (in whichever location you prefer—it makes no difference). *Do not move or remove the actual template folder from either location.* Whenever you create a new template, it will always go to the user folder as opposed to the folder located in Steinberg's Cubase 6 program folder, so it probably makes more sense to store the Cubase 6 templates within the same folder as your custom templates.

Organizing Your Plug-Ins

Since we're on the topic of organizing your template files, let's take a moment to discuss the way your plug-ins are organized. All of your plug-ins, whether they are VST instruments or effects, should be found in your Steinberg Cubase program folder. This includes any third-party plug-ins, such as Auto-Tune, Waves, Native Instruments, and so on.

Since I've been using Cubase for more than 20 years and I've been upgrading to every latest version, my folders and plug-ins have gotten more than a little messy over time. Not only do I have Cubase running on my system, but I also have WaveLab, and both share the same plug-ins. Because these plug-ins can be found in multiple locations, it can often make the job of finding and organizing them tricky.

On your local hard drive, in your Programs folder, you should be able to find your Steinberg folder. That folder contains almost everything currently running on your system that is related to any of Steinberg's programs. Your main Steinberg folder should contain a VSTPlugins folder. You should consider this folder to be the main folder in which all pre-VST3 plug-ins belong and are shared with all your Steinberg programs. If you take a few more steps and look into each folder within the Steinberg folder (Cubase, WaveLab, and so on), you may find other VST plug-in folders. Inside those folders is usually where you'll find the plug-ins that came with those particular programs. The VST3 plug-ins that come with Cubase have been bundled together into one VST3 file and are stored in their own VST3 folder. These are kept under the same Steinberg folder as your main VSTPlugins folder.

When you're installing any new plug-ins, you should pay close attention to where they are being installed on your system. For Mac users, the plug-in locations are determined by the developer and should not be relocated after installation. On a Windows system, for the plug-in to work properly in Cubase, it must be in one of the VST plug-in folders I mentioned previously. If the new plug-in is installed in another directory, you'll most likely have to move that plug-in from its installation location to the main VSTPlugins folder within the Steinberg folder on your system for it to work.

Now, let's say you have a plug-in that you really like in WaveLab, but it doesn't show up in Cubase (or vice versa). It's because that plug-in isn't located in the main Steinberg VSTPlugins folder; it's in the WaveLab folder. For it to work in both programs, you must physically move (or copy) that plug-in from the WaveLab folder to the Steinberg VSTPlugins folder. When this is done, you'll also need to restart your system. When Cubase restarts, it will see the new plug-in driver and install it within its plug-in directory so that you can access it from Cubase. Check out Figure 1.13 for a close-up of a plug-in file in Cubase from my Windows system.

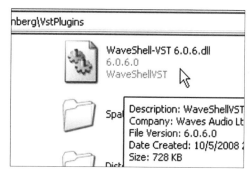

Figure 1.13 A DLL plug-in driver file for the Waves Gold Bundle found in my Steinberg VSTPlugins folder. This file contains all of my Waves plug-ins.

Within Cubase, you can also organize your plug-ins using the VST 2.x Plug-In Paths button, which is found in the Plug-In Information dialog located in the Device menu. More information is included on this in the Cubase manual, but I wanted to give you more specifics on using the "outside" approach in case you run into difficulties using this method.

Note: VST3 plug-ins are currently the latest plug-in type to work with Cubase. Older plug-in types will work as long as they're VST. VST3 plug-ins will work better and will offer a few more features than the older ones. All of Cubase 6's plug-ins will be updated to the latest version available each time you update Cubase. If you're using third-party plug-ins, you should check with their respective developers for updates in order to ensure compatibility and get the most out of them.

On a Windows system, most pre-VST3 plug-ins are DLL files and should appear as an icon with little gears. If you look up close, you'll see the name and file type, and below it you'll see the version number. If you find multiple DLL files sharing the same name, check the version number. If the version number is older, remove the driver file from your VSTPlugins folder. To be on the safe side, do not delete any file until you test run Cubase and make sure it is working properly. If there are problems after running Cubase, move the file back and try again. This process might sound a little scary for someone who's not used to digging into file systems, but it's really not that difficult.

Now that you know where all your plug-in drivers are, there's something you can do to clean them up. What I've done is simply organize the files in a way similar to organizing my samples. I put all the VST instruments under one folder and then created subfolders for them. I also did the same with my effects. Now if I'm looking for a delay, at least most of my delays are in one place. If I'm looking for a synth, all my VST synths are in one location. By grouping these in folders within the VSTPlugins folder (see Figure 1.14), I now have them organized better in my Effects and Instruments windows within Cubase (see Figure 1.15).

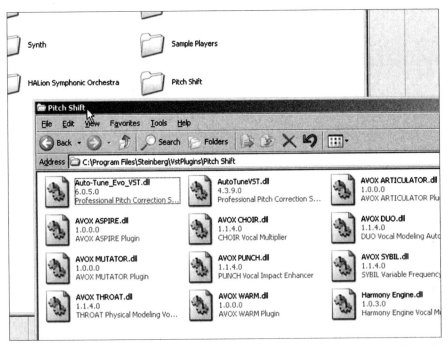

Figure 1.14 I've grouped my VST2 Auto-Tune plug-ins into a folder I named Pitch Shift.

You can name your own folders, but since Steinberg's VST3 plug-ins are bundled and not modifiable, I've chosen to name the folder for my Auto-Tune plug-ins to match Steinberg's preexisting VST3 folder. Folders with the same names will be grouped together automatically. If all your plug-ins are individual and in one location, then

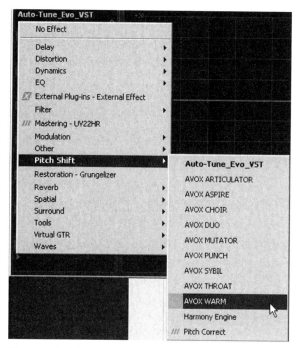

Figure 1.15 Now Steinberg's VST3 Pitch Correct processor appears with Auto-Tune's VST2 processors in Cubase.

you can name that folder whatever you want, and it will appear and work correctly in the processor list.

When you have all your VST plug-ins organized on your system the way you like, you can then optimize it by deactivating the plug-ins you don't use on a regular basis. When deactivating a plug-in, you don't actually remove it from your system or your VSTPlugins folder. By deactivating the plug-in, you're simply telling Cubase to *ignore* particular plug-ins while running. The fewer plug-ins that Cubase has to manage (especially those that are older than VST3), the better Cubase should run.

To deactivate unwanted plug-ins, select Plug-In Information from the Devices menu. Your current plug-ins will appear in a list.

Note: Notice that your plug-in list should include even more detailed information, such as a plug-in's exact location, version number, name and file type, and so on. This is a great list to have, but the reason I wanted to show you first how to organize the actual files is because if Cubase can't properly locate the driver file, chances are that it won't appear in this list.

Once the list is visible, simply uncheck the plug-ins that you don't wish to use by clicking in the left column.

Note: A new feature of VST3 technology is one that automatically disables the plug-in when it is not in use. Because of this, it's really unnecessary to deactivate any VST3 plug-ins, as doing so will not free up any extra resources for your system (which you'll learn more about in the next tutorial). You can easily identify which plug-ins are VST3 by the three slashes (///) symbol before their names in your processor/instrument lists.

Creating the Perfect "Battlefield"—Setting Your Preferences

As I mentioned previously, Cubase was designed to work the way you want it to work. It offers several different ways of doing the same thing to fit a wide variety of user types. Setting up preferences is one of the first places any serious Cubase user should look to customize the setup, but often this simple feature gets overlooked. Preferences are located under the File menu for Windows users (see Figure 1.16) and under the Cubase menu for Mac users (for those who still didn't know). In this tutorial, I'll be going over all of the preferences settings and breaking them down into two categories: modifiying the look and feel, and fine-tuning your Cubase engine.

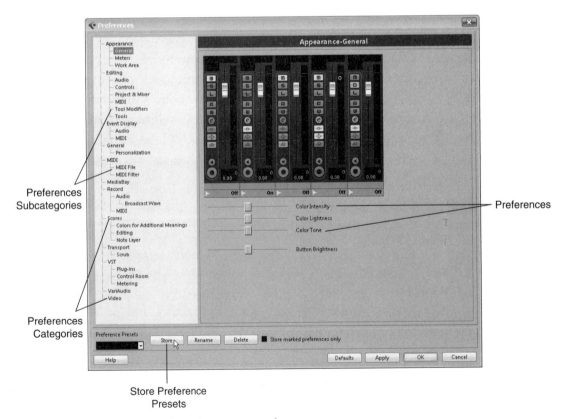

Figure 1.16 Locating and setting your preferences.

Note: References to the preferences settings are strewn all throughout the Cubase manual. This makes them a little difficult to find and learn. However, the Help menu located at the bottom of the Preferences menu contains a lot of useful information on what each setting does.

One of the coolest things about setting your preferences is that once you've made your changes, you can save your settings as a preset, and then anytime you make changes later, you can reload your own personal settings.

Modifying the Look and Feel of Cubase 6

Since there are so many preferences settings, I will break them all down page by page so it's easy to follow along. First off, I'd like to discuss changing the basic look and feel of Cubase to suit your personal needs. If you ever find yourself squinting or straining to see what you're doing in Cubase, or if you have trouble using some of the controls, it would probably be a good idea to try modifying the look and feel of Cubase.

Most of the changes to the look of Cubase come from the Appearance category in Preferences. By selecting the subcategories of General, Meters, or Work Area, you can adjust the colors and tone of your entire working environment. Using the sliders in these areas, you can control everything from the brightness and colors of the virtual controllers to the visibility of the grid lines.

Under the Event Display category, you can make modifications to the way every event is displayed in Cubase. Since every audio or MIDI recording that you'll be working with is considered an "event," this accounts for a major part of the overall look. First under the main category heading, you can choose to uncheck Show Event Names so that the individual event names are hidden from you. (By default, names are displayed.) You can uncheck Hide Truncated Names. By doing so, the event names will be displayed even when they can't be fully displayed due to the size of the event. (By default, the names are hidden when truncated.) You can choose to show overlaps (when two events cross each other, whether on purpose or accidental) when you mouse over (default) the intersection of the two events. You can also choose to always or never show overlaps.

Similar to hiding truncated names, when track heights are reduced, you can also choose whether to show event data on small track heights. By default, this option is unchecked to avoid cluttering up the view; however, if you wish to see the data no matter how small the track height is, simply check this option.

Next under the Audio subcategory (still under the Event Display category), your first option is to check or uncheck Interpolate Audio Waveforms. "Interpolating" means that Cubase will draw a waveform with a curved line as opposed to a step (binary grid–style) line when zoomed in (such as when using the Sample Editor). By checking this option, the waveform will look more like it sounds as opposed to how it is.

When normally zoomed out, the look of a waveform is automatically interpolated. You can hide event volume curves by un-checking Show Event Volume Curves Always. The only reason you might want to do this is to hide the clutter that's sometimes caused by excess data displayed within an event. Even if this is deselected, you can still modify the volume curves when the part is selected, you just can't see them when it's not selected.

In most cases, you'll want to keep Show Waveforms checked for easy audio editing and determining where the peaks and valleys of the audio recording exist. The Waveform Brightness, Waveform Outline Intensity, and Fade Handle Brightness sliders all work similarly to the slider found in the Appearance category. Each can make a huge difference on the way that waveforms are displayed.

The Background Color Modulation option is another way of viewing peaks and valleys of waveforms, since track height can determine the perception of the depth of the wave. The way this works is that the higher the peak of the waveform, the darker the shading around the waveform. I'm not a particular fan of this method because it tends to clutter the audio event display, but I could see how if you're working with a lot of audio tracks, this feature could come in handy.

Under the MIDI subcategory (still in the Event Display category), by selecting the Default Edit Action you can choose which MIDI editor to open and display when you double-click on a MIDI event. For the last 20 years, by default, the editor to open has been the Key Editor. But, if you choose, you can instead open the In-Place Editor, Drum Editor, List Editor, or Score Editor.

By default, when viewing MIDI events from within a part, they are shown as small blocks (as shown in the Key Editor). By selecting within the Part Data mode, you can choose to instead show the MIDI data in lines (flat lines that are similar to the blocks), scores (miniature notes), or drums (the same diamond shape used with the Drum Editor).

Using the same mode, you can also choose to hide the MIDI data by showing no data. You can choose whether to show controllers, which will display controller information within the part similar to the way it's displayed from within the Key Editor.

The Note Brightness and Controller Brightness sliders again work similarly to how the Waveform Brightness sliders work. "Note" brightness also means blocks or whichever way you choose to view MIDI events within a part.

The Edit as Drums when Drum Map is Assigned feature works similarly to setting the default edit action, but when there is a drum map assigned to an event, this setting will override the setting within the default edit action when the event is double-clicked. If you use the drum editor and drum maps, this is a handy feature to utilize for quick and easy access to the Drum Editor while still having quick and easy access to the Key Editor or whichever editor you choose to use on double-clicking an event.

Changing the note name style is a somewhat subtle difference you can also make but with several possibilities. The default setting is MIDI (which displays note names such as C-1). You can go further with the MIDI setting by also displaying the numeric value using the MIDI and Value setting (C-1/36). Using the DoReMi setting, notes are displayed in solfège using the fixed do method. If these three options aren't enough, you can also display the note names in the classic style or the ultra-specific classic German style.

Under the General category, you can change the language used to English, German, French, Italian, Spanish, or Japanese by selecting the desired option from the Language drop-down menu.

Show Tips is a handy little feature to have active if you're new to working with Cubase 6. By selecting this option, when you hover over a button or control with the mouse, a concise definition of what the button or control does will appear. Once you know it all, you can deactivate this option.

Run Setup on Create New Project immediately takes you to the Project Setup window when you've created a new project. This is a great feature to keep you from forgetting to make these important settings. As mentioned earlier, during the "Diving In and Taking Control of Your Templates" section, the On Startup feature allows you to start up using a default template or the Project Assistant. What I didn't mention before is that you can also choose to start up with the last project you were working on by selecting Open Last Project, or you can choose to open a preexisting project from a mini-browser by selecting Show Open Dialog. For those who prefer not to deal with any sort of automated startup procedure, you can bypass the startup by selecting Do Nothing.

Under the Personalization subcategory (still located in the General category), you can enter your name and company name, and this information will be included by default on all new projects that are created (in the project settings) and in all exported iXML data chunks.

Note: I'm aware that I skipped over the AutoSave, Backup File, and Undo steps in the General category. To learn more about these features, see the upcoming tutorial called "Saving Your Work Could Save Your Career."

Although the Editing category contains a lot of preferences that have nothing to do with look or feel, it contains many preferences that do. The Show Data in Folder

Tracks preference give you the option to display data, not display data, or show data only when the track is not expanded (which makes sense, because you will see data on the tracks that are shown once the track is expanded).

When the Link Editors preference is checked, everything you do within one editor will also reflect in the other editors. With the editors linked, your work stays consistent and organized, but if you screw up in one editor, you screw up in them all.

When the Parts Get Track Names is checked, every time you record a part, it will be named the same as the track name (with possible numbers for multiple parts on one track).

Activating Quick Zoom means less redrawing of your display. Although this saves processing power, it also means less accuracy in your zooming in and out.

Cubase offers a Drag Delay preference to differentiate between selecting an event and clicking and dragging. If you find yourself moving notes by accident when your intention was to simply select the note, you might want to try a higher Drag Delay setting.

When Track Selection Follows Event Selection is checked, as you select events in the Project window, the corresponding tracks are also selected.

Under the Audio subcategory within the Editing category, you can use the Use Mouse Wheel for Event Volume and Fades preference to tweak your mix from within the events using your mouse's wheel (that is, if you have a mouse with a wheel).

Continuing under the Controls subcategory (still in the Editing category), here you can customize the way that the sliders, knobs, and value boxes function by changing the way each type of controller functions in relation to the maneuver you make with your mouse (left/right click, rotate a knob, and so on).

Under the Project and Mixer subcategory (still in the Editing category), there are several ways to modify the look and feel. When Select Channel/Track on Solo is checked, the track/channel you solo will be selected automatically. Usually, when you solo tracks, you'll want the same tracks selected, as you are most likely going to be working with the soloed tracks, and you will not be able to hear the other tracks to make proper edits anyway. I recommend leaving this option checked, and if you ever run into difficulties regarding soloing (which is unlikely), you can uncheck this box and try again. I can only foresee possible difficulties when you're soloing several tracks at once, yet you want to focus on editing only in one track.

When Scroll to Selected Channel and/or Track is checked, your view will automatically be adjusted so that what is selected will be the center of your attention. You can customize this automatic feature to work with the Mixer only, the Project window only, both the Project window and the Mixer, or neither.

If you're more into creating tracks than making a pretty color scheme in your Project window, then Auto Track Color mode is a very handy feature. Although using different colors makes it easier to keep your work organized, it's often an afterthought in the creation process. There are several options to choose from here. I recommend using Choose Random Color for a more diverse viewing screen. When Sync Project & Mixer Selection is checked, when you select a track in the Project window, the corresponding Mixer channel will be selected automatically (and vice versa).

By using Enable Record on Selected Audio/MIDI Track, you may accidentally record on selected tracks when it's not what you intended—and it's even less likely that you'll want to enable solo on the selected track every time you select a track. Although this is a quick way to jump into recording, my suggestion is to leave both of these options unchecked and stick to activating the record or solo on the track you wish to record when you're ready to record or solo a track.

Enlarge Selected Track basically expands the selected tracks so that they appear vertically larger than the other tracks (thus making them easier to see and work with when you're using a lot of tracks). Deep Track Folding allows you to quickly open and fold multiple folders and subfolders grouped together on a track.

Skipping down to the Tools subcategory (still located in the Editing category), you'll find several preferences to change the overall look and feel of Cubase 6. When Select Tool Shows Extra Info is selected, the selection tool (mouse pointer) shows track info and time reference while mousing over the Project window.

When Warn before Switching Display Domain (Timewarp Tool) is selected, a warning will come up while you're using the Time Warp tool. As long as you're careful and understand how the Time Warp tool works, this warning is not necessary. For more information on the Time Warp tool, see Chapter 3.

With the Zoom Tool Standard Mode: Horizontal Zooming Only preference checked, when using the zoom, tracks will not be expanded vertically. (This is the normal way of zooming.) If you need to expand vertically as well as horizontally, uncheck this preference.The Pop Up Tool Box on Right Click preference is selected by default, and when you right-click, a small toolbox will appear, containing the tool buttons. To get an extended view of the tool buttons instead of the mini version, uncheck this feature.

Using the cross-hair cursor makes it even easier to find gridlines when making edits. The settings located below the preference option allow you to customize the cross hair to your liking.

Under the MediaBay category, there are a couple of different ways to change the look and feel. The first is the Maximum Items in Results List preference. This can help prevent ridiculously long lists in your results, which could result in slowing down your search. I still find that the best way is to organize your files in folders before seeking results in order to get the most out of the MediaBay, as opposed to using this "limiting" feature.

Using the Show File Extensions in Results List preference is an easy way to determine what type of file you're looking at if you're looking through multiple file types. Under the subcategory Audio located under the Record category is the Create Audio Images during Record preference. This simply means that Cubase will draw and display the waveform as the file is being created. As long as you have a fairly fast computer and hard drive, this is a nice option to utilize. If you don't, you can always uncheck this option, and Cubase will draw the waveform once the recording process is complete.

Under the Broadcast Wave subcategory, you can set your Broadcast Wave data. (There's more on this in Chapter 4.) Next, if you use the Scoring features of Cubase, you'll find a lot of different ways to modify the look of the Scoring Editor, all located under the Scoring category.

You can make quite a few modifications in the Transport category to enhance your working experience. The Playback Toggle Triggers Local Preview preference allows you to use your spacebar not only to start and stop the Transport, but also to start and stop playback of the selected event when working in the Sample Editor.

The Zoom While Locating in Time Scale preference is a quick and easy way to zoom into or out of your project. Simply click on the ruler and drag down to zoom in on your target or drag upward to zoom out.

The Cursor Width option is merely a visual modification of the cursor. (Keep in mind that the cursor is the thing that scrolls through the song, not the mouse pointer.)

The Return to Start Position on Stop option is a fast way to get back to the beginning once you hit Stop; however, this could be annoying if you're trying to work on a specific section of a song.

Stop Playback While Winding prevents the sound of scrubbing backward or forward and can enhance your system performance if it's not used. Using the Wind Speed options, you can adjust the fast-forward or rewind speed. You can also set the wind speed to adjust to zoom so that when you're zoomed in, the wind speed is slower, and vice versa.

Show Timecode Subframes only affects the display of the timecode. Your subframes are still there, even if you can't see the numbers flying by. You can also define your own subframes if necessary. When using Stationary Cursors, as the cursor arrives at the middle of the displayed Project window, it will remain centered, and the Project window will scroll to the left past the cursor. When utilizing Locate When Clicked in Empty Space, your cursor moves wherever you click (as long as the space is not occupied by an event, a part, or an automation handle).

Under the VST category, you can opt out of the Warn on Processing Overloads preference if you'd like. Obviously, you don't want overloads to occur, but if you're careful, this shouldn't happen to you.

Under the VST Plug-Ins subcategory, you can disable the Warn before Removing Modified Effects option. This warning is much more useless than the previous one. For instance, if you're changing a delay effect into a reverb effect (after making some modifications to the delay), Cubase will warn you that you're changing your effect, when 9 times out of 10 you're doing it on purpose.

By selecting Open Effect Editor after Loading It, any time you load a new effect, its related effect editor will open. When using Create MIDI Track when Loading VSTi, you have several options: to never create a MIDI track, to always create a MIDI track, or to always ask to create a MIDI track.

You can also choose to sort the VST Plug-Ins menu by vendor (which could make it easier for you to find your plug-ins in a large list), and you can make sure that plug-in editors are always on top (which means that they will not be hidden behind other windows).

Moving on to the Control Room subcategory (still within the VST category), there are several display options that can come in handy when you're using the control room features in Cubase (for monitoring while recording). The Show Control Room Volume in Transport Panel feature substitutes the Main Mix bus with the Control Room volume if selected.

Using the Signal Presence Indicators option streamlines the look of the Control Room by removing the much-larger meters. To see larger meters, deselect this option.

The Show Multi-Channel Speaker Solo, Show Downmix Presets, and Show Reference Level preferences are all selected by default. Un-checking them simply hides the feature from the Control Room.

Under the Metering subcategory (still under the VST category), the Map Input Buss Metering to Audio Track (in Direct Monitoring) option allows you to assign an input meter to the actual audio track on which you're recording. You can also customize the slow and fast fallback as well as the peak hold time of the meters.

When you've become accustomed to working with VariAudio, you can disable (by checking) the Inhibit Warning when Changing the Sample Data and Inhibit Warning when Applying Offline Processes preferences located under the VariAudio category.

Lastly, under the Video category, the Thumbnail memory cache size allows you to assign up to 128 MB of RAM memory for thumbnails captured from video. The higher the setting, the more thumbnails will be produced, but the less RAM will be available for audio processing.

Fine-Tuning Your Cubase 6 Engine

The look and feel of your working environment are important, but what I'd like to concentrate on now are the extra little tools that can save you a few steps or at least simplify the process of day-to-day tasks. These are all quick and easy settings that will get Cubase working for you in an efficient way that meets your own personal needs.

You'll find the first set of features under the Editing category. All of these preferences are related to editing in general and can help speed up your overall editing performance. The first preference in this category is Default Track Time Type. For most Cubase users, you'll want to work in Musical Time (the default). For those who work with images or timed sequences (theater cues, for example), Time Linear (Minutes and Seconds) should be your main startup format.

Selecting Follow Transport Main Display will result in the time type adjusting to Musical Time when working in bars and beats, and Linear Time when using any other time format from the Transport.

When Auto Select Events Under Cursor is checked, events (both MIDI and audio) are selected as the cursor (not the mouse pointer) moves across the timeline. This is helpful in determining which event to edit while playing back—but keep in mind that by automatically selecting events, you risk accidentally altering/moving or deleting those events.

When Cycle Follows Range Selection is checked, using the Range tool actually moves the left locator to the left side of your created range and the right locator to the right side of your created range, thus making Cubase continuously loop your selected range while in Cycle mode. This makes it easy to quickly reposition left and right locators and audition sections. However, it's not for those who prefer to use the Range tool while cycling between the locators.

When Delete Overlaps is checked, while working with multiple parts in lanes, Cubase will automatically prevent parts from overlapping so that they can be combined easily into one track. This saves you from editing but doesn't allow you to edit.

The Lock Event Attributes preference allows you to select which features of the event you would like to lock when you select to lock an event.

Utilizing the Use Up/Down Navigation Commands for Selecting Tracks Only preference allows you to use the arrow keys to scroll up and down through your track list, but it does not select the parts on the tracks. When Automation Follows Events is checked, any automation that exists on an edited track will be moved or copied along with the edit. (This prevents you from having to recopy automation-lane parts.)

You can also find the next group of features under the Editing category, but under the Audio subcategory. Each of these preferences is more specific to editing audio and can help enhance your audio-editing experience.

The first preference is to set the default Time Stretch tool algorithm for when you're performing an edit that uses the Sizing Applies Time Stretch mode. Although there are several options to try, usually the best setting to use is MPEX-Poly Musical for higher-quality processing.

When using the Treat Muted Events Like Deleted option, Cubase will treat any muted part as if it isn't there (even if it's overlapping a part that isn't muted).

When using On Import Audio Files and selecting Use Settings, you have the following options: Copy Files to Working Directory, Convert and Copy to Project If Necessary, and Split Multi-Channel Files. If Use Settings is not selected, Cubase will show a dialog box with options each and every time you import audio. If you do split multi-channel files on import, using numbers is an easy way to rename the new individual tracks. (You can rename them later.)

When using On Processing Shared Clips, you have three automatic options for this process. The default is to be prompted with a message that asks something to the effect of, "Would you like to create a new file version or write over existing files?" The other options are to create the new file versions or skip the message (which essentially would write over your existing files). The safe and easy solution would be to always create a new file when processing shared clips; that way, you can always go back to your original clips if necessary. My suggestion is to leave Assume New Versions selected.

When using Remove Regions/Markers on All Offline Processes, if you're using regions and markers while processing offline effects, only the selected regions are affected. In some cases this is the desired result, but in others it's not. I believe it's best to leave this box checked because it can be more beneficial to process only selected regions as opposed to the entire part when processing offline.

This next group focuses on MIDI editing and can be found under the MIDI subcategory located under the Editing category. The Select Controllers in Note Range: Use Extended Note Content preference allows you to select automatically controller events that occur at the same time as the notes you select within the Key Editor.

Legato Overlap allows you to define how long you would like connecting notes to overlap, and Legato Mode Selected Only means that legato settings will be applied only to the selected events.

When Split MIDI Events is checked, the MIDI note will be turned automatically into two individual notes when editing in the middle of a MIDI note. Even though this might not be the desired result in a lot of cases, at least a note-off has been created for the first note, and the second note is easy to delete if necessary. This is sort of like cutting a loaf of bread into two halves and keeping both, as opposed cutting the bread and discarding the second half in the process. Considering that the alternative is more "messy," I suggest leaving this preference checked.

Split MIDI Controllers is very similar to Split MIDI Events (except it specifies controller events), and for this reason, I recommend leaving this option checked as well. Using the tool modifiers (located in their own subcategory under the Editing category) allows you to customize which keys act as alternative functions for the tools. This can be very handy even if you memorize the default settings.

The next batch of preferences that can fine-tune your Cubase engine is located under the MIDI category in the Preferences dialog. MIDI Thru Active must be checked if you need to hear what you're playing on your MIDI keyboard while you record a MIDI part. It's very rare that you will need to have MIDI Thru Active deactivated. For this reason, just leave this checked until you have to cross that bridge.

The Reset on Stop preference is a handy feature if you have a "sticky" MIDI loop player or synth that likes to keep on going after you've stopped playback. The only thing this feature does is send a MIDI note-off command to everything in your system when you hit Stop. This command will not affect your recording in any way; however, it will reset continuous controllers (pan, volume, pitch bend, and so forth) back to zero. So if you're using these, it might be best to leave this unchecked if you run into problems. The Length Adjustment preference allows you to adjust the allotted space given after every MIDI note is played (so that notes are not connected). The default setting here is −2 ticks (which is 1/60 of 1/16 note). In most cases, this is best left as is, but depending on your recording style (for example, if you tend to hold notes a little longer than necessary), you might want to take away a few more ticks to tighten up your performance.

Chase Events allows you to customize which events you would like Cubase to "chase." *Chasing* refers to keeping track of what's happening with MIDI throughout the project. This is particularly helpful when you have multiple program changes or pitch bends on one MIDI track. As you skip around throughout the song during playback (such as when you're working on the chorus of song, then working on a bridge, and so on), Cubase will remember that the MIDI should be performed a certain way (in other words, with the program change) regardless of where you stop or start playback. For the most part, you should leave all of these boxes checked unless you need to work around some sticky MIDI devices.

Using the MIDI Display Resolution and MIDI Max Feedback preferences, you can alter the value of a MIDI 1/16 note in actual "ticks" (affecting only the display of the MIDI event) and control the amount of allowable MIDI feedback for the acoustic feedback control when auditioning MIDI events.

As with the Reset on Stop option (listed earlier), Insert Reset Events after Record is aimed at stopping those sticky MIDI notes from continuing after play has been stopped. The difference here is that you might want those sticky synths to stop before the song actually stops. To do so, record as normal; then, when you want the sticky synth to stop, hit Stop on the Transport. Doing so will cause a MIDI reset event to be written into the part being recorded. This tool can be very useful, but it's a little trickier than the simple Reset on Stop option. If you use a lot of sticky synths, I recommend checking this option; otherwise, it's probably best to leave it unchecked.

If you don't have Audition through MIDI Inserts/Sends selected when using the acoustic feedback audition feature, you will hear only the non-effected MIDI notes. Having this unchecked could be useful if you would like to concentrate on the "raw" notes recorded. However, if you would like to concentrate on each individual note as it is heard through the inserts or sends (in other words, if you would like to edit a single note while auditioning its MIDI delay), this must be checked.

The MIDI File and MIDI Filter subcategories of the MIDI category can both be used to filter MIDI information as it's imported or exported via a MIDI file or as it's received via the MIDI input in Cubase.

The MediaBay category in Preferences includes a couple more preferences that can streamline your experience when utilizing the MediaBay. When the Scan Unknown File Types preference is selected, all file types will be scanned, even if they can't be recognized. Although this is good for finding files that might otherwise be "missing," it will also create a lot of extra indexing that could prove unnecessary.

When Allow Editing in Results List is active, you can change the attributes (including renaming files) from within the Results list as opposed to being limited to changing from within the Attributes Inspector.

By selecting Scan Folders when MediaBay Is Open, you can prevent indexing from happening while the MediaBay not open. Even though Steinberg assures us that scanning does not occur while recording or playing back audio, utilizing this option makes sense because anything that's a background process could cause problems.

Under the Record category and the Audio subcategory, there is an option for setting Audio Pre-Record Seconds. This option allows you to determine a set time (buffer) for Cubase to capture before you actually record. This feature allows you to pre-record up to one minute. This is mostly useful when doing punch-in/out, as a precaution for missing part of a performance before hitting the Record button.

Under the MIDI subcategory (located under the Record category) in preferences are yet more settings that can streamline your MIDI recording experience. When the Snap MIDI Parts to Bars preference is checked, this feature lengthens MIDI parts so that they fit at bar positions. Working with partial bars is a lot trickier than working with full bars when it comes to MIDI editing, and this can help simplify the workspace.

The Solo Record in MIDI Editors preference is not to be confused with the Solo Editor feature located in the Key Editor toolbar. This is more like an automatic record-enable when you select and open a track in a MIDI Editor. This makes it easy to record new parts within the MIDI Editor, and you won't have to worry about recording on other MIDI tracks by mistake. This feature is checked by default and in most cases should remain checked.

Retrospective Record and Buffer Size is an interesting preference choice. I guess it was designed for those who thought they were recording and got the perfect take, only to realize after the fact that they forgot to push Record. If this sounds like something that might happen to you on occasion, you might want to check this feature. When you realize you forgot to record, select Retrospective Record from the Transport menu, and your recording will magically appear. For this to work, it means that Cubase is secretly recording everything you do (sort of like Big Brother!), and when you have your "oops" moment, Cubase has got your back. Because this is constantly recording, Cubase allows you to set your recording limits. The default is 10,000 events. (Keep in mind that when using continuous controllers, the event buffer can reach its limits quickly.)

The MIDI Record Catch Range setting is similar to Audio Pre-Record, except with MIDI. If you use the Replace mode, Replace Recording in Editors allows you to specify whether you would like to replace just the controller events (commonly practiced) as opposed to both the controller and note events while working in the Key Editor. Using this feature makes it easy to re-perform pitch bends or modulation on MIDI parts, and if you want to use Replace All, you can simply re-record the part as an alternative option, because it's essentially the same thing. Replace None has no effect and is used only as a safety.

When it comes to creating punch-ins/outs, there are two preference settings located in the Transport category that can help you out. When Deactivate Punch In on Stop is selected and you hit Stop (or the spacebar), your punch-in is deactivated. It makes sense to keep this one checked. Keep in mind that you will need to re-enable punch-in when you resume playback if you wish to continue performing punch-ins.

When Stop after Automatic Punch Out is checked, the playback will automatically stop after a punch-out is performed (after and post-roll settings). It also makes sense to keep this one checked.

Also, under the Transport category's Scrub subcategory, you can adjust the scrub volume, use high-quality Scrub mode (which requires more RAM but sounds better), and also use inserts while scrubbing. (Normally, to conserve CPU power, inserts are not processed while scrubbing.)

The VST category preference settings work strictly with the VST interface and affect the way that plug-ins are handled within Cubase. By selecting Connect Sends Automatically for Each Newly Created Channel, any effect sends you have created will appear in the list of available effects for any newly created track. Having this checked saves you the trouble of having to select your effects from the list of available sends when setting up a new track. I recommend having this checked because the sends are not active when the new track is created, and you still have to activate them to use the effect.

When Instruments Use Automation Read All and Write All is selected, VST instrument tracks become automation enabled. This is checked by default, and I see no reason to uncheck it unless you would like to disable automation on all Instrument tracks. No one says you have to automate anything if you don't want to.

By selecting Mute Pre-Send when Mute, whenever you mute a channel, any effect that is utilizing a pre-send will also be muted. When selecting Group Channels: Mute Sources as well, after muting a group channel, all channels that are grouped together on that channel will also become muted.

If you are experiencing latency while recording with VST instruments or processors, you can use the Delay Compensation Threshold (for Recording) setting along with the Constrain Delay Compensation button located on the toolbar. If you're having problems, activate Constrain Delay Compensation and then adjust this setting until the problem is resolved.

When selecting a Default Stereo Panner mode, you have the choice of Stereo Dual Panner (two separate controls for left and right), Stereo Combined Panner (one control for two separate linked panners), and the default Stereo Balance Panner (which is one control and most similar to the sort of standard panner you see on most common mixing consoles).

When Send Routing Panners Follow Channel Panner as Default is enabled, and the Send Routing Panners Follow Channel button (which you can find on the Edit Channel settings of multiple track types when that channel's Control Strip is displayed) is active, then the select sends on that channel will pan according to the channel's pan settings.

The Auto Monitoring preference setting gives you four options for how to monitor an input signal in Cubase. Using the Manual setting, you simply select the monitor button on the channels you need to monitor the input. Using the While Record Enabled setting, you can automatically monitor the input signal when Cubase is in record mode. When using the While Record Running setting, you will automatically monitor the input signal only when Cubase is actually recording. When using the Tapemachine Style, monitoring is similar to an analog tape recorder where you hear while record is enabled and while record is running, but you can't hear the input during playback.

Also, under the Plug-ins subcategory, there is an option to Suspend VST3 Plug-In Processing when No Audio Signals Are Received. This new optimization feature is one I'll recommend because it can save a lot of processing power. However, I'm a little suspicious (it reminds me too much of "sleeping" hard drives) because I feel as though it could cause program fluctuations that could lead to crashing while you're quickly working. I have faith that Steinberg wouldn't have released this without extensive testing, though. If you're experiencing problems with crashing and you're using a lot of VST3 plug-ins, you might want to uncheck this box. (I have a feeling that's why it's there!)

The Control Room category contains several options to enhance your experience while using the Control Room features when recording and monitoring in Cubase 6. The Disable Talkback during Recording preference prevents you from recording your Control Room talkback microphone (if used).

The Use Phones Channels as Preview Channel preference will prevent the Control Room monitors from being active while recording. The Dim Studio during Talkback option lowers the track playback volume in the monitors while you utilize the talkback microphone. The Main Dim Volume level is also set from this window.

The Exclusive Device Ports for Monitor Channels preference prevents you from using inputs and outputs on your audio interface that are meant for monitoring only. The Metronome Option in Studio Channels preference allows the metronome to play back through the studio channels, and the Metronome Option in Control Room & Phones Channels preference is necessary to monitor the metronome playback through both the Control Room monitors and the headphones.

Lastly, from the Video category, by selecting Extract Audio on Import Video File, the audio from any imported video file will be separated and imported into a stereo audio track. I recommend checking this option and always importing the audio. If necessary, you can always delete or mute the audio (as you would any audio track) without affecting the video track.

Saving Your Work Could Save Your Career

I've used both Macs and PCs, and they are both prone to crashing when you're working on complex programs, such as Cubase. But this probably isn't news to you. I regularly save files and back up my computer now. I have multiple hard drives, and I copy each drive to a completely clean backup drive every month. I have battery backups so I will have time to save and shut down my system to avoid a devastating crash in case the power suddenly goes out. But even with all this, I still lost one month's worth of work one year during a power failure. There's no insurance for this kind of loss, and when it comes to tax write-offs, this sort of thing doesn't even make the list. The work and time are gone, and the only thing that can replace them is more work and time, whether that time is paid or unpaid. Always expect and be prepared for the worst.

I'm not going to preach anymore about backup hard drives and battery backups. I would like to focus on the simple task of saving your work and discuss saving methods that will hopefully (if you practice) help you avoid some of the pain I've gone through in my career.

First, let's talk about the Auto Save features that come in Cubase. When I first started using Cubase and learned about the Auto Save feature, I thought, "Perfect! I hate having to save often. This thing will do it for me, and I'll be safe!" Then I learned that Auto Save was saving over my old files and preventing me from going back and correcting things if I ran into problems down the road. It was a nightmare. Well, Auto Save has gotten better. Now, Cubase saves the file under a new file type (BAK) and under a modified name (with numbers), and it saves only when changes have been made. I have tested this operation, and it works.

You can locate and activate the Auto Save preferences from within the General category of the Preference settings (see Figure 1.17). Here, you can set the maximum backup projects (the default setting is 10) and set the interval of how often the backup occurs (the default being every 15 minutes).

Note: Mac users should take note that if you plan to open your projects on a Windows system (ever), you should remember to select the Use File Extension in File Dialog option, also located in Preferences.

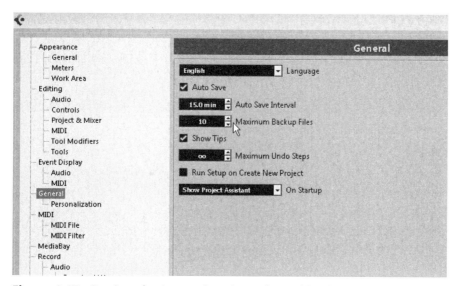

Figure 1.17 Setting the interval and number of backups.

When Cubase reaches its maximum number of backups for the project you're working on, it will replace the earliest saved backup. Auto Save occurs as a background process while you're working. This is the reason why a lot of users do not use Auto Save (thinking that it could cause problems while recording, importing, exporting, and so on).

I have never witnessed any such problems while using Cubase 6. Steinberg claims that this background service never occurs while recording or processing audio. When using Auto Save, Cubase 6 will save the backup project to the project folder you have created if you have set up a project folder and saved the project to it. Otherwise, Cubase 6 will save the project as an untitled project (if the project has not yet been named) to the default project folder location (located in My Documents on a Windows system or the Cubase Projects folder within the Music folder on a Mac). You can change the default location by opening the Project Assistant and setting a new default location, as shown in Figure 1.18. This, of course, allows you to select an external drive as opposed to the same hard drive from which Cubase is running.

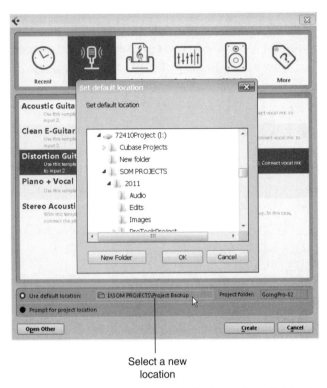

Select a new
location

Figure 1.18 Setting a new default project folder location.

> **Note:** The default setting of the Maximum Undo Step Preference in Cubase is the symbol for infinity. There's no reason to change this unless for some reason you want to limit your undo history while working in Cubase. It should not affect the performance of your system either way.

You should still back up your projects regularly using Save or Save As throughout the recording process. When you're working away on a project, you should save at least once every hour and/or immediately after you've captured an amazing performance. When you save, I never recommend just selecting Save from the File menu; instead, select Save As and then create a new name for your file. For instance, I'm recording my latest hit, "Stevesong." I will be working on this over the next few days, so today I will name it Stevesong5-15-11 (including the date) as soon as I get my project setup taken care of. In one hour, I've already done a lot of MIDI work, and now I will save it as Stevesong5-15-11a in the same project folder. Tomorrow, I'll end the day saving as Stevesong5-16-11g (after working for seven hours on the project), and the next day I'll end with a final mix and save the song as StevesongFINALMIX5-17-11 when I'm through. By the time I get to my final mix, I have about 20 different project names for "Stevesong," and I can go back into the song at any of those stages of production in case something goes wrong or I decide to make some major changes later on. Don't worry if you miss saving after one or two hours during the process of working. Just do yourself a favor and try to save as often as possible.

There's another, easier way to do this, although it isn't quite as thorough. This function is called Save New Version, and it creates a new version of your current project name. But instead of getting into so much detail (as I did in my "Stevesong" example), it simply uses the same name and puts a new number at the end (such as Stevesong-17). It doesn't take a brain surgeon to figure out that Stevesong-04 was one of the early stages of my work and Stevesong-16 was one of the latter, but the more info you can put in the name, (hopefully) the less time you'll waste when you actually want to find the version you need. To try the Save New Version method, simply press Ctrl+Alt+S on your Windows keyboard (or Command+Option+S for Macs) when you reach a good save point. This file will be created in the same project folder as your original file.

Project files don't require a lot of hard drive space. The actual audio files are the real space hogs. If you are working on a project where you've recorded a lot of audio, and you're paranoid about a hard drive crash that could wipe out all of your irreplaceable recordings, then I recommend at the end of each day (before you power down the system), you do a project backup. This process takes a little longer than a basic save because every audio file becomes duplicated in the process. The process isn't much different from just dragging your project folder (using Windows Explorer or Mac OS Finder) to another hard drive. What's better about using the backup feature in Cubase is that you can exclude certain things and sort of "clean up" your project by copying only what's really important during the backup process.

Note: A lot of people don't seem to understand that if you're going to back up your project, it does you absolutely no good to back up to the same hard drive. The whole purpose of backing up is to protect you from hard-drive failure. If you don't have another hard drive, back up to a DVD or CD. When you've done your backup, load your new backup into Cubase to make sure that it is working correctly. This takes only a moment, and it's better to do at that time than to discover later there was a problem when you were really counting on that backup to work.

To utilize Cubase's project backup feature, select Back Up Project from the File menu. (Remember to select a different drive location from the one where your original project already exists!) Enter a new project name. (I suggest including the date because you'll probably have multiple backups.) Only check the option boxes if you feel it's necessary or if you want to clean up your project, and always remember to test your backup before calling it a day.

One more thing—if your system *does* crash while you're in the middle of a recording, Steinberg claims (along with a little disclaimer) that your audio file will still be saved. The file would be in the Audio subfolder of your project folder. I personally wouldn't bet my life or my career on it. (For more information on this, see the Cubase 6 manual in the chapter labeled "Recording.")

I'll end this section with one more tip (from a guy who thought all his bases were covered). *Always shut down your system before you step away from it.* This includes external hard drives. The reason I lost one month's worth of work was because I left my office for 20 minutes, and I came back to find that the power had gone out, as well as the power on my battery backup. This resulted in a hard-drive failure on a drive I had not had a chance to back up. Ouch! Lesson learned.

Time-Saving Steps—Setting Up Key Commands and Macros

Cubase has offered key commands and macros in their software for quite some time, but a majority of users don't even know what they are, let alone utilize them.

Key commands can involve almost *any* single function in Cubase. You can custom-assign this function to any key on your QWERTY keyboard and then use that key to save yourself time. Setting up these key commands is much easier than setting up any other sort of MIDI controller, and it can save you loads of time in the studio. For less than $20, you can even find somebody out there to sell you stickers to make your computer keyboard look like an extension of Cubase. (Try Googling "Cubase sticker.")

Note: For those who aren't into customizing key commands, the pre-configured commands can also come in handy. To learn the pre-configured commands, you can reference the handy list in Chapter 44 of the Cubase manual.

To jump in and start setting up your own personal key commands, select Key Commands from the File menu. When you open the Key Commands window, you should see folders upon folders of commands appearing as they would in Windows Explorer or Mac OS Finder. You can browse through these folders and open them by selecting the plus (+) sign next to them to locate the command you would like to utilize.

Obviously, there are more commands in this list than you can fit on one keyboard. The idea is not to put every command on your keyboard, but only the commands you use on a regular basis and that are time-consuming to access.

If you don't feel like browsing through the folders, you can use the Search function to find the command you're looking for. Just enter the name of the command (usually provided somewhere in the program) and then select the Search button (magnifying glass), and it will most likely appear. If there is more than one command with a similar name, just keep selecting Search until the desired result appears. (They appear one at a time.)

When you've found the command you want, it's time to assign a key. In the Type in Key field, type the single keystroke or combination of keys that you would like to utilize for the selected command. In this example, I have decided to create an Add Audio Track command. I want to use the letter A, so I type the letter in the field and select Assign. When I do this, a warning comes up telling me that the A has been used for another command (see Figure 1.19).

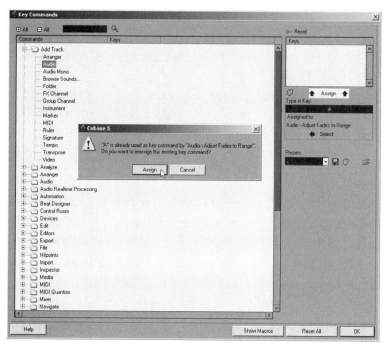

Figure 1.19 The A has already been used.

Note: You shouldn't let this warning stop you from using the keys you want to use. Most likely, all the keys have been pre-assigned to other commands. What's important is that you choose the commands that will make your life easier, and choose keys that will make it easy for you to remember. The best plan is to make a list of all the commands that you want to use and then lay them out on the computer keyboard, the same as you would design a layout for a MIDI controller. Once you have the "map" put together, you're ready to turn your QWERTY keyboard into your dream controller.

If you don't get a warning, your key selection will be assigned automatically to the command. If you *do* get a warning, simply select Assign, and your key will be assigned as you wish.

While you're browsing through the list of commands, you'll probably notice that some of them already have a letter value in the Keys column. That is because they have already been assigned by default. When you're finished making your assignments, the keys you have assigned will also be located next to their proper commands. You can use this list to refresh your memory of which key is what command at any time.

Note: Besides using single keystrokes for one command, you can also combine keys (such as Shift+A) to create more command-placement options. The key commands are not stored within individual projects, but within the Cubase program folder. Once you create a command, it will work with any and all projects you work with in Cubase.

You can save key-command setups into different presets. That way, you can create a particular key-command setup based around recording, another based around editing audio, and another based around editing MIDI (and so on) if you desire. When you need to use a previous specific setup, simply load it using the Import Key Command File button located in the Key Commands window.

Macro commands take key commands to another level. With macros, you can combine multiple commands on one key to get to the end result. Unfortunately, you can't get too specific in your commands (such as pitch shift up one octave) because you can't enter in specific values (such as the one octave). If you include a process that requires a value, your processor will appear and allow you to enter the required value, and then when you complete the process, the next process will appear. Although this can still save time, it isn't nearly as practical as setting up macro commands so that the entire process is completed in one simple keystroke. An example of this might be creating a duplicate event that is reversed to follow a selected event (to sort of get a quick "push/pull" audio effect).

To make a macro command such as the one stated in my example, select the Show Macros button to open the Macros section of the Key Commands window. Next, create a name for the macro by selecting New Macro and entering a name that describes your command (in this example, Duplicate and Reverse). Next, with the new macro selected, find each of the commands in the list above that is necessary to complete the new macro command. When you find each command, click Add Command while it is highlighted, and it will appear below your new macro name. When you have all of the necessary commands under your macro, click Okay.

Your new macro is now ready for you to assign a keystroke to it. Locate the Macro folder in the list of command folders. Your new macro command should be in that folder. Assign a keystroke to the macro using the same method you used to assign any key command and then click OK. Your new macro should be ready to go. This is one of those things that you have to double-check in Cubase and possibly make alterations if necessary. If you *do* need to make alterations, just click the Show Macros button again.

You can delete commands (by clicking Delete) that don't work and/or add new commands to the existing macros. Just remember to click OK to exit. Figure 1.20 shows my new macro in its creation stage.

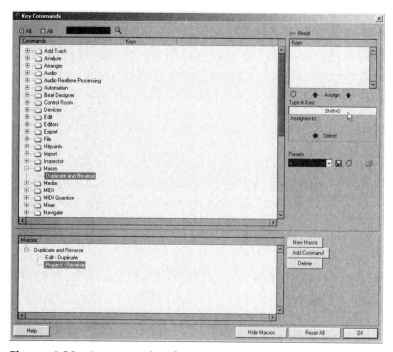

Figure 1.20 An example of a macro command being created.

Juggling Windows When the Pressure Is On

When I started using Cubase in 1990, there was one window allowed on the screen at a time. Back then, it was all my poor little Atari computer could handle. Now, there can be so many things happening at once in Cubase that you need 20 different windows open at once just to figure out what you're doing.

The growing number of windows you need to use is spreading like a disease, and I doubt it's going to get any better, since our demands are getting higher and higher. The only problem with having too many windows open at once is that it makes for a ridiculously messy workspace. The last thing you need in the middle of a session (when the musicians are ready and psyched to perform) is to stop the show and make everyone wait because you can't find your Transport.

The key to proper window juggling is (like everything else I've gone over so far) proper organization. Sure, it definitely helps to have a multi-monitor display, but even if you're using multiple monitors, you need an organized workspace at all times. (Cubase refers to the arrangement of your windows as a *workspace*.) You might laugh about the example I used regarding the missing Transport window, but I bet you've all been there before.

To properly organize your windows, you need to have a generalized idea of editors or controls you'll need to have at your fingertips to perform a certain task (whether it's working with your virtual synths, mixing, recording vocals, and so on). Then you need to arrange those in your workspace in the way that works best for you when performing those tasks.

Your workspace appears the moment you start up Cubase. Even though the display might look like a blank canvas, it's still considered a workspace. When you save your project, it saves it the way you left it. If you have multiple editors spread out across the workspace when you save a project, that will be what you see when you load that project the next time.

Workspaces affect only the appearance of Cubase. If you were to close a few open windows and resave your project, it would make only a *visual* difference in your project. (For instance, if you closed a window for a delay plug-in, you'd still have that delay in your project.)

Cubase allows you to save workspaces and recall them when needed. This is sort of like taking a snapshot of your setup, then rearranging your setup, and then recalling that original snapshot again. Just to show you what this workspace might look like, Figure 1.21 shows a workspace that I have set up for recording vocals.

Figure 1.21 A snapshot of my vocal-recording workspace.

Now that I've arranged all of my controls the way I like them, saving the workspace is easy. From the Window menu, select New Workspace, enter a name (such as "Vocal Recording"), and click OK. After you've created the new workspace, you can view it by selecting Organize from the Workspace menu (located in the Window menu). When the Organize Workspace dialog appears, select the square under the Locked column that corresponds to your new workspace. By locking this workspace, every time you select it, it will appear just as you have set it up.

There are two types of workspaces you can set up. The default is the workspace that is saved with your project and is unique to the particular project on which you are working. A *global* workspace is one that you can open in any project, and it will work. A global workspace will not remember your actual settings, but it will remember the layout of the windows and their customized size (if applicable). Keep in mind this means that if your processors aren't loaded or you don't have your tracks created, you won't see anything when using a global preset workspace.

To turn your project workspace into a global workspace, select Organize from the Workspace menu located under the Window menu. The Organize Workspaces dialog box will appear (see Figure 1.22). From the Workspaces list on the left, select the project workspace that you would like to make into a global workspace and then select the right arrow button (located between the two lists). Your project workspace has now become a global workspace preset. Now it exists as both a project workspace and a global workspace.

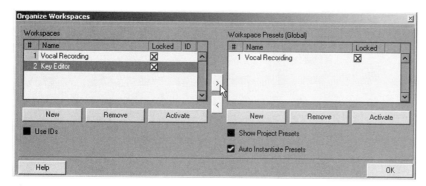

Figure 1.22 Organizing the workspace presets.

At this point, you can delete the project workspace (if you would like to clean up your existing project workspaces) by selecting it and clicking Remove. The global preset will remain intact during this process. The global presets are saved in your system and in the project (in case you open your project on another system). You can copy global presets back into the project by selecting the global workspace from the right side of the dialog and moving it to the left side using the left arrow button in the center. At this point, you are able to unlock and store them with that particular project with the settings still intact (effects settings, presets, levels, and so on). To automatically copy the global presets into the project from the beginning, check the Auto Instantiate Presets box.

Note: Another handy feature is that you can assign key commands to each global workspace preset to quickly adjust your views in Cubase. Just reference the corresponding preset number and the workspace presets commands located in the Workspace folder in the Key Commands window.

Besides using workspaces, if for some reason you run into problems, you can find all currently active windows listed at the bottom of the Window menu. With regard to the Transport (as in the earlier example), if you can't find it under the Window menu, it probably was closed by accident. You can always reopen it from the Devices menu. Most windows have an Always on Top feature, which can also prevent windows from getting buried in the heap (see Figure 1.23). Just right-click on the upper-left corner of the window to open the context menu. Even though it says Always on Top, keep in mind that there can be only one "king of the hill" window at one time!

> Note: Just for the record, by default Cubase is set up so that you can hide and display the Transport by using the F2 key command.

Figure 1.23 The Always on Top option.

More Steps to Save Yourself a Few Headaches

I've covered quite a lot in this chapter with regard to streamlining Cubase so that it fits your needs like a glove, but there are still quite a few things you can do to take it even further. First of all, there are even more ways to customize Cubase:

- **Customizing the toolbar.** This one's super easy to do, but it is often overlooked. Are there items on the toolbar that you never use and have no intention of using? Or maybe you can't even see all the tools that exist for you. If you right-click on the toolbar (above the ruler), a list of tools will appear with check marks. If you're still using the default settings, guess what—you're not seeing all the tools. Take this opportunity to place a check next to tools that you could be using and uncheck tools that will just get in your way. Also, if you run into tools you don't understand, take the time to read up on them in the manual. Did you know that each editor has its own set of tools on the toolbar? Cubase is a deep program, and it's easy to miss things if you're not using it to its full potential every day.

- **Customizing the track display.** You can also add and remove buttons from each track. Cubase comes with a factory default setup, but there's a lot more you can do with it. (For example, if you're not into using lanes or drum maps, why clutter your tracks with them?) Also, have you ever run out of space when typing in a track name and just abbreviated it? You can lengthen the name field in the same place. Right-click on any track in an empty area within the track display and select Track Control Settings to make your adjustments. Keep in mind that each track type has its own display settings.

- **Customizing the Transport.** Are you using the Transport to its full potential? Right-click on the Transport and select Show All. The Transport has become massive, as it now also contains a mini keyboard. There are so many useful features right at your fingertips, and you might not even know they exist if you just started using Cubase right out of the box.

- **Customizing the Inspector.** If you right-click at the top of the Inspector when it's open, you'll get a list of everything in the Inspector. You can check or uncheck anything that you want to appear or disappear from view. Some people don't even use the Inspector because it's hidden almost too well. If you don't know what the Inspector is, you should check it out in the Cubase manual.

- **Customizing the Mixer.** The Mixer can be full of detail. Are you getting what you need out of it? Take the time to explore the Mixer to its fullest and customize the views to fit your needs.

- **Customizing the Edit Audio/MIDI Channel Setting display.** That handy little "e" button located on each channel brings up one of the most useful tools in Cubase: the Edit Channel Settings display. This display offers more features than most are aware of, and you can expose them by right-clicking almost anywhere in the display.

- **Taking advantage of using the Quick Controls.** The Quick Controls are easy to set up using the Learn feature. With them, you can use any (generic) control surface (as well as the virtual controls) to control the definable parameters in Cubase. For more information, search the Cubase Manual for Quick Controls. I discuss using the Quick Controls with HALion Sonic SE in Chapter 2.

- **Checking out and using the new Set Up Window Layout button.** In an effort to combat the ever-increasing number of windows, Cubase 6 utilizes a new way to hide/display windows (see Figure 1.24). This Set Up Window Layout button appears on the toolbar and also in the bottom-left corner of the MediaBay. You can use it with different windows to show or hide other windows that you regularly use or don't use. When first selected, it displays a gray option window option box, and this box closes on its own after a short time.

Of course, general computer maintenance is always important when it comes to using Cubase. Keep those hard drives defragged. Disable your hard drives from entering "sleep" mode if possible. Keep updating your operating system. Keep checking with www.steinberg.net for updates. Cubase 6 comes with a lot of new little features that

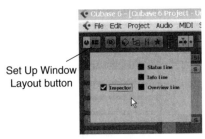

Set Up Window
Layout button

Figure 1.24 The new Set Up Window Layout button, as shown from the Project Window toolbar.

were not around in previous versions. I try to cover most of them in this book, but if you see something new that you don't recognize, check the manual for more information. All of this is important. If you need more information on optimizing your computer system, please check out another one of my books, *Your Cubase Studio* (Course Technology PTR, 2008), or refer to Steinberg's web support at www.steinberg.net.

2 Maximizing MIDI in Cubase 6

There are plenty of pros working in the world who don't use MIDI during the recording process. MIDI is what Cubase was built on and where it truly shines as a DAW. For me, the MIDI features in Cubase are the key ingredients for how I make my living as a composer/producer. If you're one of the pros who isn't a keyboard player, don't let that stop you from exploring the world of MIDI. It's really not as difficult as some might think.

> **Note:** I encourage those who aren't familiar with MIDI to read my book, *MIDI Editing in Cubase: Skill Pack* (Course Technology PTR, 2007). The book was written for beginners, but it also summarizes the vast world of MIDI in Cubase, and you can use the included CD-ROM to follow along with some exercises. The CD-ROM is revolutionary for Cubase training because you can actually hear, see, touch, and alter the MIDI, unlike with most books that make you start from scratch. Even though the book and CD-ROM were written for Cubase 4, they work and hold up well with Cubase 6.

Primarily, this chapter's main goal is to go over MIDI features that often get overlooked or are too difficult for most MIDI novices to learn. I'll also be going over the new MIDI features included in Cubase 6.

Taking MIDI to New Levels with Note Expression

I've heard some people say that MIDI is dying or that it's on its way out. Of course, I've already discussed how important MIDI is to me, and I dismiss all of these rumors. That being said, one thing I've noticed is that even though MIDI and Cubase have both been around for nearly 30 years, the way we work with MIDI (besides the addition of VST instruments) hasn't really changed dramatically in the last 20 years.

Leave it to Steinberg to once again approach MIDI with an open mind and reinvent MIDI with their addition of Note Expression in Cubase 6. VST Expression was introduced in Cubase 5. Even though VST Expression is a very cool feature (particularly for those who utilize the scoring tools in Cubase), Note Expression opens up new doors to *anyone* who uses MIDI.

> **Note:** To summarize, VST Expression has to do with creating audible dynamics (utilizing MIDI controllers) by using standardized musical articulations (such as the symbols for forte, piano, staccato, legato, and so on). To make the most out of VST Expression, you can set up expression maps within Cubase that translate those age-old, tried-and-true musical commands into real working MIDI controller commands. If you're utilizing the scoring features and not yet using VST Expression, you're missing out. I'll touch on VST Expression and Expression Maps in this chapter, but to learn more about VST Expression, go to Help/Documentation/Operation Manual/Part 1/Expression Maps in Cubase.

For anyone who's ever used or edited MIDI controller data in Cubase, Note Expression offers a whole new world of possibilities. In the past, we'd been limited to utilizing and editing MIDI controllers in controller lanes. Obviously, we've been able to do quite a bit under those limitations, because we've been using controller lanes for years with no major complaints.

One of the big issues with controller data is that it's sent out as channel-specific data. What this means in layman's terms is that if you were adding, for example, pitch-bend controller data to a MIDI track that contained several notes that were played simultaneously, such as those in a four-note chord, the pitch-bend data would be applied to the entire chord as opposed to maybe one or two notes from that chord.

We've found ways of working around this in the past. Perhaps we would record part of the chord from another "copy" of that instrument and then pitch-bend that single note as a completely separate MIDI track/channel. Note Expression offers a new, simple approach to this. Using Note Expression, we can apply these controller commands to the individual notes as opposed to the entire track. This means you can add pitch bend, volume changes, panning, and so on to each individual note on your track as opposed to simply applying it on every note within that track.

But wait! There's a catch. MIDI was not really designed to do this. In order for Steinberg to make these advances, they had to reinvent MIDI to a certain degree. This means that old synths will *not* recognize this new data. This "new" MIDI is available in instruments that utilize VST3.5 (invented by Steinberg) technology. VST3.5 not only allows instruments to respond to note-specific controller data, but also expands the original MIDI range (0–127) and makes for much more natural-sounding data curves.

Since the range has increased, you no longer have major jumps in volume/pitch changes between each increment. Old synths will still respond to MIDI controllers from within Note Expression, but it will affect the rest of the notes that are playing simultaneously alongside the edited note (within the same track), just as if the controller was applied in a controller lane. But don't throw out your old synths to replace them all with VST3.5

instruments just yet, because they're still great. Steinberg recommends that you continue to utilize controller lanes for these synths, just as you have done in the past.

The good news is that Cubase 6 comes with one VST instrument (HALion Sonic SE) that is already set up with VST3.5 technology. HALion Sonic SE is sort of a cross between HALion One and its bigger brother, HALion 3. There's also a 45-day demo trial for the full-blown version of HALion Sonic. (The full upgrade is currently available through Steinberg for $199, which is a great deal considering the large library of programs/sounds that you get with it.)

I'm not going to go into a lot of detail on HALion Sonic SE because the manual (located at Help/Documentation/HALion Sonic SE) is quite detailed. HALion Sonic is multi-timbral (which means it can load up to 16 programs/sounds at once), and it can export key-switch maps (maps are automatically created to match musical articulations).

HALion Sonic SE and HALion Sonic are currently the *only* VST3.5 instruments that we have available to work with. Knowing Steinberg, we're sure to see some more powerful VST3.5 (and greater) instruments to come in the near future.

Utilizing VST3.5 with HALion Sonic SE

Cubase 6 offers a detailed tutorial on using Note Expression (located at Help/Documentation/Operation Manual/ Part 1/Note Expression). The manual goes into specifics on how you can record Note Expression via MIDI or by using controller surfaces and so on. Because VST3.5 is new, and currently the only available instrument is HALion Sonic SE, I'm simply going to show you how to utilize Note Expression the same way you would edit from within a controller lane and focus on the parameters that are included in some HALion Sonic SE programs. Just keep in mind that even though I believe I'm demonstrating what seems to be the most practical way of utilizing Note Expression, there are other ways to work with it.

> **Note:** The VST3.5 parameters that you can work with in Note Expression depend on the available parameters of the instrument itself (not Cubase). Not all programs that come with HALion Sonic SE share the same Note Expression parameters (as I will demonstrate in the tutorial).

There are a couple of ways to open HALion Sonic SE in Cubase 6. You can open it from VST instruments or by double-clicking on a sound/program from within the MediaBay. By double-clicking in the MediaBay, you'll be creating an Instrument track, and all programs loaded on that instance of HALion Sonic SE will be routed through its stereo outputs. Because this is the easiest way to route, it's the way I'll choose for this example.

Note: HALion Sonic SE should be located under your VST Instruments/Synths heading after installing Cubase 6. For some reason, it wasn't available when I first installed Cubase 6 on my setup. This could be some sort of bug in the installer and may be specific to my setup. If it isn't installed yet on your system, you can find the setup programs on the Cubase 6 installer disc from the Windows or Mac folder /Additional Content/VST Sound. From within the VST Sound folder, install both the HALion Sonic SE (64-bit if you're working on a 64-bit version of Cubase) and HALion Sonic SE content before continuing. Also, if you want, you can install the demo version of the full-blown HALion Sonic as well. Using the HALion Sonic demo, you get access to more sounds and some other features for a limited time.

Open the MediaBay and locate the VST Sound folder in the browser. Open the VST Sound folder, locate the HALion Sonic SE Common Presets folder, and select the folder so that all of the HALion Sonic SE programs are located in the Results window. From the Results window, locate the programs called Natural Nylon NoteExp, Clean Blues Harp NoteExp, and Phasing Clavinet. Double-click on each program so that an Instrument track is created for each instrument in the Project window.

Record some MIDI on each track with each instrument. Make sure to include some chords. You can mute each separate track, if necessary, once you've recorded it. In this example, we're going to be looking at each track and its Note Expression one at a time.

When you have MIDI recorded on all three tracks, select one of the tracks and also select the Note Expression tab from the Inspector, as shown in Figure 2.1.

Closely examine the Note Expression data in the Inspector and alternate Instrument tracks so that you can see the differences between the three instruments. (You can compare them to Figure 2.2.) First examine Phasing Clavinet. Notice that it contains three solid boxes, colored red, orange, and yellow, and they are labeled Volume, Pan, and Tuning. These boxes are solid because they represent the VST3.5 parameters that are available for this program.

The multicolored empty boxes below the solid-colored boxes represent standard MIDI controllers. Those particular MIDI controllers behave the exact same way as if they were created in controller lanes. The only difference with them is that having them here allows you to assign the controllers to specific notes.

As mentioned before, MIDI controllers will affect every note on the channel, so if you were to use one of these controllers on one note at a time at the same time as there are other notes playing on the same track, the MIDI controller would affect the other notes as well. For this reason, I suggest that you use only the VST3.5 parameters (solid boxes) for now and stick to editing MIDI controllers using the controller lanes below, just as you would if Note Expression never existed.

Figure 2.1   Selecting Note Expression from the Inspector on a HALion Sonic SE Instrument track.

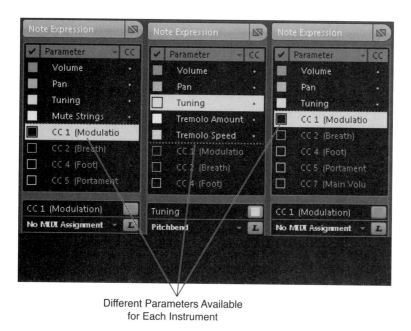

Different Parameters Available
for Each Instrument

Figure 2.2   A closer look at the Note Expression tab in the Inspector (edited to fit into one image).

Examining the Natural Nylon NoteExp, you'll notice that it has one more VST3.5 parameter that Phasing Clavinet doesn't have: Mute Strings. Examining Clean Blues Harp NoteExp, you'll notice that it has two additional VST3.5 parameters that Phasing Clavinet does not have: Tremolo Amount and Tremolo Speed.

Note: Just for the record, every program in HALion Sonic SE contains VST3.5 parameters for Volume, Pan, and Tuning. Every program that contains NoteExp in its name contains *extra* parameters.

Now, double-click on the MIDI part that you recorded for the Clean Blues Harp Note-Exp. Doing so will open the MIDI part in the Key Editor. Open the Inspector in the Key Editor once again so that you can select the Note Expression tab for the Instrument track, as you did in the previous step. Next, locate and activate the Show Note Expression button. This button looks similar to the Bypass Note Expression button found on the Note Expression tab in the Inspector. It is located on the toolbar between the Auto Select Controllers button and Show Part Borders button (shown in Figure 2.3).

Figure 2.3 The Show Note Expression button on the toolbar.

Notice the small slider to the right of the button. You can use this slider later to change the zoom on your Note Expression data so that it is easily viewable from within the Key Editor. Next, select the Tuning parameter from within the Note Expression tab in the Inspector so that it is highlighted. Now double-click on one of the notes in a chord that you created so that the Note Expression Editor opens up on the selected note (as shown in Figure 2.4).

The Note Expression Editor might appear somewhat small at first. You can change the zoom from within the Key Editor to zoom in closer on the note you're working with. You can also expand/contract the height of the Note Expression Editor by selecting the = symbol at the bottom and dragging up or down.

You cannot adjust the length of the editor beyond the normal zooming from within the Key Editor. When you're editing from within the Note Expression Editor, you mostly use the same editing tools (Pencil tool, Line tool, and so on) that you would normally use from within the Key Editor. The Note Expression Editor also comes with its own (almost hidden) tools, as shown in Figure 2.5.

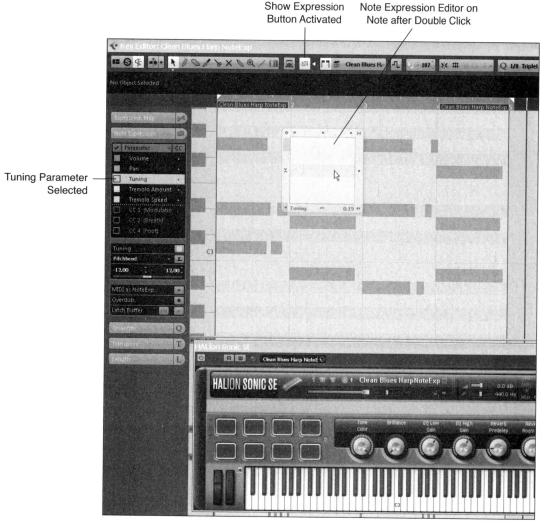

Figure 2.4 Opening the Note Expression Editor from within the Key Editor.

Vertical Snap and Horizontal Snap are both useful when creating edits that are in step increments. Vertical Snap affects pitch steps, and Horizontal Snap affects time steps in the same way that snap in any editor works with the quantize settings. Using both of these snap functions together is a great way to create pitched "steps" using the Tuning parameter.

One-Shot mode is to help you create a straight line. This is useful when you're editing a fixed value (such as if you want a note to be one particular volume level from the start to the end of the note).

The Value display is useful for determining the value of the parameter you're working with. When you're working with pitch, for example, it displays semitones and cents.

The Release Length feature is useful for when you need your controller data to go beyond the length of a note to obtain a more natural-sounding affect.

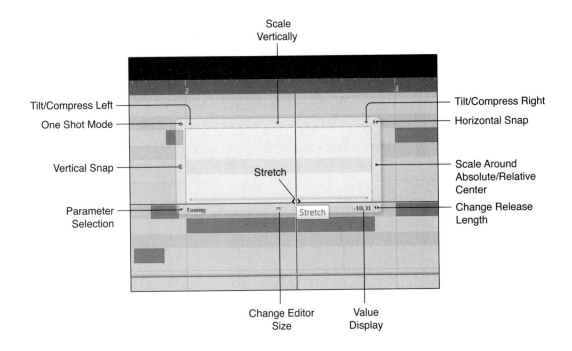

Figure 2.5 A close-up of the tools in the Note Expression Editor.

The rest of the tools are referred to as *smart spots*. Move Vertically allows you to move the controller data up or down within the Editor without affecting the curve. Scale Vertically allows you to adjust the overall size of the curve without changing the actual curve itself. Stretch works sort of like Time Stretch and allows you to expand or contract the length of the data, which in turn affects the length of the curve. Scale Around Absolute/Relative Center and Tilt/Compress Left/Right are six other ways to modify the curve. To access the alternate controls, hold down Alt/Option while selecting the type. All of these tools alter the curve using similar methods as the scale and stretch tools, with slight variations.

Since you've selected Tuning from within Note Expression tab, select the Vertical Snap and Horizontal Snap (make sure One-Shot mode is *not* active) and, using the Pencil tool, create a four-stair-step pitch shift on your note so that its pitch is two whole steps higher at the end of the note (as shown in Figure 2.6).

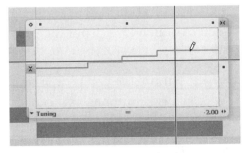

Figure 2.6 Creating pitch change steps on one note in a chord.

After you've made your changes, play the track back and listen. Notice that the only note that's pitch-shifted is the note you singled out. This is thanks to VST3.5 technology and would not be possible when using standard MIDI pitch bend controllers.

Now select the Tremolo Amount parameter from the Note Expression tab and deselect the Vertical Snap and Horizontal Snap tools. Select the One-Shot Mode tool and, using the Line tool, create a line from left to right at the top of the editor. (This raises the tremolo amount.)

Next, select the Tremolo Speed parameter and, using the Pencil tool, draw a curve that goes from the bottom left to the top of the editor and then back down to the bottom right. If your acoustic feedback is active, you should hear the tremolo speed increase and then decrease on the note as you draw the line.

Examine the bottom-left corner by placing the mouse pointer at the arrow pointing down (see Figure 2.7). All three parameters that you've used should be listed here. If you need to re-edit one of the parameters, you can select it from this list and proceed with editing. Play back your track and listen to your note with its new VST expression!

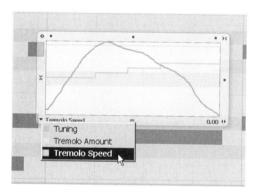

Figure 2.7   Three different Note Expression edits on the same note.

If you need to delete the Note Expression you've created, you can select Remove Note Expression from the Note Expression heading located under the MIDI menu. This command will remove only the Note Expression from the selected note.

You can copy and paste a Note Expression from one note to another, as well as select and simultaneously edit multiple notes at once using multiple methods, including the standard commands. Also, if you find that you need to narrow or widen the editing range for each parameter (such as setting your tuning range to 12 semitones as opposed to 2 semitones), you can adjust the range where the currently selected parameter is listed on the Note Expression tab in the Inspector (see Figure 2.8).

There's a lot more to cover on Note Expression, but this should be plenty to get you started. For more information, such as using controllers, recording Expression via

Figure 2.8 Adjusting the parameter's range.

MIDI, or transforming Note Expression data, please refer to the Cubase manual, as I mentioned at the start of this chapter.

Utilizing VST Expression in the Key Editor

As I mentioned earlier, VST Expression was introduced in Cubase 5 and was accessible from within the Score Editor. Now, along with Note Expression, VST Expression can be utilized from within the Key Editor. This tutorial will pick up where we left off in demonstrating Note Expression in the previous tutorial and will demonstrate how you can utilize VST3.5 instruments with VST Expression from within the Key Editor.

First of all, I'd like to take a moment to explain why VST Expression is important even for those who do not concentrate on scoring and notation in Cubase. Most acoustic instruments sound different when they're played certain ways. The dynamics at which an instrument is played change the tonality and sound of the instrument itself. For instance, a saxophone that is overblown will sound a lot different than a soft, breathy sax.

For this reason, we often have sample libraries that reflect different tonalities of the same instrument. Most advanced sample libraries might contain multiple samples on each key for when the instrument is played with different dynamics. In other words, when you press a controller key softly, a soft dynamic of the instrument will be heard, and vice versa when you press down hard on that key. This process of assigning different tonal samples to different keyboard velocities is referred to as *velocity mapping*.

Also, acoustic instruments are often played in ways that are impossible to replicate using a MIDI keyboard. For instance, a sax note fall-off could somewhat be duplicated with a pitch-bend wheel and a keyboard, but chances are it will not sound natural. Because of this, key switching has also become an important feature in working with sample libraries.

Key switching works fairly simply. When you select a certain designated key from the keyboard, the sample that is currently selected will switch to a completely different sample. This makes it easy to quickly change from a straight-played saxophone to a saxophone played with fall-offs or a saxophone played staccato (short) or legato (long).

For a long time, it has also been difficult, particularly for long sustained parts (such as strings), to have dynamics that constantly change throughout the performance. Using a similar concept to velocity mapping, you can now utilize VST Expression to not only trigger certain dynamics at the start of the note, but actually trigger all of the available dynamics and then crossfade between those dynamics as the note is sustained. This, for instance, makes crescendos and decrescendos sound much more realistic.

The biggest problem with utilizing these dynamics in the past was that there is no such thing as standardized dynamic settings for different sample libraries. This meant that if you decided a particular sample wasn't working for you and you switched to another, your dynamic changes and key switching all would have to be reprogrammed via MIDI editing.

Utilizing the Expression Maps in Cubase, you can now specify your sampler's instrument settings so that you never have to alter the programmed dynamic changes again (see Figure 2.9). Setting up Expression Maps can become a little tedious, but once your maps are set up, creating expressive musical arrangements is a breeze.

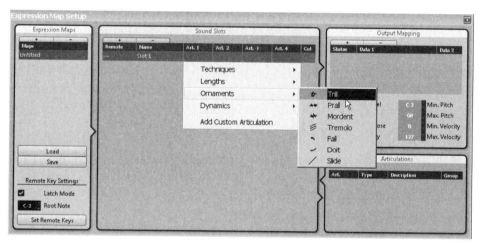

Figure 2.9 Creating Expression Maps in the Expression Map Setup window.

Another great thing about VST3.5 instruments is that sometimes you don't even have to set up the Expression Maps yourself. Going back to our Note Expression tutorial, refer to the Natural Nylon NoteExp track from within the Project window. Select the Expression Maps tab from the Inspector while the Instrument track for Natural Nylon NoteExp is selected. Click where it reads "No Expression Map" from within the Expression Maps tab. From there, select Import Key Switches, as shown in Figure 2.10.

Once the key switches are imported, you will notice that there are four separate articulations included with that particular instrument: Open, Whole Hammer On, Semi Slide Up, and Harmonics.

Now double-click on your MIDI part so that the Key Editor opens. From the bottom, right-click in any existing controller lane and create a new lane using Create Controller

Figure 2.10 Importing pre-configured key switches for a program from HALion Sonic SE.

Lane. After creating a new controller lane, select Articulations/Dynamics from the list of controllers, as shown in Figure 2.11. After you've created the articulations/dynamics lane, you might want to expand the view in the lane so that you can easily read the key switches and the word "Dynamics" from within the lane.

You can now easily insert key switches and dynamic changes from within the Key Editor. Start by using the Draw tool at the beginning of the part next to the dynamics lane within the articulations/dynamics lane.

When you first create dynamics, the default dynamic is *mf*. You can change this easily by using the drop-down menu at the top of the dynamics lane. To make a dynamics change, simply use the Pencil tool once again at another place and create a new dynamic.

Listen back to your changes. Depending on how extensive the dynamics mapping is (in the case of this particular instrument, it's not that extensive), you can get very detailed in the dynamics (from *pppp* to *ffff*). You can also add crescendos and decrescendos.

Next, use the Pencil tool to create articulations in the nylon-string guitar part. Start by selecting the open lane (which is the standard-sounding nylon-string guitar sample). Then later, switch to any one of the other key-switch lanes to hear how the sound has changed to a different articulation (see Figure 2.12).

Note: When creating dynamics/articulation events, the event will be continuous from the start to the end of the part. This is because you cannot have more than one dynamic or one articulation occurring at the same time within one MIDI part.

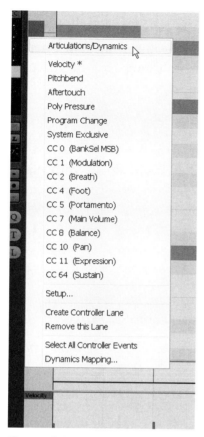

Figure 2.11 Creating an articulations/dynamics lane within the Key Editor.

Figure 2.12 Editing dynamics and articulations from within the articulations/dynamics lane.

As you can see, utilizing dynamics and articulations can be beneficial for all MIDI programmers. As I mentioned before, the Cubase manual goes into a lot more detail about how to create your own maps for your existing sample library so that you can take full advantage of Cubase 6 and all of your preexisting instruments.

Using Quick Controls with HALion Sonic SE

One of the great new features of using HALion Sonic SE in Cubase 6 is easy access to its Quick Controls. Every program in HALion Sonic SE has been set up with eight easily controllable parameters that can greatly affect the overall sound of the program when altered. The parameters are then added automatically to the Instrument track's Quick Controls, which are easily accessible from within the Project window. This means you can easily tweak your sounds from within the Project window without having to open the HALion Sonic SE VST instrument panel.

To view the Quick Controls, open the Quick Controls tab from within the Inspector on any selected HALion Sonic SE Instrument track (as shown in Figure 2.13).

From the Quick Controls panel, you can easily make changes to HALion Sonic's program and also automate the parameters.

Monitoring Raw MIDI

When it comes to seeing MIDI data being received into Cubase, most users refer to the MIDI activity indicator on the track or Transport. When you see the indicator bouncing as you hit a key on the keyboard, you know you're receiving a MIDI signal. If you wanted to know more details (such as the particular key that was pressed, how hard it was pressed, controller info, and so on) before the signal is actually recorded, you've been out of luck and had to use other software, such as MIDI-OX (a third-party freeware MIDI utility program for Windows), to see what was truly going on with your MIDI.

In Cubase 5, Steinberg integrated a MIDI plug-in so that you can monitor the raw MIDI signal in a more detailed fashion (see Figure 2.14) without having to exit Cubase.

To access the MIDI Monitor, select any MIDI track and then select MIDI Monitor from the list of insert effects. With the MIDI Monitor, you can see live events as they happen directly from the output to the input of Cubase. You can filter the view of certain data without affecting the data itself by using any of the preset filter tabs on the effect. Even though this new utility doesn't quite have the capabilities that MIDI-OX has, it's simple and very effective. The primary need for the MIDI Monitor is to analyze data, and it helps in troubleshooting.

Using the New Virtual Keyboard

While we're on the subject of utilities and monitoring, let's take a moment to go over the new virtual keyboard located on the Transport panel (see Figure 2.15). As a keyboardist, my first reaction to this new feature was, "Huh? Why would we need

Figure 2.13   Accessing HALion Sonic SE's Quick Controls.

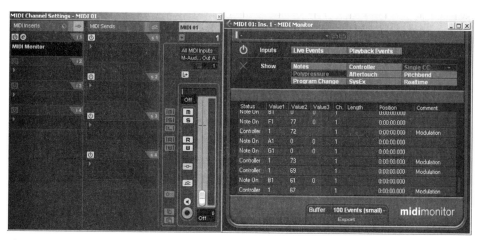

Figure 2.14   The MIDI Monitor insert effect in Cubase 6.

something silly like that when we've got a real keyboard?" It's by no means a replacement for a MIDI keyboard, especially if you're a keyboard player. But what's great about the virtual keyboard is that now (if you're not a keyboard player and you want to add some MIDI notes to your recording) you can type in your notes rather than drawing them in. This is a huge timesaver for non-keyboard-player programmers who still have a basic understanding of the octave range on a piano keyboard.

Figure 2.15   The virtual keyboard on the Transport in QWERTY mode.

The best part is that you don't even need to have a MIDI keyboard connected to input real MIDI data in real time; you can use this virtual keyboard as a quick alternative MIDI tester to make sure that your VST instruments are working correctly and there's not just some other MIDI communication issue from your controller to the MIDI input in Cubase.

To view the virtual keyboard, select it from the Transport's display menu by right-clicking on the Transport and then selecting Virtual Keyboard from the top of the menu or by selecting it from the Devices menu. By default, the keyboard appears in what I call *QWERTY mode*. In this view, you see your QWERTY keyboard laid out in a pattern similar to that of a piano keyboard. The letter Q represents the pitch C, the number 2 represents C sharp, and so on through to the letter I, which represents one octave above the original C.

Numbers 1, 4, and 8 are irrelevant on the QWERTY keyboard because they fall in non-piano-keyboard-like places. This means when you type a Q on your QWERTY keyboard, you should hear (and input) a C-pitched note.

You can adjust the single octave to focus on any of the seven octaves in the keyboard's seven-octave range (C1 through C5) by using the virtual buttons located just below the virtual keyboard. You can adjust the input velocity by using the slider on the right of the keyboard. You can also switch the view to a keyboard that has more of a piano-style look.

Keep in mind that with this display you still can only utilize the same keys on your QWERTY keyboard, but you can also use your mouse to play other keys (or perhaps do one of those Jerry Lee Lewis piano slides). Also, when using your QWERTY keyboard, notes are all entered at the fixed default velocity. This means that performances will not be touch-sensitive, as they would be when using a touch-sensitive MIDI keyboard.

Of course, in order to hear anything, you'll need to have a MIDI track with its output selected to an activated VST instrument (or external synth). You also can use this virtual keyboard to audition your synths when using the MediaBay. So even though this little keyboard is limiting, it can be a handy feature to have at your disposal (especially for the ever-expanding group of laptop DAW users out there).

Advanced Quantize and Groove Features

Cubase has always been great about giving you multiple ways to quantize MIDI in order to give you your desired grooves. Even with all of these tools available, there are times when simply *not* quantizing your MIDI is the best way to preserve a groove. The "human" factor is extremely hard to calculate, and even though we work so hard to obtain a "tight" live performance, it's the little imperfections from each individual player that give the groove its particular "color."

Quantizing MIDI has changed slightly from Version 5 to Version 6. Now, due to the extensive work in quantizing audio in Cubase 6, the quantize functions are located under the Edit menu (as opposed to the MIDI menu). And now it's simply named Quantize as opposed to Over Quantize.

To undo the quantization, you select Reset Quantize instead of Undo. You can switch easily from the standard Quantize to Iterative Quantize from the Quantize display by selecting the Q or iQ. You also can easily open the Quantize panel (to make your Iterative Quantize setting) by selecting the small arrow on the right side of the toolbar's Quantize display. The Advanced MIDI Quantize features, such as Quantize Lengths, Quantize Ends, and Freeze Quantize, are now also located under the Edit menu and contain the word MIDI in their name (because these special quantize features are not yet available for audio quantizing).

Another major difference in Cubase 6 is the quantize grid itself. Now, you can adjust more accurately the grid to match your complex quantize settings (such as 1/4 triplet, 1/2 dotted, and so on). Simply select Use Quantize when setting your grid and select the appropriate quantize setting from the Quantize display. The Key Editor and the Drum Editor also contain a Quantize tab in each of their Inspectors with all MIDI Quantize options.

Quantizing MIDI Parts to an Audio Groove

Whether you use a loop or a drum recording, if you record drums (or any instrument, for that matter) without using MIDI, you are going to be working with an *audio groove*. Quantizing MIDI to an audio groove actually has become a somewhat simple process in Cubase 6, but it's still not quite a perfect science, as it is when working only with MIDI.

The first step in the process is to analyze the audio groove and create hitpoints.

Note: *Hitpoints* are virtual markers in Cubase that are used to identify where the accents of the groove (or beat) are. In a way, hitpoints are there to create a MIDI representation of the audio groove. You can use hitpoints not only to create a MIDI "map" for your other parts, but also to quantize and alter the tempo (as you would a REX file) of your audio groove.

Before creating hitpoints, you want to make sure that your audio groove is locked to the tempo and is edited to start at the beginning of a measure. The goal is to capture the main groove of the audio file (not necessarily the entire audio part), so cut your audio groove to fit between two or four measures to keep it from getting too complicated. This preparation makes your job a lot easier.

Cubase 6 has added a new feature that automatically calculates hitpoints in an audio groove and then creates a MIDI groove from those hitpoints. To use this feature, first select the audio groove and then select Create Groove Quantize Preset, located in the Edit menu under Advanced Quantize.

This new automated feature can save you a couple of steps, but sometimes automated features don't work like they're supposed to. For this reason, I'm going to take you through the process so that you can modify the automatic calculations if necessary.

Select and open the audio file in the Sample Editor by double-clicking on the audio track in the Project window. When you open your file in the Sample Editor, you should see the two- or four-measure groove highlighted, as well as any audio that happens before and after your selected groove.

Make sure the Inspector is showing within the Sample Editor window by selecting Show Inspector from the toolbar located just below the menus. Once the Inspector is showing on the left of the Sample Editor window, select the Hitpoints tab from the left of the window. Next, activate Edit Hitpoints.

Because you selected Create Groove Quantize Preset as your first step, hitpoints have been automatically created on the transient attacks of the audio groove. If for some reason some of the transient attacks do not contain hitpoints, you can adjust the hitpoint calculation by holding down the mouse and dragging from left to right under the Threshold setting (see Figure 2.16). This might take a little tweaking to get right, depending on the actual recording and groove.

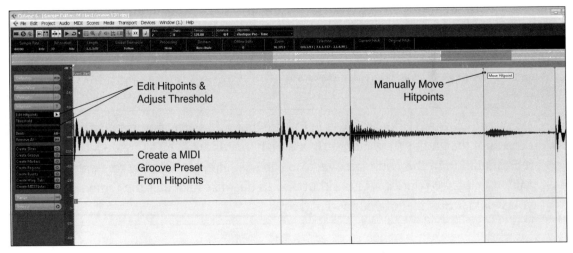

Figure 2.16 Editing hitpoints in the Sample Editor for my audio groove.

You can also audition each section (between hitpoints) by clicking in that section using the Audition tool. This can help you determine whether you are spreading enough hitpoints across your groove. If you need to make minor adjustments to the location of the hitpoint, you can do so by selecting the hitpoint event (located at the top, by the ruler) and moving it left or right on the ruler timeline. You can also disable the hitpoint by selecting the *x* at the top of the hitpoint. Disabling a hitpoint is something you'd want to do only if there were too many hitpoints created for one particular hit on the groove.

Technically, by utilizing the Create Groove Quantize Preset feature, you have already created a quantize preset from the audio groove. However, if you have modified that hitpoint map from its original state, you will have to re-save the groove. Simply select the button named Create Groove (located in the Inspector of the Sample Editor).

Nothing exciting appears to happen when you've selected the button, but minimize the Sample Editor window and examine the Quantize display on the toolbar of the Project window, and you'll find a new quantize type in the list named after your actual audio file (see Figure 2.17). If you did not alter the hitpoint map, then you could have skipped these steps from within the Sample Editor and moved ahead to locate your new groove from within the Quantize display.

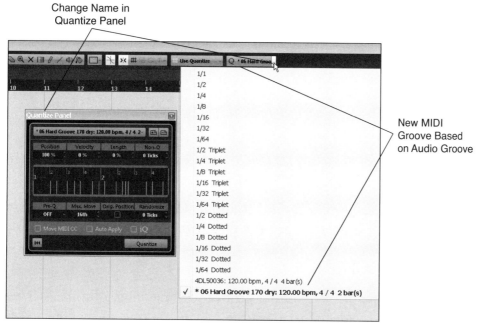

Figure 2.17 Your new groove is now located in the Quantize Type menu.

Now you can select your other non-quantized MIDI tracks, select the new quantize groove from the Quantize drop-down menu, and then select Quantize to make your MIDI track match the groove of your audio track.

As I mentioned before, this is not a perfect science. In some cases, it's best if you use the Snap feature and manually move notes to the correct positions on the quantize groove. It all depends on how well your hitpoints are set up in the previous step and how well you performed on your un-quantized MIDI tracks.

In Figure 2.18, you'll see how the bass note has been quantized to match the imperfect timing of the kick drum in the audio groove. This type of quantize would not work with your standard quantize selections. If you're having problems, un-quantize your original MIDI tracks by using Reset Quantize and then go back into the Sample Editor screen and adjust your hitpoints, create a new quantize groove, and try it again.

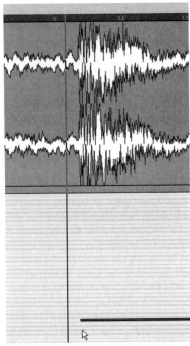

Figure 2.18 The bass now matches the slightly off kick drum from the audio groove.

If you plan on using this quantize groove a lot, I recommend saving it as a permanent setting in your quantize setup. To do so, open the Quantize panel from the Quantize display on the toolbar while your quantize groove is still selected in the Quantize drop-down menu and then select Save Preset.

I recommend changing the name of the quantize groove to something a little easier to remember, as opposed to using the default name given by Cubase (the audio file name). To rename the quantize groove, click on the text within the Name field, select Rename Preset, and type in something you'll remember. That new quantize groove will stay in the Cubase Quantize drop-down menu permanently (even on new projects).

If for some reason you don't save your new quantize groove, Cubase will just write over it the next time you create a new quantize groove from hitpoints.

You can also use the Create Groove Quantize Preset option to copy a groove from a MIDI part and add it to your Quantize display menu. With this option, you'll be able to achieve the exact opposite of what you've done in the previous exercise and instead be able to quantize your audio groove to match your MIDI parts. I will discuss more quantizing features in Chapter 3, "Taking Audio to the Limit in Cubase 6."

Adjusting the Quantization and Feel of the Groove in Real Time

Sometimes quantizing can have annoying side effects and cause you not only to lose your groove, but also to change the groove so that it just doesn't work. Going back and forth between quantizing, adjusting your quantize, and then undoing your quantize can become tedious when trying to find that magic quantize combination for complex grooves. Grooves that swing (in particular) can be a real test of your patience.

In these special cases, real-time quantization might be in order. To get real-time quantization, unlike groove quantization, I recommend starting with a pre-quantized part. This means if your part is supposed to have a 1/16-note swing feel, try quantizing it to either swung or straight 1/16 notes first. This will get the quantization in the ballpark (even if this means losing some of the feel) using the regular automatic quantize methods. Keep in mind that you can always undo your quantization if this isn't working for you.

Next, select the "e" on the MIDI track to bring up the MIDI Channel Settings window. From one of the Inserts drop-down menus, select Quantizer (as shown in Figure 2.19).

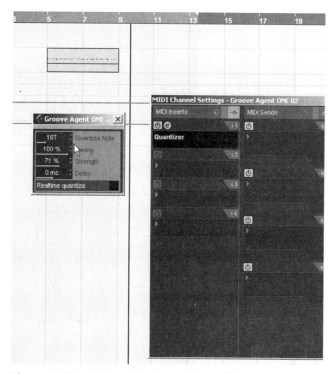

Figure 2.19 Using the Quantizer effect as a real-time quantizer.

As your MIDI events pass through the Quantizer effect, they will be repositioned automatically according to the settings of the Quantizer. This means you can adjust your settings as you play back.

Try to get your feel back by first setting the Quantizer to your ballpark setting and then adjusting the Swing and Strength fields while playing back. The Swing field adjusts the grid-lines position, whereas the Strength field adjusts the distance between the actual note position and the grid position (the grid position being at 100% and the real position being at 0%). Both are important factors in determining the feel of your groove.

If it's still not working for you, go back and undo your original quantize and try once again with the Quantizer's Swing and Strength settings set at 0%, and then gradually adjust them while playing back. Many times you can at least get close to where you need to be with your quantization using these two methods.

When you're happy with your effects settings, I suggest duplicating your original part and then making the setting permanent (by using the Freeze MIDI Modifiers command from the MIDI menu) in the original file. Duplicating your original part prevents you from losing your original performance. And, by "bouncing" your real-time MIDI effect, you'll save your system's processor some work. Once the effected part is bounced, you'll actually be able to see the MIDI events in their new quantized positions. You'll learn how to bounce these parts a little later in this chapter, in the section entitled "Creating Editable MIDI Parts from MIDI Effects."

Note: If you would like to have your notes quantized as you play live, check the box next to Realtime Quantize. Keep in mind that even though what you'll be hearing will be quantized, the actual performance is what will be recorded. This features works sort of like auto-tune for the rhythmically challenged (as opposed to the pitch-challenged).

Advanced MIDI Effects and Modifiers

Since we're on the subject of MIDI effects, I'd like to mention that the actual MIDI effects in Cubase 6 have become more intuitive and user-friendly than they were in earlier versions. For those who are new to using MIDI effects and/or MIDI modifiers, let me explain by saying that these processors treat MIDI in a similar way to how an audio processor treats an audio signal. Using MIDI effects, you can create a new sound that can always be bypassed or altered and does not affect the original MIDI data.

Even though the look and user appeal has been jazzed up a notch in Cubase 6, there's not a lot that's new in terms of added effects. The main new addition is the Beat Designer, which I will go over in a lot more detail later in this chapter. (You can find more instruction on these plug-ins by selecting Plug-In Reference from the Documentation option of the Help menu.)

Because the list of effects is long, I'm going to separate them into categories: MIDI modifiers, musical and tonal altering effects, MIDI tools and controls, and programmers.

Before I begin, I think it's important to understand the differences between a MIDI track send and an audio track send. A MIDI insert works only on the MIDI track on which you are activating the insert effect (very similar to the way that an audio insert functions), but a MIDI send transfers the effected data to another MIDI channel or instrument. This means it's not designed to group or bus several instruments under the same send and share the same effect (as an audio send functions).

An example of a MIDI send would be if you wanted to output a MIDI delay to another instrument so that the sound of the delay was played on an instrument other than the original MIDI track (such as making the delay of a guitar a violin sound instead, and it plays the same note 1/16 note after each guitar note is played). It's not as common to work with MIDI sends, but they can be used to create some really interesting effects.

Category 1: The MIDI Modifiers

I've categorized these effects into one location because they are used primarily to make slight adjustments to the main MIDI part. These are mostly effects you could do with some simple editing; however, they automate the process and do not affect the contents of the original part. The effects that make up this category are the MIDI modifiers' effects: Compress, Context Gate, and Quantizer. I've already discussed the Quantizer, so here's a brief explanation of the others.

The first and foremost in my MIDI modifiers category is the MIDI effect that's appropriately named MIDI Modifiers. Not only can you find this in the insert or send effect drop-down menu, but you can also locate the main elements from it in the Inspector. The only difference between using MIDI Modifiers in the two separate locations is that the insert/send effect option of the MIDI Modifiers includes a couple of extra features that the Inspector version of the MIDI Modifiers doesn't (scale and delay features). Out of all of the MIDI effects, this is probably the most basic and useful real-time effect you can use.

The Transpose feature allows you to shift the pitch of the MIDI notes (on the entire track) up or down by up to 127 half steps. The Velocity Shift feature raises or lowers the velocities of the entire track without affecting each individual note's relative velocity (meaning that all velocities increase or decrease in the same increment). Keep in mind that the original notes will not be modified in any way and that you'll only be hearing the result, as opposed to seeing the result.

The Velocity Compression feature is a useful effect when it comes to limiting the range of velocity on the MIDI track. Again, the actual velocities will not be affected, and you will only be hearing the result. Length Compression is a quick and easy way to tighten up a performance. This is a great effect to use on instruments such as bass or strings, which have a tendency to overlap on occasion during a performance or recording.

The Range filters and limiters allow you to set a low note/velocity and high note/velocity and either limit the playing of the notes/filters within your specified range or remove any notes/velocities that fall within a specified range. There are many ways you can utilize this effect. For instance, you can use it to remove ghost notes (low velocities) on drum parts, notes outside of an instrument's range, and so on.

The Scale feature (located in the plug-in effect only) allows you to quantize your pitches set to a musical scale. This means that if you want all your notes to fall within a C minor scale, you can set the scale to C minor, and any note that doesn't fit within that scale will be transposed to the closest note within your scale setting. This does not affect the timing of the MIDI part in any way.

The Delay feature simply pulls the whole track forward or backward and can be very useful when it comes to tightening a mix where samples are used that have a delayed attack, and so on. This delay is not to be confused with your standard echo effect, although it could be used in such a manner if you're using it on a duplicated track.

> **Note:** Even though the Random features are included in the MIDI Modifiers, they are covered in the following section, "Category 2: Musical and Tonal Altering Effects."

The Compressor MIDI effect is not much different from the compressor section located within the MIDI Modifier effect or the Inspector. The main difference is that it offers a slightly more "classic" representation of an audio compressor. Depending on the MIDI track or instrument you're working with, it might work a little better for you than the alternative.

The Context Gate MIDI effect is very similar to using the Range filter/limiter from the MIDI Modifier effect. The main differences are the snazzy look of the effect and the fact that you can filter and limit chords as well as mono parts. This is a great way to quickly restrict the polyphony of the MIDI track (for instance, change a track to a mono instrument as opposed to a polyphonic instrument).

Category 2: Musical and Tonal Altering Effects

These are the effects that the computer/dance-music creators love. Most of these effects offer ways to allow the computer to randomly write the music for you. Although these effects can be a lot of fun, I thought they should be separated. If you're not into this particular type of music, then chances are you'll rarely use these effects. The components in this category include Arpache 5 and SX, Auto LFO, Chorder, Note 2 CC, Density, Random effect modifiers, and MIDI Echo.

The Arpache 5 and Arpache SX are both arpeggiator effects. When using these effects, holding a sustained chord will result in each note of that chord being played individually in either an up-and-down pattern or even one that you can program yourself. You can also adjust the speed and note length as each note is played. The Arpache 5 is a slightly slimmed-down version of the SX. This MIDI effect lets you reproduce the classic Giorgio Moroder synth effect we all have a soft spot for.

Next, the Auto LFO in Cubase 6 replaced the previous Autopan MIDI effect. The name changed because now the effect not only offers the possibilities of setting up an automated MIDI pan, but it also allows you to specify any MIDI controller (volume, brightness, velocity) and has the same basic effect of automatically turning a virtual knob back and forth. The effect allows you to control the range of the affected notes, waveform, density, and wavelength. This can get very complex to program due to the fact that different synths respond differently to the effect (due to parameters that aren't supported by the plug-ins). Cubase suggests you have your MIDI implementation charts on hand for your hardware synths, but even I had some difficulties using this with some of the virtual synths within Cubase.

The Chorder is an interesting effect that gives you the opportunity to lay out several chords across individual keys and even change chords, depending on the velocities of the individual notes. This is a great way to set up sounds like Wendy Carlos' *TRON* soundtrack and could be used as an easy way to enter chords for non-keyboard players out there.

The Note 2 CC effect is sort of like a very simple Auto LFO effect, but instead of having an automatic virtual knob turning back and forth, its action is more like a virtual switch flipping back and forth, and that effect happens when each MIDI note occurs in sequence. This was designed to work with monophonic parts because polyphonic parts (chords and so on) could lead to mass Cubase confusion due to the nature of this effect. Again, like the Auto LFO, different synths are going to react differently to this effect, so it might take a little tweaking to get it right. This could be a great effect for panning each individual hi-hat hard left and right between every hit.

The Density effect is also interesting and unique. You have the option of either removing MIDI notes at random or adding MIDI notes at random from your part. Anything below 100% will have notes removed. (The less density, the more notes are removed.) Anything above 100% will have random notes added. (The greater the density, the more notes are added.)

When discussing the Random features (located under the MIDI Modifier effect or in the Inspector) in the "Category 1" section, I mentioned that I felt they belonged more in this category. That's because they're designed to create a random effect similar to the way the Density effect works. Using this modifier, you can let Cubase decide at random how to alter a note's pitch, velocity, position, or length. Depending on the way you change these settings, Cubase could write a completely different part than what you currently have. This could be similar to having a musician play some sheet music that has been turned upside down!

MIDI Echo has to be the most commonly used MIDI effect out of all of the effects. The new MIDI Echo in Cubase is quite advanced and packed with more features than previous versions of MIDI Echo. Now you can set the effect to echo other random notes, control the velocity of the echoes, and adjust the timing, length, and decay. Keep in mind that each echo is actually a played note, and all of this action can cause strange things to happen occasionally if you're pushing your system. For most simple delays, I still prefer the audio effect as opposed to the MIDI effect, but there are plenty of creative things that you can do using this effect as opposed to using an audio effect.

Category 3: MIDI Tool and Controls

I separated these MIDI "effects" into their own category because they're not really effects at all. They're tools and controls. They are only MIDI utilities, or they only affect MIDI like a control surface. The components of this category include the Micro Tuner, MIDI Control, Track Control, and MIDI Monitor. Since I've already discussed the MIDI Monitor, following is a brief explanation of the other three controls.

First off, I consider the Micro Tuner to be a utility, even though it could be used in a creative way. Its main purpose is to tune or detune instruments, and it can be used to tune or detune individual pitches within the 12 steps of a piano keyboard. This tool is almost a necessity for some types of instruments and music that step outside the 12-tone scale (such as some instruments and music from India or the Far East).

Having MIDI Control is like having a virtual controller to manage particular CC events without actually affecting the pre-recorded events. This is similar to playing back a MIDI track and using your pitch-bend wheel from your controller keyboard without recording the track. The difference is that this is a virtual controller, and it can be automated and designed to fit your specific needs.

The Track Control MIDI effect is a visual interface designed to work specifically with synths that utilize the GS and XG standards (Roland, Yamaha, VST instruments, and many others). This is a pretty self-explanatory control that is specific to these particular external synths parameters. If your synth is not affected by using this effect, it's probably not set up to GS or XG standards.

Category 4: Programmers

This category is for another group that I don't really consider as effects. However, if anything, they resemble musical and tonal altering effects. The last of the MIDI effects are the Step Designer, Beat Designer, and Transformer. The Beat Designer was introduced in Cubase 5, and I'll go over it in more detail later in this chapter, in the tutorial called "Step Programming Drum Beats with Beat Designer."

Step Designer and Beat Designer both have similar design concepts. The idea goes back to the old-school way of programming in step sequence (as used with drum machines) as opposed to using a MIDI controller keyboard or similar to enter the events. Step Designer doesn't take it quite as far as Beat Designer, though. You can use Step Designer to create small sequences (in step time) and trigger those sequences with other MIDI notes to create a variety of patterns that will play back on command via performed or pre-recorded notes. This is similar to the Arpache 5 or SX but more specific when it comes to programming sequences.

The Transformer effect is similar to the Logical Editor, except it acts as a real-time effect as opposed to an editor. Even though this effect is completely different from Step Designer and Beat Designer, it still involves a lot of programming skills to get anything to work. Because this effect is so similar to the Logical Editor, you should be able to get a basic understanding from the section entitled "Utilizing the List and Logical Editors" later in this chapter.

Creating Editable MIDI Parts from MIDI Effects

When you have the MIDI effect sounding exactly the way you want it to, I recommend turning the MIDI part into one that represents what's happening with the MIDI and the effect so that you can lighten the burden on your system, and you are able to edit the notes that didn't exist (before the effect was added) in more detail.

The way to do this is to "freeze" the MIDI part with the MIDI effects (modifiers). I recommend duplicating your MIDI track so that you always have the original track to go back to, in case you change your mind about something down the road. You can always mute the duplicate track and keep it muted for the rest of your project. When you're ready to "marry" the effect to MIDI (similar to bouncing audio tracks or effects), select the MIDI part and track you want to freeze and then, from the MIDI menu, select Freeze MIDI Modifiers. (This will "freeze" the MIDI effects, not the VST Instrument track.)

Keep in mind that once you have frozen your MIDI modifiers and effects, your MIDI data may look a lot different, but it might not jump out at you as a major change, depending on the sort of effect you're using. For example, a frozen Arpache effect will show dramatic changes, whereas it might be hard to spot any changes in a frozen Track Control effect. For the most part, it's probably in your best interest to freeze parts that create new notes or contain a lot of velocity or CC data and to leave the other types of parts with effects unfrozen, because there's not much benefit to freezing tracks that don't change. Of course, once you've frozen your tracks, you can go back to throwing more effects on the new tracks if you so desire. Figure 2.20 shows an example of a MIDI track before and after freezing a MIDI Echo effect on the part.

Advanced MIDI Functions

Cubase contains an extensive list of edit functions located under the MIDI menu. Although I went over them pretty extensively in my book *MIDI Editing in Cubase: Skill Pack* (Course Technology PTR, 2007), I think they are important enough to

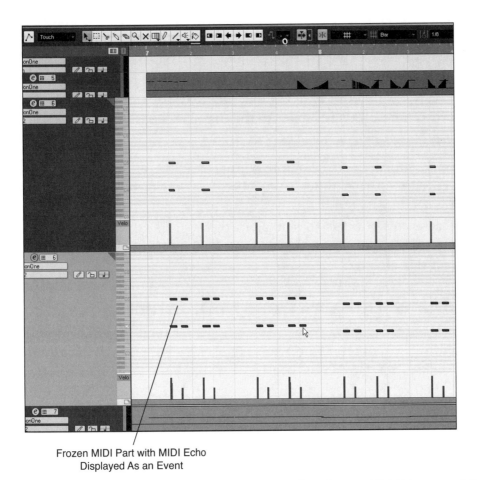

Frozen MIDI Part with MIDI Echo
Displayed As an Event

Figure 2.20 Before and after processing and freezing a MIDI Echo on a MIDI track.

touch on briefly in this book for those who have skipped over them in the past. I will not provide any walkthroughs for them, but instead I'll give a brief explanation as to what each function does.

To explore the MIDI functions, select the Functions option under the MIDI menu. The options listed there are Legato, Fixed Lengths, Delete Doubles, Delete Controllers, Delete Continuous Controllers, Delete Notes, Restrict Polyphony, Pedals to Note Length, Delete Overlaps (Mono and Poly), Velocity and Fixed Velocity, Thin Out Data, Extract MIDI Automation, Reverse, and Merge Tempo from Tapping. These have not changed since Cubase 4, so if you're already familiar with them, feel free to skip this section.

■ **Legato.** This function works just as you'd think it would if you're familiar with the musical terminology (played smoothly, tied together). Upon using legato, the selected note end will extend into the start of each following note. This is a great way to clean up a legato performance because often you'll have notes that overlap or are just a little shy of reaching the following note. Keep in mind that your samples from your instrument will hold only as long as the sample length, and there is no special MIDI magic that's going to change it.

- **Fixed Lengths.** This function is a quick way to make all your notes the same length. In many cases, there's no better way to tighten up a performance than to make those note lengths match. I find this particularly useful for MIDI bass.

- **Delete Doubles.** This function does exactly what you'd think: It gets rid of any note that may have been doubled accidentally during a captured performance or after quantizing. Doubled notes are often hard to detect because visually they look like one note. If you hear one note or drum sound that jumps out in the mix even though the velocity appears the same as the other notes, chances are it has been doubled. This function will clean up that problem.

- **Delete Controllers and Delete Continuous Controllers.** These functions are pretty straightforward as well. Using either function, you can eliminate any controller data without affecting the rest of the MIDI data and without having to open a controller lane to examine the data in the Key Editor. Once you've deleted the controller data, it's easy to overdub new controller data over the same track. Velocity, however, is not affected by this function.

- **Delete Notes.** This function is much more complex than it sounds. With this function, you can set up parameters that define which notes you would like to delete from a group of selected notes. The parameter options include note length and note velocity (see Figure 2.21). This is another great tool for getting rid of pesky little ghost notes that were recorded during a performance.

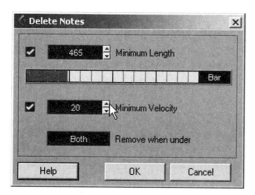

Figure 2.21 The Delete Notes dialog box.

- **Restrict Polyphony.** This function allows you to put a limit on the notes that can occur simultaneously in the recorded MIDI part (usually as a chord). In the limiting process, it removes the notes starting from the bottom of the chord and works its way up to the top. This means that if you have a four-note chord and you want to restrict it to only two notes, only the top two notes will remain after this function has been applied.

■ **Pedals to Note Length.** This function converts sustain-pedal controller events into note events by lengthening the notes that are sustained to the point where the pedal is released. This function is a little shaky because not only does it alter the sound of the recording, but it also works depending on how good your performance was with the foot pedal. However, in some cases it may be necessary to do this conversion (such as when you're using a synth that doesn't recognize sustain after recording with another MIDI controller and a sustain pedal).

■ **Delete Overlaps.** This function is similar to Legato, but it does not lengthen notes. Instead, it only shortens notes that extend past the start of following notes. The Mono Delete Overlaps function specifically shortens notes of the same pitch, whereas the Poly Delete Overlaps function specifically shortens notes that are on different pitches.

■ **Velocity and Fixed Velocity.** These functions are two quick and easy ways to change the velocities of your selected notes. To correct velocities so that they are all the same (great for drum parts or bass), set the velocity that you'd like the notes to be at in the Insert Velocity box on the toolbar. Once set, use the Fixed Velocity function to bring all of the events to that particular velocity. The Velocity dialog box offers several ways to adjust the velocity (similar to the effects discussed earlier). You can add/subtract (raise or lower) the velocity, compress/expand, or limit it by setting a velocity range.

■ **Thin Out Data.** This function's main purpose is to compress the data from continuous controller events. Because there are so many events that get recorded during a volume change or pitch shift (for instance) that are mostly inaudible, Thin Out Data erases a portion of the unnecessary data to save on valuable processing power, which can prevent system crashes. But this sort of a clean-up function isn't really necessary unless you are recording a lot of CC events and having system issues.

■ **Extract MIDI Automation.** This function's purpose is to convert events, such as panning controllers or volume controllers, into automation lanes that work under your MIDI track in the Project window. Automation lanes are usually easier to work with than controller lanes and can also save some system resources. Once the controller lanes have been converted to automation lanes, they are removed from the original MIDI part. Because of this, I recommend duplicating your part as a backup before utilizing this function.

■ **Reverse.** This is sort of a fun function that takes everything selected and swaps the direction of the events. (Multiple events are necessary to detect the change.) Unlike audio, you won't hear any backward instrument sounds. This is more like a piano player reading and playing music from the end to the beginning, as opposed to beginning to end.

■ **Merge Tempo from Tapping.** This function is much different from the rest of the functions. Its main purpose is to create a tempo track for an audio recording that fluctuates in tempo by tapping along with the recording while listening back. Because of Cubase 6's new Advanced Tempo Detection, this tool that was once useful is now becoming more obsolete. For more information, refer to the Cubase manual.

Utilizing the List and Logical Editors

You can easily work through a ton of projects without ever opening the List or Logical Editor in Cubase. Both of these editors are very technical and appear to have no real musical appeal. However, if you're a dedicated programmer, both offer possibilities that none of the other editors can match.

List Editor

The List Editor contains a list of every single MIDI message recorded in the selected part in the order that it happens. This includes note-on and note-off events, pitch-bend or aftertouch MIDI messages, and so on. You can edit the data within the editor, but because it's so detailed, you should limit yourself to editing here only if you're looking for very specific events.

I believe the main reason to use the List Editor is for inserting or modifying program change messages, for inserting text, and for editing SysEx and SMF data. It's by far the easiest and most precise way to deal with any of these advanced MIDI events.

You can create program changes in the other editors, but I find the List Editor to be one of the best editors to perform the task. To create a program change (or, in layman's terms, to change sounds during playback of a MIDI part), you simply need to find the exact location where you would like the program change (usually about a half bar before the sound starts, so that you can give your synths some time to play catch-up). Then change the insert type to Program Change, and use the Pencil tool to create a program change event in the desired location (see Figure 2.22). When you have this event in place, you need to assign the new program number.

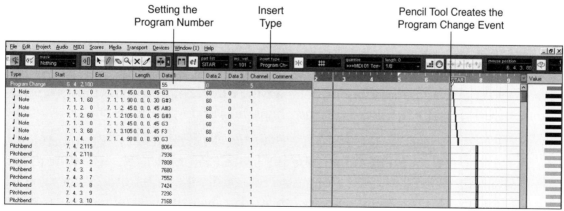

Figure 2.22 Creating a synth program change from within the List Editor.

Note: Program numbers can be confusing to work with because the numbers that are represented in your synth's patch bank usually don't match their actual program number. I find that an easy way to get around the mathematical conversions is to simply watch your synth while you scroll through the numbers in the program change Data Field 1. The programs should change on the synth as you scroll if your MIDI is set up correctly. And once you find the correct patch on your synth, you'll also have the correct MIDI program number in Cubase.

Also, keep in mind that if you create a program change event anywhere in the middle of a song, it's a good idea to have an initial program change event at the start of the song that includes program data for the first half of your song. The reason is that once you change your sound in the second half of your song, you'll be stuck with that sound every time you replay the song if you don't have the initial program set up.

If you're using a lot of external synths, using SysEx events at the start of your project will speed up your startup time. The reason why is that you can store all of your synths' program information and other data in Cubase so that you don't have to reprogram or set up each individual synth separately. Also, depending on which external synth you're using, you may be able to record the parameter controls of your synth (such as adjusting the LFO knob) during a performance. Recording SysEx events is not much different from capturing a performance (it can be accomplished on any MIDI track in the Project window), but actually viewing or tweaking the SysEx data is easiest in the List Editor or the SysEx Editor.

The process of recording SysEx messages usually involves recording in Cubase on the synth's MIDI track while manually sending a bulk SysEx dump from the synth. When recording any SysEx dump, it's always a good idea to leave ample room (several measures) before starting the song after the SysEx event; once your setup has been loaded, you should try to avoid constantly replaying the song over the SysEx event.

The reason for all of this is that when a synth gets a SysEx message, it can be sort of like giving birth to a MIDI baby and could disrupt your system. If you want to go "super MIDI nerd" with SysEx, the MIDI SysEx Editor is the place to shine when using your MIDI Hex conversions. Of course, to do this properly, you'll need to get your hands on your synth's MIDI implementation charts. To open the SysEx Editor, select it from the Comments column on the SysEx message from within the List Editor. Again, the SysEx Editor is not necessary for most programmers, but if you're having trouble getting things to work properly with regard to SysEx, it allows you the option of working with the raw data.

Adding text (lyrics, notes, and so on) along with the MIDI tracks is not something I personally do a lot of, but if you don't use the Score Editor and you just want to get some lyrics or other phrases placed along with the music, the List Editor allows you to add text in a similar fashion as adding any other event (using the Pencil tool). It's a very basic text editor—don't expect Microsoft Word. You can, however, copy and paste words from another document type (such as Word) into the text input box. Even though you can add text here, I think it's easiest to work with text from within the Score Editor if that is an option for you.

SMF (*Standard MIDI File*) data is important when creating SMFs that are going to be shared universally. In the List Editor, you can specify up to 128 specific types of data, including sequence number, copyright information, track name, instrument name, lyric, marker info, cue points, key signature, and MIDI channel. If you're working with videogame developers, websites, cell phone companies, or toy manufacturers, SMF data could be a very important piece to the final MIDI file you create, and this is the only place you can work with that particular data from within Cubase.

Logical Editor

Working with the Logical Editor is only slightly easier than working with MIDI Hexadecimal from within the SysEx Editor in the List Editor. First, you should understand that the Logical Editor, Transformer (MIDI effect), and MIDI Input Transformer are all very similar, to the point that if you know one of them, you can know and understand them all. The main difference is that the Transformer and MIDI Input Transformer operate in real time.

Anyway, if you like math, algebra, calculators, and that sort of thing, the Logical Editor is for you. Working in the Logical Editor is similar to working with a basic computer language. It's a way to program very particular automatic edits that aren't included in your standard Cubase list of functions and editor tools. The Logical Editor in Cubase 5 received a facelift from its original look. This editor is much different from any other editor in Cubase, and its access is located toward the bottom of the MIDI menu.

You might be wondering, "Why on earth would I ever need to edit beyond using the many ready and available tools in Cubase?" The simple answer is that you don't have to even bother using the Logical Editor. It's designed for people who want to take editing to the max. Most likely, it would be less common for someone to start programming the Logical Editor in the middle of a recording/editing session. Using the Logical Editor is similar to setting up macros. If you're always taking the same steps when editing to get to one result, it might be easier for you to turn those multiple steps into one function in the Logical Editor. Whereas using macros can help in this matter, the Logical Editor takes it several steps beyond the limitations of macros.

By examining the presets from within the Logical Editor (see Figure 2.23), you'll see new and interesting functions that you won't see in any other editor. For instance, Delete Black Keys is found under the Experimental menu option. When using this preset function, all the notes found on black keys on the piano keyboard will be removed from the selected part.

You can look at the Logical Editor as another completely different program within Cubase. It's a program designed to create edit functions. If you just want to experiment

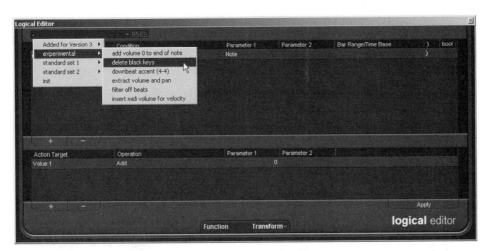

Figure 2.23 The presets found in the Logical Editor.

with creating some new functions, I recommend starting with some of the presets that are already available and adjusting the variables found within them. The Cubase manual has a whole chapter dedicated to this editor, so you can find more details there if you would like to dive deeper into this powerful tool.

Just as most prefer working in Windows to working in DOS, any edit you can perform in the Logical Editor can be performed by using the other editors. It's just that it might be faster and easier to achieve results (including real-time results) by using the Logical Editor (or Transformer) if you have a preset function created to do the monotonous work for you. All that being said, if you get a headache even thinking about the Logical Editor (don't worry, you're not alone), then maybe you're better off sticking to editing without the shortcuts that the Logical Editor can provide. There is no right or wrong way to work in Cubase. As mentioned before, there are just different ways to get to the same result.

Automating MIDI in the Project Window

Because you're probably already familiar with mixing in Cubase, you most likely are also familiar with the automation lanes in the Project window. If you're not, you will learn a little more about them in Chapter 4, "Mastering the Art of Mixing in Cubase 6." What you might not have known is that these same lanes are available for automating changes in your MIDI tracks as well. I mentioned earlier how you can use the Extract MIDI automation function to convert your MIDI data into automation tracks. Now, you're going to get a closer look at how to utilize those MIDI automation tracks and create more as you need them.

I'm sure you've probably figured out by now that the Project window is where you'll be spending the most time while working on your project. Because this is the case, why not utilize all the features you can without having to open other editors? The automation lanes for MIDI tracks replace almost everything you need to do in a standard controller lane within the Key Editor and make it easier to compare alongside your audio tracks, all from within the Project window. Once you've mastered the automation lanes, you'll probably spend a lot less time looking at controller lanes.

By default, after selecting Show/Hide Automation under a MIDI track in the Project window, you should see the MIDI volume automation lane. To see even more MIDI automation lanes, simply add more lanes by selecting the plus sign (+) located on each additional lane (see Figure 2.24).

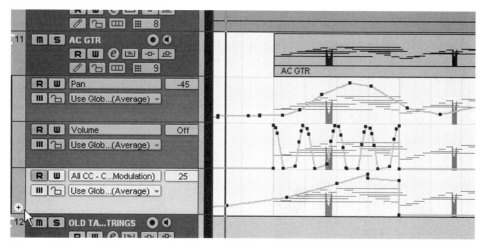

Figure 2.24 Adding MIDI track automation lanes in the Project window.

MIDI parts can have controller events (such as pitch bend, volume changes, or panning) recorded along with them. This makes working with automation in the Project window a little confusing because you can have a combination of parts that already contain controller events mixed with newly created track automation from within the Project window. This can confuse the program when it comes to calculating accurate results.

Because of this, you need to define how you would like Cubase to handle the automation. You have five options. By using global settings, you can preset particular controllers to always default to a certain setup in the MIDI Controller Automation Setup dialog box, which is found by selecting CC Automation Setup from the MIDI menu. Selecting Global Settings will default to the methods listed at the top of the MIDI Controller Automation Setup window.

If you choose not to default to the global settings, you can choose from four other methods. By using Replace 1- Part Range, you can choose to have Cubase respond to the part automation as a priority and then abruptly switch to track automation when you go past the part borders and vice versa. Using Replace 2- Last Value Continues works similarly to Replace 1, but it works when the controller kicks in instead of at the part border. Average is a hybrid method that calculates an average combination between the part's controller data and track automation. Modulation acts as a combination of the two types (similar to Average) so that the automation track lane accentuates the part automation if it's adjusted.

It's confusing, I know. Unfortunately, there's no simple answer as to which mode you should always use, because it really depends on what you've already recorded and the type of controller events you've used. Some methods simply work better than others for certain controller types, and if you have automation on the track as well as the part, there can be conflicts if your settings aren't adjusted.

All of the options should work to some degree, no matter which you choose (especially if you try hard to limit yourself in recording with controller data). If you're not too picky, you could probably get by just using the Average setting most of the time. Select one of these five options from the Automation Merge Mode located within the MIDI Controller Automation Setup (see Figure 2.25).

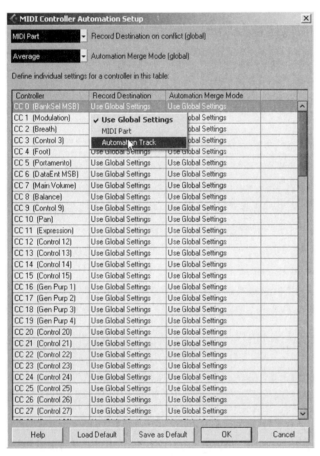

Figure 2.25 Automation Merge Mode within the MIDI Controller Automation Setup window.

Using the Controller Selection drop-down menu, you'll be able to automate any standard controller as well as the MIDI Modifier, and even the parameters of the MIDI effects. Figure 2.26 shows two examples of editing within an automation lane when working with a panning MIDI controller and the step size of the Arpache 5 MIDI effect.

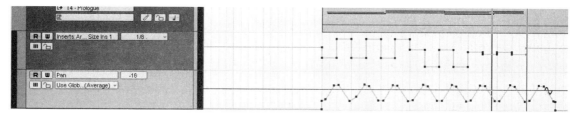

Figure 2.26 Automating a MIDI effect and pan effect in automation lanes for a MIDI track.

Note: Unfortunately, you'll still find it easier to edit pitch bend and individual note velocities from within the Key Editor's controller lanes.

Taking Giant Leaps with LoopMash 2

Cubase 5 introduced its users to a new toy, particularly for those who can't get enough out of their loop library. LoopMash is similar to a multitrack REX player. It's like taking your old loops and throwing them into a blender to make a new, weird beat cocktail.

LoopMash not only has the ability to instantly convert any audio file into a sliced file, but it also analyzes the beat and sound of the file. When dropping in multiple audio loops, it considers one loop to be the master loop and then uses elements from the other loops to change the color of the sound of the original loop. It actually tries to replace snare drums with other snare drums or sounds in the same general timbre, and it tries to find similar grooves from other files to replace the original grooves. Even though it appears to be a pretty simple toy, a lot of thought went into its design.

LoopMash 2 has now been introduced in Cubase 6 and has opened up a whole new world of possibilities for those users who enjoyed the original LoopMash. LoopMash 2 provides users with much greater control in the groove-creation process and might even completely do away with the need to ever use REX files again. Personally, I enjoyed the original LoopMash, but I could not find a lot of practical use for it. Now, I see how it can become an almost invaluable tool for those creating dance/electronic music tracks and the like.

Note: Even though Steinberg and I have referred to it as LoopMash 2 because it's the second version of LoopMash, the program and manual refer to it simply as LoopMash in some places and as LoopMash 2 in others. There is no such thing as LoopMash 1 in Cubase 6. To keep things from getting too confusing I will refer to LoopMash 2 simply as LoopMash from now on. Also, for those who own an iPhone, LoopMash is available as a downloadable app (visit Apple's App Store), which means that you can easily take LoopMash with you wherever you go.

Now, keep in mind that throwing an old shoe, a can of spinach, and a frog into a blender might not make a delicious piña colada in the end. The art of using LoopMash is similar to the art of cooking—it's all about using the right ingredients and how you mix them. If you want to read more about LoopMash from the Cubase manual before you start my walkthrough, you can find a couple of pages of info in the Help menu: Select Documentation > Plug-In Reference > The Included VST Instruments > LoopMash.

Editing Loops in LoopMash

The easiest way to open LoopMash is from within VST Instruments. Locate and create an instance of LoopMash and also create an Instrument/MIDI track. Next, open the MediaBay; from the VST Sound folder, locate and open the LoopMash 2 folder. Locate Beat_Phunky.4 in the MediaBay. You can audition the loop in the MediaBay if you'd like. Next, drag and drop the loop into the first track of LoopMash, as shown in Figure 2.27.

Drag and Drop Loops from MediaBay into LoopMash

Figure 2.27 Dragging a loop from the MediaBay into LoopMash.

> **Note:** For this tutorial, I'll be demonstrating using the included LoopMash library. Keep in mind that you're not limited to using the LoopMash library. You can use *any* audio loop. The only thing you need to consider is that the loop is edited to a one- to four-bar phrase and is already cut to loop.

For this example, select the button labled Sync so that it is *not* highlighted and press the Play button. If you auditioned the loop in the MediaBay, you will notice that it sounds pretty much identical at this point, being played from within LoopMash. Also, as quickly as you have transferred the file from the MediaBay to LoopMash, LoopMash has already sliced the loops and analyzed their rhythm and sounds.

Prior to all of this, I had already decided that I liked the feel of this particular groove. Because of that, I want to make this the master groove. The master groove defines the main feel of the groove. Any other grooves that I decide to add should mostly affect the tonality of the groove.

When selecting the master groove, keep in mind that it does not have to be a drum loop. Even a vocal track could be used to capture a groove. Examine the groove closely as it plays. Notice the outlined box that moves across the groove. This box defines the current location during playback. Also notice the range markers above the loop lane. This defines the length of the groove. Because this groove is two bars long, the range markers have been set automatically at two bars. By dragging either the start or the end range marker inward, you can easily shorten the length of a groove in beats.

The slider to the left of the groove is referred to as the *similarity gain slider*. You can use these similarity gain sliders in a way similar to a mixing console. The more the slider is moved to the right, the more the sounds from the loop are used to fit the master groove. This means that if your similarity gain slider is positioned all the way to the right for your master groove, you will hear only the original master groove.

Right above the top similarity gain slider is a small arrow pointing down, and below the bottom similarity gain slider, there is another arrow pointing upward. Dragging this arrow to the left or right determines the threshold of all of the similarity sliders. This threshold is a new feature in LoopMash and offers you a little more control over all the sliders.

Stop playback on LoopMash and use your cursor to select one of the 16 slices from the master groove. When a slice is selected, LoopMash will audition the slice. You can also use the Step Left/Right buttons (located on the LoopMash Transport) to audition each slice one at a time, moving forward or backward on the loop.

To the right of the loop lane, there are two other controls: Transpose and Gain. You can use the Transpose simply to alter the tone of the loop or to match the keys from the various loops you use. When using the Transpose feature, the timing of the loop will not be affected. The Gain control can help control loops that are louder or softer than others. You can adjust the Gain up to +6 dB, so be careful not to abuse this and clip your output level and cause digital distortion.

Near the LoopMash Transport at the bottom of the player are three field buttons: Slice Selection, Audio Parameters, and Performance Controls. By default, Slice Selection is open when LoopMash first launches, and it displays Number of Voices, Voices per Track, Selection Offset, Random Selection, Selection Grid, and Similarity Method. Each of these settings affects how LoopMash treats all of the slices that it plays. Simple changes here can even affect one single master loop. Press Play again so that your master loop is looping while you adjust the controls, so that you can hear what's happening.

The Number of Voices and Voices per Track definition settings sort of work together. Number of Voices defines how many slices can be audible at one time (up to four). Voices per Track defines how many slices you can use from each track at once (up to four). The default setting is to have one voice per track at one voice at a time. By simply selecting two voices per track and two voices at one time, you can hear changes within one loop. This is because LoopMash is taking slices from other places within the loop and layering them with the slice that's currently playing back.

Now, once again, restrict the voices to one voice per track and one voice at a time and slowly move the Selection Offset slider to the right. What's happening now is that LoopMash is replacing slices with slices that sound less similar from within the groove the farther you move the slider to the right. Because your voice is limited to one voice at a time, you should be hearing only a loop that is altered from the original loop, and the alterations should increase the farther the slider is moved to the right.

Random Selection works similarly to Selection Offset, but instead of selecting slices based on the polar opposite of what's happening with the original groove, it selects slices at random, thus creating a slightly different effect.

Setting the selection grid affects how often changes occur. With its default setting at Level 1, the selection grid replaces every slice from the master groove with another slice. If switched to Level 2, the selection grid replaces every other slice from the master groove. If switched to Level 3, the selection grid replaces every fourth slice. Finally, if switched to Level 4, the selection grid replaces every eighth slice. This means that the higher the level of the selection grid, the less variation you will notice.

Lastly, adjusting the similarity method can also greatly affect the sound. The default method is set to Standard. If you are more interested in replacing instruments with other instruments of their same type (for example, replacing a kick drum with a different kick drum), you might want to try the Relative setting. If you're interested in replacing slices based on their sound more than on their rhythm, you can try utilizing the Harmonic setting.

One of the coolest new features in LoopMash 2 is the ability to edit and create loops using the slices in LoopMash. With this option, you aren't limited to what LoopMash decides fits into your groove. You can manipulate the slices yourself and put them where *you* want them to go.

To demonstrate this, drag the slice at Beat 1 so that it's at Beat 2 in the measure. Dragging the slice creates a copy. When you drop the slice, LoopMash brings up a dialog box asking "Make Track 1 Composite?" Select OK, and a new slice composite track will be created. Now, by using Track 1 as a composite track, you can rearrange any of the slices as needed. If you had other loops loaded, you can also drag and drop slices from other loop lanes. This makes editing loops a breeze. See Figure 2.28.

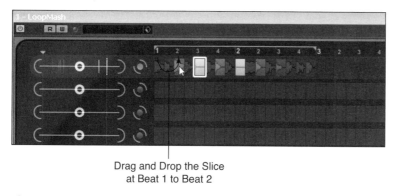

Drag and Drop the Slice
at Beat 1 to Beat 2

Figure 2.28 Copy and pasting slices within a composite track in LoopMash.

The other new and exciting feature in LoopMash 2 is the addition of slice effects. Slice effects allow you to manipulate each audio slice using standard effects that most DJs use. The new LoopMash comes standard with 17 DJ-type effects that you can add to every individual slice. To access these effects, right-click on the slice before (the eighth-note pickup before) Beat 4 and select the backwards R (reverse). Play back your loop and listen to how the beat has been reversed, creating a new sound. Also note that a symbol has been placed on the slice to indicate that an effect has been used on it (see Figure 2.29).

Figure 2.29 Creating a reverse effect in a slice.

The other effects, besides reverse, include mute, staccato (shortens the slice), two different scratch effects (using the audio slice), a backspin (lasting four slices), slowdown, tapestart, two different tapestops, two slurs (stretches the slice over two or four slices), and five various stutters of different degrees. Using the slice selection modifiers, located at the top of the context menu, you can also set up your slices so that LoopMash will affect them in the way you want them to be affected.

The first two of these modifiers are available only on the master track slices. Selecting Always on a slice means that it will always be played. Selecting Always Solo on a slice means that it will always be played and nothing else will be played (even when using multiple voice tracks) while it is playing. Selecting Exclude will keep LoopMash from using the slice anywhere in the mix. Finally, selecting Boost will make a slice more prone to being utilized by LoopMash while it's mashing up slices. If for some reason you decide to change your mind later, you can always remove the modifier or effect by selecting the related Clear command at the bottom of the context menu or by selecting None on the currently selected slice.

With all of these features in the new LoopMash, you almost don't even have to add additional loops to the mix. Adding extra loops is easy, though. Just drag and drop a couple more loops from the MediaBay to some of the other lanes in LoopMash. If you decide later on that you would like to make a different loop the master loop, all you need to do is select the Master Track button next to the other loop that you would like to have as the master from the track display. Changing the master loop can greatly affect the overall sound of LoopMash.

Go ahead and add a couple of loops and have fun making adjustments until your new beat cocktail starts to have the taste you've longed for. Remember to use the similarity gain sliders to mix between the master and slave loops. I consider the Audio Parameter tab to contain a little extra "glue" that helps tighten your new groove. Select the Audio Parameter tab so that the control panel is available (as shown in Figure 2.30).

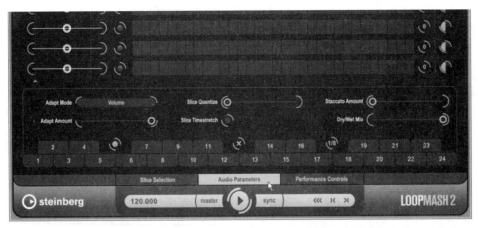

Figure 2.30 Preparing to adjust the audio parameters in LoopMash.

Adapt Mode and Adapt Amount work together to help blend the various sounding slices together. To get a better understanding of Adapt Mode, first slide the Adapt amount all the way to the right. When the Adapt Mode is set to Volume, LoopMash matches the volumes of the various slices almost as if they were going through a compressor effect.

Envelope mode is similar to Volume except it maintains more of the dynamics from the master loop. Spectrum ignores volume changes and simply focuses on the tonality. EQ is added to make slices resemble the tone of the original master loop's slices. Env + Spectrum is simply a combination of the two Adapt modes.

If your master loop is not quantized, the Slice Quantize feature acts as real-time quantization. The farther the slider is moved to the right, the more the beats will move to the eight-note grid.

In most cases, Slice Timestretch should be active. Without Slice Timestretch, there could be gaps or overlaps between slices if there are changes made to the original loop tempos. Only disable Slice Timestretch if you intend not to change tempos or if your computer is having trouble processing this real-time effect.

Staccato Amount is a way to tighten your slices by making them shorter in length. The effect of the Staccato Amount is similar to using a tight audio noise gate. For the most part, you'll want to keep the Dry/Wet Mix slider positioned all the way to the right. This ensures that all the processing achieved by LoopMash will be front and center. Moving the slider all the way to the left will leave you with only hearing the original master loop.

Recording and Sequencing LoopMash Grooves

Programming LoopMash is similar to programming an old drum machine. You set up patterns (similar to what you've done so far in the previous tutorial) as a "scene" and then store that collection of patterns as a LoopMash preset. You can store 24 patterns per instance of LoopMash (meaning you can have 24 preset rhythm changes). Because 24 just happens to be the magic number for two piano octaves, you can also trigger these patterns from any MIDI keyboard (or even easier, the virtual keyboard). The scenes are visible when the Slice Selection tab is selected.

The concept in programming these preset patterns is simple: You edit until the pattern sounds the way you want it, select the Record button (the red dot), and then select one of the 24 pads where you'd like to store the patterns. You can then double-click on that same pad and name it something that helps you to identify that groove. Continue doing this until you have all the patterns you want. If you need to delete a pattern from one of the buttons, select the X button and then select the pad you would like to delete.

When you have all your patterns set up, you should save your new program as a preset using the Save/Load Preset icon located at the top of the LoopMash window. You're now ready to record your new groove track.

There are multiple ways to record a groove track. I've decided to show you two completely different ways because neither of them is exactly a piece of cake, and they both have their pros and cons.

Figure 2.31 Programming patterns in LoopMash.

Recording LoopMash via Automation

If you would like to use the virtual pads on LoopMash to perform your groove (by selecting patterns via the Scene buttons manually during playback), you can use the W (or Write Automation) button (the W turns red when it's active) at the top of LoopMash. Simply select the W button, push Play on the Transport, and play the Scene buttons along with the song. When you're finished, deselect the W button and select the R button next to it. (It turns green when selected.) Now you should be able to hear and see your performance as LoopMash plays back through your sequenced scene changes.

You can edit your performance by bringing up the automation lane of LoopMash. To find the automation lane, open the folder called VST Instruments on the track display and then open the LoopMash folder to add automation lanes. From the list of controls, select Recall Scene. The events should be viewable on the lane, as shown in Figure 2.32. Here you can modify or erase the events if necessary, and you can also re-record or add events. You can automate every feature in the LoopMash and edit its lane using a similar method. The benefits of recording via automation are that you don't need to use MIDI, and it's also very easy. On the flip side, it's a little trickier to work with and edit in an automation lane than it is to use the Key Editor.

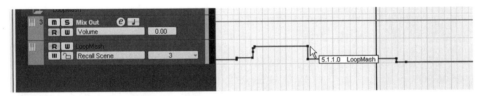

Figure 2.32 Editing from within the LoopMash automation lanes.

> **Note:** A *jump interval* is used to determine when you want the loop pattern (scene) to change during playback. This is particularly useful when programming via automation or playing LoopMash live. You can change the jump interval during playback or simply set it up before you start programming scene changes. The jump interval control's default setting is a 1/8 delay (meaning changes

happen the same instant when the pads are selected). When you use a longer jump interval, the pad flashes to indicate the change is coming and the change will occur at the time according to your interval setting (next measure, half measure, and so on).

Recording LoopMash via MIDI

If you want to record via MIDI, you can't use the fancy pads on LoopMash. Instead, you must use your MIDI controller keyboard (or the virtual keyboard) if you want to record the pattern changes on the fly. To do this, set up your keyboard so that it's triggering the pads from the LoopMash and then record your MIDI as you would any MIDI track. When you're finished, simply treat the scene (pattern) changes as notes and edit them as you would any note in the MIDI Editor.

There are many advantages to recording with MIDI, and for LoopMash in particular, having the ability to quantize your changes and move your notes on the grid in the Key Editor is really handy (see Figure 2.33). If you don't need to record your changes on the fly, then you can just create a blank part on the LoopMash track (using the Pencil tool) and then open that part in the Key Editor and pencil in where you want your changes. Recording via MIDI might seem a little awkward to some, but because of its editing features, it's definitely the most exact and detailed form of recording.

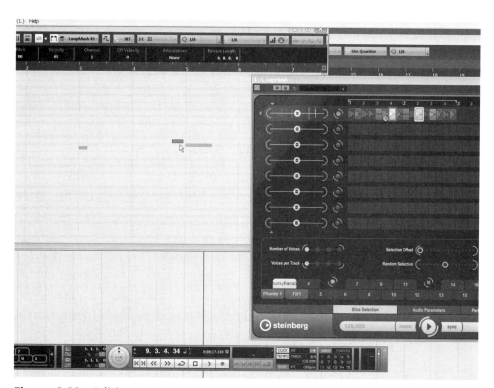

Figure 2.33   Editing LoopMash patterns in the Key Editor.

Performing Live with LoopMash

As you may have noticed already, LoopMash works best while its parameters are being tweaked. Steinberg is well aware that a growing number of live performers are utilizing software such as LoopMash for live performances.

Besides assigning scenes to pads and manipulating controls in real time, LoopMash also has a complete set of live-performance controls available by selecting the Performance Controls tab located above the LoopMash Transport (see Figure 2.34).

Figure 2.34 The live-performance controls in LoopMash.

The performance controls might look pretty familiar already. That's because they are simply representations of the DJ-style effects that were located when right-clicking on an individual slice. By selecting these performance pads, you have easy access to the DJ effects while performing on the fly. You can, of course, also record these effects live via MIDI or automation, as discussed earlier.

Note: To synchronize LoopMash playback to any existing projects, simply select the Sync button on the Transport. LoopMash's Transport controls will not work when in Sync mode. The Transport is controlled via the main Transport in Cubase.

Using Groove Agent ONE with the MediaBay

Since we're on the topic of drums, let's take a closer look at the Groove Agent ONE VST instrument. If you're familiar with the other Groove Agents, they're a lot different than Groove Agent ONE. Groove Agent ONE is simply a sample player with an emphasis on drum sounds. Unlike a drum machine, it doesn't include patterns, and you can't create patterns with it as you can when using LoopMash. Like LoopMash and the other VST instruments, Groove Agent ONE comes with a nice assortment of presets that can come in really handy throughout the creative process. You can read quite a bit more about Groove Agent ONE in the Help menu: Select Documentation > Plug-In Reference > The Included VST Instruments > Groove Agent ONE.

As I briefly mentioned in Chapter 1, you can do amazing things using the MediaBay along with Groove Agent to get the most out of any sample library. Now I'm going to show you how to transfer files to the Groove Agent from MediaBay, how to spread loops across the pads of Groove Agent ONE as individual sounds, and how to quickly create a MIDI groove out of an audio loop to take your audio loops to a new place.

Dropping Individual Drum Samples into Groove Agent ONE

With the MediaBay and Groove Agent ONE both open, locate the drum sample you would like to utilize in Groove Agent ONE from within the MediaBay (for example, a snare-drum sound, a kick drum, a hi-hat, and so on). Keep in mind that you can audition your samples from within the MediaBay if necessary. Once you've located the drum sample, simply select it in the MediaBay and drag and drop it on any pad in Groove Agent ONE. Voilà! Select that pad to hear your drum sample being triggered from within Groove Agent ONE. It doesn't get any easier than that! Now you can fill in all the pads with other drum sounds and then save it as one of the preset drum kits.

You can also drag and drop entire custom-made non-formatted drum kits into the MediaBay. First, start with a new blank (empty) Groove Agent ONE. If you have a folder already set up that contains all the samples of a full drum kit, select that folder in the MediaBay and then select the samples that make up that entire kit. (Use the Ctrl key for multiple selections.)

When you have all the samples selected, click and drag the group of samples over to the E-2 pad of Group 1 on Groove Agent ONE. While pressing the Shift key on your QWERTY keyboard, drop the entire selected batch of samples onto the pad. Your samples will automatically be assigned to individual drum pads. This is a super slick and fast way to use your custom sample library (see Figure 2.35).

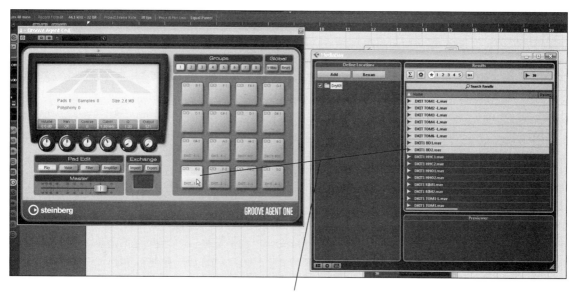

Drag and Drop Entire Custom
Drum Kits from MediaBay into
Groove Agent ONE

Figure 2.35 Transferring multiple samples from the MediaBay to Groove Agent ONE.

Note: I suggested the E-2 pad of Group 1 because if there are more than 16 samples in your selection, the remaining samples will spill over into the next sequential group due to the fact that there are only 16 pads per group.

Transferring an Audio Drum Loop via Slices into Groove Agent ONE

Now you can take your audio drum loops a few steps further by taking the individual sounds from within the loop and spreading them across Groove Agent ONE. By doing this, you'll have the ability to actually reprogram the original audio drum loop using MIDI.

The first step is to slice the drum loop that you want to trigger from Groove Agent ONE. Again, have both the MediaBay and Groove Agent ONE open and ready. In the MediaBay, locate the drum loop that you would like to slice from your sample library. Select and drag the desired loop to either a blank audio track or an empty spot below the tracks in the Project window. (The latter choice will create a new audio track.)

Note: For this exercise, make sure that you are not using the Align Beats to Project feature in the MediaBay before dragging your loop into the project. This means you'll be working at the loop's original tempo. Once the loop is transferred into the project, you should manually adjust the project tempo to match the loop. For tips on how to do this, refer to Chapter 3.

Double-click the loop when it appears in the audio track. (This should open the Sample Editor.) In the Sample Editor, create hitpoints for the loop (much like I described earlier in this chapter when quantizing MIDI to an audio groove). When you've set up your hitpoints correctly, click the button next to Create Slices in the Sample Editor's Inspector.

The Sample Editor will close when the slices are created. Double-click the part again. This time, it should bring up the Part Editor. The Part Editor contains several individual sample slices (audio events), as shown in Figure 2.36. If the slices are not touching each other, it means that your project tempo is not set correctly. Try adjusting the project tempo until the slices appear as they are in Figure 2.36.

Select all of these slices of the audio loop and then drag and drop them onto the bottom-left pad (while holding the Shift key) of a fresh instance of Groove Agent ONE, as explained in the previous walkthrough. Your slices will then become individual sounds on the Groove Agent ONE pads. You can delete or mute the original drum loop that you imported into the project, because you won't need it again (unless you feel you need to redo the slicing).

You can now audition each slice of your original audio loop using the Groove Agent ONE pads. Although this might not seem entirely practical, from here you can substitute individual sounds from your groove if necessary. This might not make complete

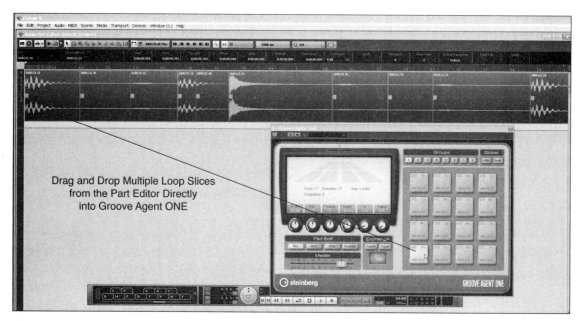

Figure 2.36 Spreading a sampled drum loop over Groove Agent ONE.

sense to you yet, but I will explain in the next section how you can now edit the audio groove using MIDI.

Note: You can also drag and drop individual slices from LoopMash into Groove Agent ONE. This tutorial is much more focused on transferring the whole drum loop via slices, but if you're just looking for one particular sound from the loop, utilizing LoopMash to slice the loop and then drag the slice from the LoopMash loop lane to a pad in Groove Agent ONE (similar to creating a composite track in LoopMash) might be the easiest way to go.

Creating a MIDI Track to Trigger a Sliced and Imported Audio Loop

For a finishing touch, you're going to take your newly converted loop in Groove Agent ONE another step further by creating a MIDI groove from it, which can be used to trigger the audio slices within Groove Agent ONE. This will allow you to work with the sliced audio file you created in the previous exercise in a way similar to using Loop-Mash, but using Groove Agent ONE instead.

First, create a new MIDI track for Groove Agent ONE in the Project window. Next, using Groove Agent ONE with your newly imported sliced drum loop, locate and select the arrow graphic under the Import button (it should be glowing) and drag and drop the arrow into your new MIDI track. This arrow-dragging action will create a MIDI representation of the sliced audio loops groove.

Now you can use this new MIDI groove to trigger the individual audio slices in Groove Agent ONE. To play back the slices as if the loop was still intact, assign the MIDI track to the VST instrument instance of Groove Agent ONE that contains the audio loop slices (see Figure 2.37).

Figure 2.37   Assigning the new MIDI groove track to the new sliced loop in Groove Agent ONE.

After you've properly assigned the MIDI track to Groove Agent ONE, clicking Play on the Transport should result in you hearing the sound of your audio loop again. The difference is that this time your loop is actually a MIDI part triggering your audio slices in Groove Agent ONE. (Note the flashing pads.) Now that the slices are being triggered by a MIDI part, you can easily quantize or remove any part of the groove (see Figure 2.38) simply by editing the MIDI. If you would like, you can also replace certain drum sounds with new samples by changing the sample on the pad triggered within Groove Agent ONE. The MIDI track will trigger the new samples just as it triggered the old samples.

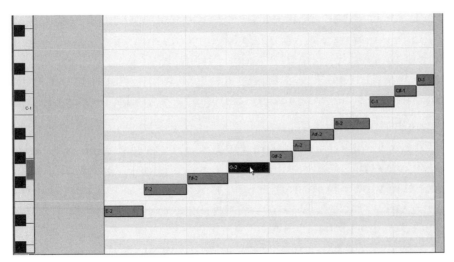

Figure 2.38   Moving a beat within the MIDI groove of the new sliced audio file.

However, make sure to replace all of the correct samples, because the MIDI track might be playing multiple samples of the same sound from within Groove Agent ONE.

Step Programming Drum Beats with Beat Designer

As I mentioned earlier, Beat Designer is one of the newest MIDI effect additions to Cubase, but it's not really an effect at all. It is its own program within Cubase and much more similar to a drum editor than an actual effect.

Beat Designer takes us back to the old-school approach of programming beats (similar to the Roland TR-808 and TR-909 drum machines, for those familiar with the good old days). Because I have gone over multiple ways to create beats already, you don't need to use Beat Designer to make your beats; it's just another option.

Beat Designer handles beats differently from any other method in Cubase. It's similar to ReDrum in Reason. Obviously, this way of programming has been "reborn," because a lot of people understand its simple-to-use control surface. Beat Designer does not actually contain any drum sounds; therefore, you need to use a source (most likely Groove Agent ONE) to trigger sounds from. To do that, create a MIDI track and load in Groove Agent ONE as a VST instrument. Afterward, load one of the preset banks from Groove Agent ONE (so that you have some sounds to work with). Next, from the Inspector of your selected MIDI track, choose Beat Designer as an insert effect. Your setup should look similar to that shown in Figure 2.39.

Figure 2.39 The Beat Designer is now active on a Groove Agent ONE MIDI track.

You can easily load pattern banks for Beat Designer from the Load/Save pop-up menu at the top of the Beat Designer window. As an alternative way of working with the pattern banks in Beat Designer, you also can locate these pattern banks in the Media-Bay and then audition them from there.

The fact that you can audition patterns through the MediaBay without having to load them is a real bonus when you're searching for the perfect premade beat (or at least something close to perfect). After you've found the pattern you're looking for, just double-click the pattern, and an Instrument track with all of its pre-saved settings and an instance of Groove Agent ONE will be loaded automatically.

Because you're dealing with a pattern-based drum machine format, the concept is that you create multiple patterns and assign them to keys, which you trigger via MIDI to capture a performance. This sequencing method is very similar to working with Loop-Mash scenes. If you follow my simple instructions from the LoopMash walkthroughs, along with the extra info in the Cubase manual (located in Help > Documentation > Plug-In Reference > Midi Effects > Beat Designer), programming your sequence should be a piece of cake. The main difference is that to trigger and record the changes, you need to activate Jump mode, which is located in the top-right corner of Beat Designer. Unlike the LoopMash's jump-interval feature, you only have the option of changing patterns for every bar, as opposed to making half-bar jumps and so on. Also, you can have up to 48 patterns per instance in Beat Designer, because it uses four banks of 12 pads (four octaves) as opposed to having access only to 24 pads total when using LoopMash.

When it comes to actually programming the beat in Beat Designer, it doesn't really get much easier. The default is set to one measure of 1/16 notes per pattern; if you want to change that, you can do so by changing the settings at the top left. To select the sounds in your pattern, click each sound in the list on the left to open a list of sounds available.

Drawing in patterns is easy. Just click in the space where you want a beat. To create an accented beat (louder), click toward the top half of the sound's track. Or, to create a beat with the normal input velocity, select toward the bottom of the sound's track. If you change your mind, click on the note again, and it'll be gone.

You can solo each sound's track while playing the pattern to focus on the particular sound you're working with. You can insert up to three flams within each beat to give certain beats that extra little punch by clicking in the lower-left portion of each beat. The flam's position and level are adjustable by using the sliders located at the bottom left.

One super cool feature is the ability to have two different swing settings. Then, on top of that, you have the ability to adjust each individual sound in the pattern's swing. This can really add some character to the overall groove (see Figure 2.40).

You have more options available in the top-left menu (the arrow pointing down) in Beat Designer (see Figure 2.41). Most of these are fairly straightforward, but here's a quick breakdown as to what each function does:

- **Shift Left.** This simply moves the entire groove to the left one increment. The first beat moves to the last position. This is great for repositioning the start and end of the pattern loop.

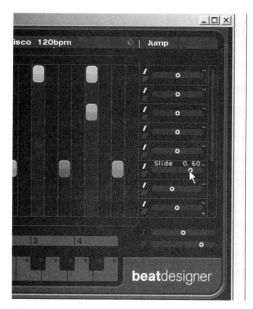

Figure 2.40 Adding some swing to the hi-hats in a preset groove.

- **Shift Right.** This is the exact opposite of Shift Left.

- **Reverse.** Similar to the MIDI function, this just flips the events around and starts with the events at the end. It does not create backward-sounding samples.

- **Copy Pattern.** This is exactly as it sounds—it makes a duplicate of the entire pattern to the Clipboard for pasting.

- **Paste Pattern.** This allows you to put your duplicate in a new location.

- **Clear Pattern.** This wipes the pattern you're viewing clean so you can start fresh.

- **Insert Pattern at Cursor.** This handy little feature takes the pattern that is currently visible and creates either a MIDI part representation on the MIDI track (if you're working on a MIDI track) or an audio part representation on the VST Instrument track (if you used the VST instrument method). This allows you to easily edit the loop like any MIDI part. Using this method, the one-bar pattern is placed at the cursor location on the track you're using.

- **Insert Subbank at Cursor.** This is even more useful than Insert Pattern at Cursor because it inserts every pattern that is within the currently selected bank (up to 12 patterns total) into the MIDI or VST Instrument track at the cursor location. When all your patterns are located on a MIDI track, you can edit their arrangement however you like without the need for programming changes.

- **Insert Pattern at Left Locator.** This is exactly the same as Insert Pattern at Cursor, except it puts the pattern start at the left locator.

- **Insert Subbank at Left Locator.** This is exactly the same as Insert Subbank at Cursor, except it puts the pattern start at the left locator.

- **Fill Loop with Pattern.** This fills the MIDI or VST Instrument track with the currently selected Beat Designer pattern from the left locator to the right locator.

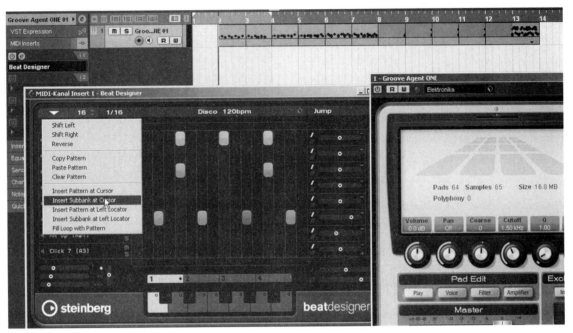

Figure 2.41 Inserting Beat Designer patterns into a VST Instrument track using Insert Subbank at Cursor.

VST Instruments in Cubase 6

So far, as VST instruments are concerned, you've familiarized yourself with Groove Agent ONE and LoopMash. You've learned a lot about drum instruments. Cubase also has a great arsenal of included synths, on which I could write a whole book. If you're into synths, Prologue provides excellent classic subtractive synthesis. Spector uses a spectrum filter to create some very rich sound pads and textures. Mystic also makes some rich-sounding textures using comb filters. Embracer works very nicely for synth pads, and when it comes to mono leads and bass lines, Monologue is usually the way to go.

Whenever I need a synth sound, I'm fairly confident that I can find or create what I need with this collection alone. If for some reason I can't find or create what I need, I use a sample of a synth in HALion ONE or its big brother, HALion Sonic SE.

HALion ONE is a very useful but simple sample player. You can consider it to be sort of a mini version of HALion Sonic SE. Even though it isn't multi-timbral like HALion Sonic SE, you can use multiple instances of it to get the same effect.

Note: I've mentioned the term "instances" a few times in this book. As this pertains to VST instruments, it means having several of the same instruments loaded. For example, you can have a rack full of eight HALion ONE sample players even though there is only one HALion ONE VST plug-in. Just load another *instance* of HALion ONE.

The HALion Symphonic Orchestra is a great library of sounds, and Cubase 6 comes with a trial version of the instrument, just as it also came with Cubase 5. The cost to upgrade and own the full orchestra is only $99—an amazing bargain. If you purchase the license, you can utilize the sounds with HALion Sonic SE as well as with its own HALion Symphonic Orchestra player. Using HALion Sonic SE makes it even easier to utilize the VST Expression that the Symphonic Orchestra provides.

Figure 2.42   The HALion Symphonic Orchestra utilized from within HALion Sonic SE.

Note: Before you rush out to purchase HALion Sonic, you might want to wait for the release of HALion 4 (coming soon). I have used HALion 3 for years. I'm certain that the VST sampler HALion 4 will offer even more flexibility than HALion Sonic and will have a lot of the same (and possibly more) new VST3.5 features.

The only argument for the HALion Sonic instrument is its massive library of easily accessible sounds.

Tips When Using VST Instruments

The VST3.5 platform is brand new at this point. Most third-party companies are still scrambling to come out with a VST3 version of their plug-ins. Even if you can get your hands on a VST3 version of any plug-in, you'll be better off working with it in Cubase 6. You can save system resources, automate them more easily, and have overall better compatibility.

I've never had to use VST System Link or run my VST instruments through another computer. If you're doing some heavy-duty live recordings, I could possibly see the need to use VST System Link down the road, but I don't think most users ever need to worry about syncing two computers together in this way. Computers are getting faster, RAM and hard drives are getting cheaper, and I've had enough experience with syncing things in the past to really allow me to appreciate the fact that I can have everything in one "box." If you need to save system resources, just do what I've been doing for years, when there was no such thing as system resources: Bounce your VST instruments down to audio tracks and then disable the instrument, or use the Freeze function. You can always reactivate your instrument down the road if you need to correct something in the mix. You'll save yourself a lot of headaches and never have to worry about sync issues or system resources.

VST instruments can cause major technical issues in Cubase—especially ones by third-party developers. The more instruments you pile into your system at once, the more you can expect your system to crash. Be careful when opening too many at once, and always save your work before loading instruments, just to be safe.

If you ever get a stuck MIDI note on one of your VSTs (or external synths), try to first implement the MIDI reset, which is found at the bottom of the MIDI menu. This little feature can come in really handy. Using this reset won't do anything harmful to your system or project. It was designed solely to kill that stuck MIDI note.

Whenever you load a VST instrument, a VST Instrument track is created for it. This is where you can find everything that has to do with the automation of the plug-in as well its audio output. If you want to hear your VST instrument through one of the audio plug-in effects, you can do so by activating the "e" (*edit instrument channel settings*) on the channel that reads Volume. (This is the output routing of the instrument.) Once you have that setting open and available, you can adjust your effects or EQ if necessary.

Keep in mind that routing an effect this way will cause the effect to be recorded to the audio track if you bounce down the instrument. It can be a little tricky trying to audition the playback of the VST instrument while you're making adjustments to your instrument audio settings because both the VST Instrument track and the MIDI track need to be selected, and they have a tendency to cancel each other out. It might be frustrating at times, but it is possible. Remember to use the Ctrl/Command key while selecting multiple tracks at once.

You can also select which audio output you want to use for whatever instance of your VST instrument you're using from within the VST Instruments panel. Just click the last icon on the left side of the instrument and select the output you would like. Using multiple outputs is great if you want to get a great mix without bouncing the instrument to an audio track first, and this is a quick and easy way to define how many outs should appear in the Project window. When using multiple outputs, remember that you still have to define which sounds are routed to each individual output from within the VST instrument.

External synths and other MIDI devices can be controlled in similar ways to virtual instruments. You can control the parameters of the synths via panels from within Cubase. If you use a particular external synth frequently, I recommend setting up a control panel for it. It's not exactly a simple process, but taking the extra time could help you get the most out of your external device. For more on external MIDI devices, refer to the Cubase 6 manual. Designing a control panel can become tedious and similar to designing a website, but both the device panels and the smaller user panels (within the Inspector) can make it really easy to automate those external synths (see Figure 2.43).

Figure 2.43 Using a device panel for an external Roland MC-303 in Cubase.

3 Taking Audio to the Limit in Cubase 6

MIDI is where Cubase started, but the powerful audio recording and editing tools available today make it a DAW that is just as professional as Nuendo and Pro Tools.

In this chapter, I will be going over some of the new audio editing features in Cubase 6, such as Advanced Tempo Detection, grouping and editing multiple audio tracks (such as live acoustic drum kits), and the new VST Amp Rack. Along with these new features, I will also discuss important features that are still somewhat new, such as vocal pitch correction using VariAudio, the offline process history, and a general overview of how to work with audio in Cubase.

I'll also discuss the Steinberg MR816 CSX audio interface that was specifically designed for use with Cubase in mind in order to maximize its audio possibilities. There are a lot of choices out there for audio interfaces, but if you're a serious Cubase user, this choice can be a very attractive one (even if only for the fact that the MR816 CSX is an audio interface that is manufactured and fully supported by Steinberg).

Grouping and Editing Live Acoustic Drums

Regardless of whether you record live drums, you can get something out of this tutorial. You can apply the all-new process of grouping and editing grouped tracks to any group of audio and/or MIDI tracks. The reason I've decided to title this tutorial "Grouping and Editing Live Acoustic Drums" is because it's a very common practice to edit multiple drum tracks simultaneously, because each individual track (hi-hat, snare, kick, and so on) is really just a small piece of the big drum puzzle.

Even if you're not set up to record live acoustic drums, you're in luck. Steinberg has included a full-blown band demo that includes tracks of a drum kit, and I'll be using it as an example not only for this tutorial, but also for the tutorials on the VST Amp rack and vocal pitch correction later in this chapter.

To open this demo, you'll need to transfer its project folder from your Cubase 6 installation disc to your hard drive. You can find the folder by viewing the contents of the disc, opening the Cubase 6 for Windows (or Mac) folder, then opening the Additional

Content folder, and finally the Demo Projects folder. Here you should see a folder labeled Cubase 6 - Live Forever. Drag this folder over to the hard drive where you store all of your Cubase projects.

Note: The Live Forever demo also contains a QuickTime video. Depending on the transfer rate of your hard drive and your computer, you may have trouble playing back the project (due to the video). If so, you can try removing the Live Forever QuickTime file from the project or perhaps move the Live Forever QuickTime file to another hard drive (removing it from the original folder). After you move the QuickTime file, when you load the project, the QuickTime file will show as *missing* from your project. If you want to ignore the video, just skip the search for the missing file. If you'd like to try to view the video, you can try to select it from another hard drive. Selecting the video from another drive takes a lot of pressure off your project hard drive, and it could work. Also, make sure you have the latest version of QuickTime installed on your system (download it for free from QuickTime.com) if you plan to watch the demo video. Keep in mind that the demo video is just for show and is not required for the walk-throughs in this chapter.

After you've transferred the Live Forever demo to your project drive, launch Cubase, select Open from the File menu, and navigate Cubase to the copied Live Forever project on your project drive. When loaded, it should look similar to Figure 3.1.

Figure 3.1 Steinberg's Live Forever project in Cubase 6.

> **Note:** If you've removed the QuickTime video or altered its location, it's a good idea to choose Save As and rename the project so that you don't have to deal with the missing-file issue every time you reload this demo project.

The click (metronome) can be a useful tool when editing timing, but it's not active on this project's output. Select VST Connections and then select the Output tab and click in the Click column just to the right of the Device Port column (as shown in Figure 3.2). Now you should be able to hear the audio click at 130 bpm, along with the "Live Forever" song.

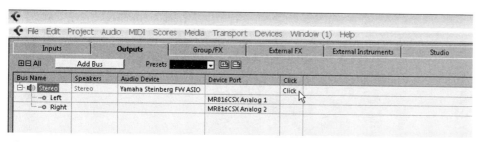

Figure 3.2 Activating the click in the Cubase project.

Go ahead and listen through the song and solo individual drum tracks (such as the kick or snare) as you listen back. Notice how you can hear some of the snare and cymbals on the kick-drum track. This is a common occurrence that's hard to control when you're recording a full live acoustic drum kit with microphones.

Notice that there is a track simply named Drums. This is a Folder track. Even though these drums were all recorded separately on individual audio tracks, this Folder track was created later, as a container for all of the individual tracks.

You also might have noticed that some of the audio tracks (such as Bass Drum In and Bass Drum Out) have been grouped into Group Channel tracks, and those tracks are also included within the Drums Folder track. The Group Channel tracks were created so that the similar tracks could share the same output (typically known as *bussing* tracks). If you select the "e" (edit channel settings) on either the Bass Drum In or the Bass Drum Out track, you can see that the output has been directed to the Bass Drum Group Channel track, as shown in Figure 3.3. This technique makes it easier to control the level of the bass drum through one audio channel, as opposed to trying to control it from multiple tracks at the same time.

There is also a shared limiter effect on the Group Channel as opposed to the individual channels. If you try to solo either one of the Bass Drum tracks, the Group Channel track will also be soloed because it contains the audio output. Soloing only the Bass Drum Group Channel track will result in nothing being heard because both Bass Drum tracks will be muted. Although this is a good example of using a Group Channel track,

Edit Channel Settings Button
Reveals the Routing for Each Track

Bass Drums Group
Channel Track

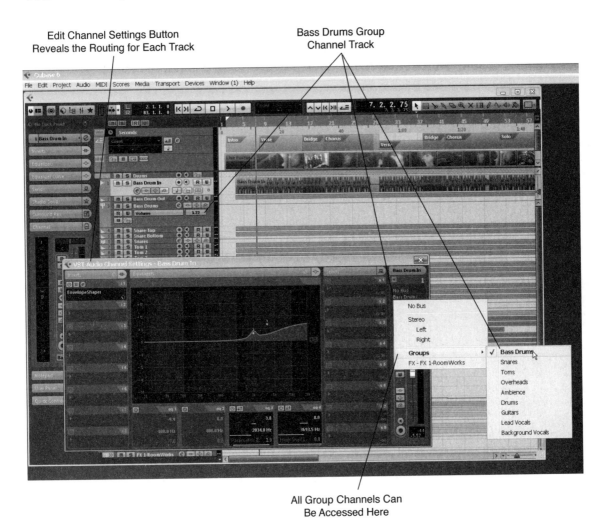

All Group Channels Can
Be Accessed Here

Figure 3.3 Utilizing Group Channel tracks on similar instruments.

it should also be noted that it's not absolutely necessary to group audio tracks in this manner when creating a mix.

Note: To create a new Group Channel track or a Folder track, simply select the option from the Add Track function in the Project menu.

A Folder track is also used for grouping, but in a completely different way than that of using a Group Channel. Instead of bussing outputs, a Folder track simply allows you to edit a group of tracks together instead of individually. This means if you want to edit the drums as a whole group, you can simply edit the Folder track as opposed to each of the individual tracks.

Select Solo on the Drums Folder track. Notice how *all* the individual drum audio tracks (and Group Channel tracks) within the Folder track have now been soloed (meaning that only drums can be heard in the mix). Now, let's say that I wanted to change the groove in Measures 4–8 to sound identical to that of the drum groove from Measures 8–12. Instead of editing the individual tracks, I can simply edit the Folder track, just as I would if it were a stereo mix of the drums. Go ahead and cut the Folder track with the Split tool so that Bars 4–8 and Bars 8–12 are split (remember to set your snap at bar, your snap settings at grid, and your ruler at bars and beats for an easy edit) and then delete the edited Folder track part at Bars 4–8. Notice how all of the individual audio tracks contained in the Folder track were split and later deleted as you edited the Folder track. Next, copy and paste Bars 8–12 of the Folder track into Bars 4–8, as shown in Figure 3.4. Now that's an easy way to cut and paste a bunch of tracks!

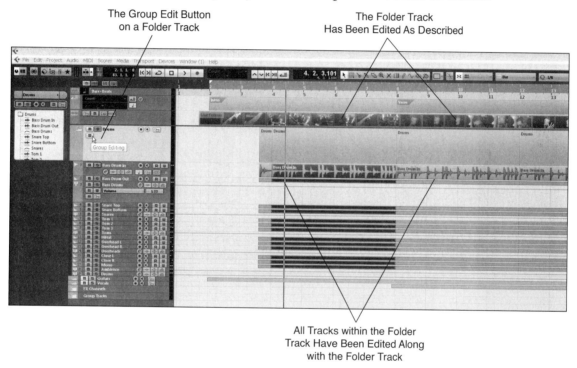

Figure 3.4 Editing the drum Folder track.

Take note of the = sign button on the Folder track. This button is also known as the Group Edit button. When this button is active, selecting any track within the Folder track will automatically select any other track that shares the exact same start and end point within the group. In most cases, this will be all the tracks included in the folder, unless the tracks have been edited individually as well as in the group.

Note: When a track within the Folder track has been edited individually, it can no longer be considered a part of the group for group editing. If you try to edit a Folder track that has been compromised in this way, you will also get a warning that there could be sync issues after editing the Folder track. To prevent this, you should make all group edits *before* making any individual edits—or, if necessary, you can remove the track you wish to edit individually from the Folder track.

Making an edit to a track within the Folder track while the Group Edit button is active will also apply the edit to the other selected (grouped) tracks, including the Folder track itself.

> **Note:** Because individual tracks that have been edited previously will not be included in the group, selecting and editing another (previously unedited) audio track (while the Group Edit button is active) is a good way to focus on the group tracks without affecting the sync of the previously edited track.

Quantizing Live Acoustic Drums

Quantizing live drums on multiple audio tracks is slightly different from simply quantizing a stereo mix of drums. The reason is that all of the individual tracks need to be edited as one track so that there aren't any sync issues later.

Using the Folder track and the Group Edit button (as mentioned in the previous tutorial) is the first step in quantizing live acoustic drums. Next, you need to determine how to slice all of your tracks so that they groove the way you want them to.

> **Note:** Instead of trying to quantize the entire drum track in one pass, edit the Drum Folder track so that just the chorus is isolated from the rest of the song (Measures 20–30).

The first step is to set the hitpoints for the individual audio tracks. (You cannot set hitpoints as a group edit.) You don't have to set hitpoints for *every* track in the Folder track, though. Setting the hitpoints on the tracks that contain the main groove is enough. Go ahead and determine hitpoints on the individual tracks for the Bass Drum In, Snare Top, and Hi Hat tracks using the same methods as discussed in Chapter 2, in the "Quantizing MIDI Parts to an Audio Groove" section. There's no need to create a groove from the hitpoints at this time (as you did in Chapter 2).

After you've set your hitpoints, activate the Group Edit button on the Drums Folder track and then select the Bass Drum In track and open the Quantize panel from the Edit menu (as shown in Figure 3.5). The three tracks for which you created hitpoints should be listed under the Slice Rules Hitpoint Tracks.

Notice that there is a priority ranking next to each of the hitpoint tracks. The higher the star rating, the more important the track is in determining the groove. In this case, the bass drum is set at the highest priority, with the other tracks having a lower rating. If your tracks are not ranked in this priority, adjust them to match Figure 3.5 by clicking on the stars.

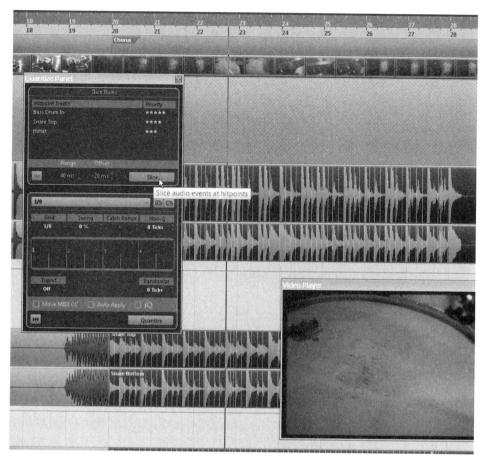

Figure 3.5 Setting up the slice rules in the Quantize panel.

You can use the Range control to minimize slices in a similar way to how the Threshold feature controls the number of hitpoints created. The Offset control helps prevent cutting off signals on tracks that do not contain hitpoints and can also help when crossfading slices (discussed a little later in this tutorial). Using both the Range and Offset controls is a little tricky, and you'll probably find that it's best just to use the trial-and-error method.

When you have a setting, select the Slice button, and all of the grouped tracks will be sliced accordingly. If you're not happy with the way the audio was sliced, select the Reset button (to the left of the Range control), adjust the Range, Offset, or Priority, and then re-slice by selecting the Slice button again.

At this point, even though all of your drum's audio tracks have been sliced, the actual groove of the drums should not be altered. This is because you have not yet applied quantization. Up until this point, you've merely *prepared* the drums for quantization.

This particular track sticks to a basic straight eighth-note feel, so go ahead and set your quantize to 1/8. Quantize as you would any MIDI or audio part (adjusting the swing, iterative quantize, and so on as necessary).

> **Note:** At this point, you can also use a groove you've created from another audio or MIDI track, as discussed in Chapter 2. Using this method, you can quantize the drums to the bass guitar track or perhaps a MIDI click track if necessary.

When you quantize the drums, you'll probably notice gaps or overlaps in the audio where the drums have been sliced and repositioned. This is normal. The Crossfades section of the Quantize panel (which opens when the audio track has been sliced) is designed to fix those gaps and overlaps. The Crossfade Editor (the "e" button) allows you to specify the curve type. To create less space in the gaps or remove overlaps, add length to or subtract it from crossfades under the Length parameter. Use the Nudge tool buttons to reposition the location where the crossfade occurs (left or right). When you've made your settings, select the Crossfade button.

> **Note:** Even though the Crossfade Editor is a nice addition, I sometimes find that manually expanding a single slice (selected with the Object Selection tool) past the following slice for crossfading is easier in certain circumstances. In this example, there are a couple of tricky spots where the automated crossfade option does not work well. For an easy fix, simply drag the right side of the slice before the gap across the gap (with Group Editing still active) until it extends past the next slice and select "x" for crossfade.

Quick and Easy Live Drum Replacement

There's nothing quite like capturing a live drummer's performance and the sound of a fully miked acoustic drum kit. Recording in this manner sometimes comes with a few catches, though. Not only do you have to have a great drummer and a great-sounding kit, you also must have a great live acoustic recording room, the right microphones, a multi-input audio interface or mixer, and a great engineer. As you can see, there are a lot of places where recording live acoustic drums can go wrong.

There's also another problem with recording live drums. This is a problem that sometimes goes unnoticed until the final mixing starts. The problem could actually be the captured *sound* of the actual drums. Keep in mind that this is also after the drummer has finished recording, packed up his/her drum kit, and called it a day. Not only that, there's a good chance that the final mix is being done at a completely separate location from where the original drums were recorded. Calling the drummer in to re-record the drums might not even be an option.

So, let's say you're mixing down this Live Forever track in your studio. You're now in *your* studio, and you don't have a live drum room. The drum performance is perfect, but you can't seem to get the snare drum to have the same crisp bite in the recording that it normally has. Or maybe you're a producer, and upon listening back to the track, you're thinking that the sound of the snare overpowers the vocals at the start of the song. How do you fix it?

For many years, MIDI and samplers have come to the aid of engineers and producers in this scenario for what is known as *drum replacement* or *enhancement*. During drum replacement, a drum sample is triggered from a sampler via MIDI, and the original drum is muted from the track (meaning the original sound is completely eliminated from the mix). In drum enhancement, the original drum is left, but a sampled drum is also layered and mixed with the original to add to the quality of the overall sound.

Cubase 6 comes with a super-easy way to replace or enhance drum tracks. Because Groove Agent ONE comes with Cubase, you already have a built-in sampler and a library of drum replacement sounds. The next obstacle is capturing the performance of the drummer. In the previous tutorial, you adjusted and created hitpoints for the snare. These hitpoints are actually MIDI representations of the actual drum hits. Hitpoints have no sound, but because they represent hit locations on the grid, all Cubase really needs to do is to assign note information to the hitpoint so that it actually becomes a MIDI note. Once it becomes a MIDI note, the MIDI note can be used to trigger *any* MIDI source.

For this tutorial, refer to the first verse of the song "Live Forever." Let's replace the sound of the snare drum with a sample of a snare rim to change the overall tone of the first verse. Work with the original copy of the Live Forever track so that there are no previous edits. Make sure the Group Edit button is disabled. Split the Snare Top track so that it ends right before the double snare hit before Bar 16 and then do the same with the Snare Bottom track. Double-click on the Snare Top track so that the Sample Editor is visible. There should be hitpoints created, but if not, create hitpoints. Next, select Create MIDI Notes from the Sample Editor's Inspector under the Hitpoints tab. The Convert Hitpoints to MIDI Notes dialog box will appear, as shown in Figure 3.6.

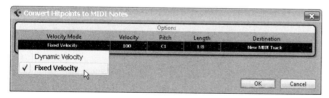

Figure 3.6 The Convert Hitpoints to MIDI Notes dialog box.

This is a very simple conversion tool to help you create the ideal MIDI track for your drums. The first field allows you to choose how Cubase handles the dynamics of the tracks. Cubase will attempt to translate the audio data's dynamics (the loudness or softness of the transient attacks on the actual drum tracks) into MIDI data if Dynamic Velocity is selected under Velocity mode.

This is not a perfect science. First, you must realize that just because the dynamics are somewhat captured, a sampler will only respond to certain dynamic changes. (For example, if the translated dynamic isn't at 80 but instead is at 81, then you may not hear any difference in sound.)

The other option is to create your notes at a fixed velocity. Next to the Velocity Mode column is a column for setting a fixed velocity. This means that every note created will have this velocity setting. Either of these settings will work, and you can always edit the dynamics via the Key Editor, In-Place Editor, or Drum Editor later on so that you get the most out of the sampler you're using.

The Pitch column simply defines the note you will create from the hitpoint information. Again, you can change this note later via MIDI editing to match the sample pad on Groove Agent ONE.

The Note Length setting depends on the feel of the track. If the track has a quarter-note feel, set it to 1/4 notes. If it has a 1/16-note feel, set the note length to 1/16. The longer you can set the note, the more sustain you'll get from your sampled MIDI drum.

Finally, the Destination defines where you want the MIDI track to go when it's created. The first choice is the first selected track. If you've previously set up a MIDI track with a sampler, it might be a good idea to select that track before taking these steps for a quick and easy conversion. If you haven't prepared a MIDI track yet, then selecting New MIDI Track will automatically create a new track for you. If you would like to just copy the data to the virtual clipboard so you can paste it where you need it later, select Project Clipboard.

For this tutorial, select Fixed Velocity, set the Velocity at 100, and set the Pitch at C-1, the Note Length at 1/8, and the Destination to New MIDI Track. Click OK.

Next, close the Sample Editor and scroll to the bottom of the track list in the Project window to find your newly created MIDI track for your snare drum part. Now, open Groove Agent ONE from VST Instruments under the Devices menu. (If you're asked to create a new MIDI track, select Cancel.)

From the Preset menu (located at the top of Groove Agent ONE), select Brush Kit. With your new MIDI track selected, change the output of your MIDI track to Groove Agent ONE from the Inspector (as shown in Figure 3.7). Now solo the MIDI track and click Play on the Transport. You should hear your snare part being played on a kick drum. This is because we created the MIDI note at C-1, and on this particular kit, C-1 happens to be a kick drum.

To fix this, click and drag the Rim pad to the Kick 2 pad. This will correct the problem. Now when you play back your MIDI track, you should hear the Rim sound you're looking for.

Groove Agent ONE Active on the Drum
Replacement MIDI Track Output

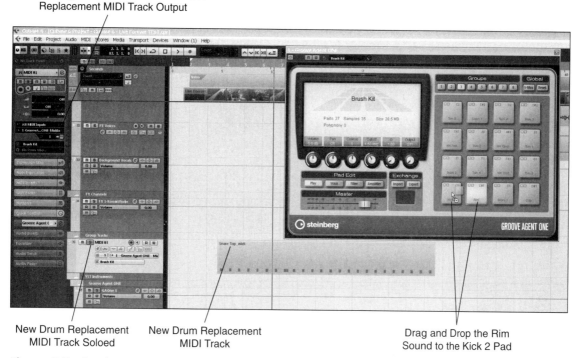

New Drum Replacement   New Drum Replacement   Drag and Drop the Rim
MIDI Track Soloed   MIDI Track   Sound to the Kick 2 Pad

Figure 3.7 Setting up Groove Agent ONE with your new MIDI track.

Last but not least, un-solo your MIDI track and mute both the Snare Top and Snare Bottom parts that you split earlier. Now when you play back your track, you will hear the new Rim sound, and the sound of the originally recorded snare will be gone. The snare will come back in at the pre-chorus, where we want it, and the Rim will disappear. It's like magic!

Of course, you don't have to stick with that particular Rim sound. Now that you're working with MIDI and samples, changing sounds is a breeze. You can even sample the same exact snare you used originally by recording a hit (in your studio or wherever) and then assigning that edited audio "snare hit" to a pad on Groove Agent ONE, as I demonstrated in Chapter 2. The possibilities are endless. To enhance the drum sound, simply un-mute the original track and mix and blend between the new MIDI track and the old audio track.

Working with the MR816 CSX

As I mentioned earlier, recording live drums usually requires a multi-input audio interface. In the case of the Live Forever demo, there were 13 live drum tracks recorded simultaneously. This means that they had to utilize a soundcard that had multiple inputs. Because Steinberg's flagship audio interface is the MR816 CSX, I'm sure that they used at least two of these interfaces linked together so that they could record the entire band in one pass.

There are two slightly different models of the MR816: the MR816 X and the MR816 CSX. Both are very similar, with the only significant difference being that the MR816 CSX includes a Sweet Spot Morphing Channel Strip (see Figure 3.8).

Figure 3.8 The Steinberg MR816 CSX.

The price of the MR816 CSX is a little higher than many other audio interfaces, but because we are talking about going pro, an audio interface should be judged on how well it fits in the professional scheme, as opposed to its price. Like the CC121 discussed in Chapter 1, the MR816 CSX was built around Cubase; that's what makes this audio interface stand out in the oversaturated world of pro audio interfaces.

The most important aspect of any audio interface is the audio quality, and the MR816 CSX definitely delivers. When I first made the adjustment from another interface, which I liked and had gotten used to, I was disappointed in the sound at first. Then I realized that the sound from the MR816 CSX was less "colored" (distorted) than the other interface. After making adjustments to my mixes, not only was the sound better on my system, but my mixes sounded great on other systems as well.

The MR816 CSX is definitely designed for professional studio use, and you can interface up to eight analog XLR/TRS connectors. As with several other interfaces on the market, you can also chain up to three units together to add the possibility of recording up to 48 tracks simultaneously (or 24 tracks using only the analog inputs). In your chain, you can mix the different versions of the MR816 with no headaches. The feel of the MR816 CSX is full-on professional. Steinberg didn't skimp with cheap buttons, knobs, and connectors. This audio interface is just as professional as any gear that Yamaha (the parent company of Steinberg) creates.

If you've recorded a lot of vocals with other audio interfaces without using direct monitoring, you might have noticed there's a little noticeable latency. Using direct monitoring with most interfaces will solve the latency issue, but because direct monitoring means that you're bypassing the VST engine, you will not be able to use your plug-in effects or monitor with effects. If your singer needed to monitor her vocal performance with effects (such as reverb), the process could be a little tricky. The MR816 CSX uses direct monitoring as well, but by using its built-in reverb and compressor DSP (unlike using a plug-in effect), you can achieve zero latency—and monitoring with reverb is painless.

Keep in mind that when you monitor a performance using direct monitoring, you are not really listening to a true representation of what is being recorded. This is because when utilizing direct monitoring, you will be hearing the input bus as opposed to the output bus (which explains why you can't utilize the VST effects when using direct monitoring). If hearing a true representation of the output is a must (for instance, if there was a plug-in that you absolutely had to hear while recording), the MR816 can achieve latency as low as 1.188 ms (very low).

Remember that achieving this sort of latency will put a tremendous strain on your system. This means that the more you have going on in your mix (such as VST effects, EQ, several tracks, and so on), the less likely you'll be able to have extremely low latency. Although using the Constrain Delay Compensation (found on the toolbar) can help in controlling the latency when you're not utilizing direct monitoring, it also can impose more strain on your system. The MR816 and Cubase 6 are both capable of running on a 64-bit system. If you choose to go down the 64-bit road, you can utilize more RAM on your system. More RAM means that you'll be more likely to achieve lower latency without using direct monitoring.

Unless you're recording some experimental vocals, most of the time a little reverb (in the headphones) and some EQ and compression are all that you're going to need. The MR816 CSX has that covered. The included reverb is very simple, but it should cover all your bases when it comes to having a basic "recording" reverb. The Sweet Spot Morphing Channel Strip comes in handy as an alternative to using another outboard compressor/EQ on input, except you can easily bypass or simply monitor the effect as well as record the effect while tracking. Another advantage to having these two effects in the MR816 CSX is that you can use them both during a mix (as opposed to using them only during recording and monitoring). You can also save their settings along with the project (just as you would an internal VST3 plug-in).

Getting back to the idea that the MR816 CSX was built around Cubase, the element that truly sets it apart from other audio interfaces is the Cubase *link*. This link I'm referring to gives you the ability to bus your audio inputs to your audio tracks (using what Steinberg refers to as the *Quick Connect* feature) without having to continuously reset your ins and outs in the Inspector or Device Setup window. This is an indispensable tool for speeding up the process of capturing live takes in the studio. To set up your tracks, all you have to do is select the track on which you would like to record in the Cubase project and then select the input button of the MR816 that you'd like to bus (see Figure 3.9).

In a case where you might want to bus multiple inputs to a stereo track (for instance, eight individual acoustic drum mics coming into the MR816 but recorded into one stereo track in Cubase), you'll need to first set up your mix in the VST mixer in Cubase in its input section and then manually create a stereo bus (under VST Connections). Afterwards, you simply send the signal from each input channel's sends to the new bus. When the signal from the desired inputs has been routed to the appropriate bus, you can select that bus as your input under a stereo track in the Project window. This

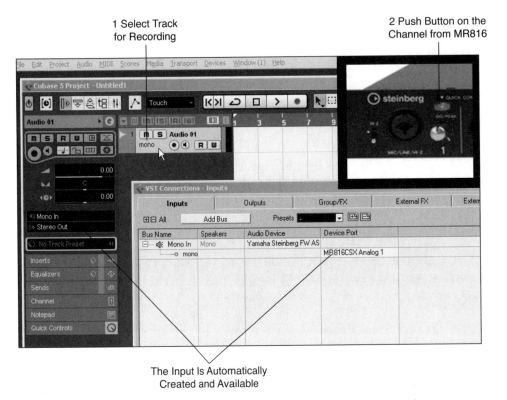

Figure 3.9 Bussing an audio input of the MR816 to an audio track.

method isn't quite as simple and automated, but it *is* effective, and it beats having to use an external submixer.

Lastly, the MR816 also allows the possibility for setting up two separate latency-free headphone mixes by using the monitoring section in Cubase along with the studio sends and MR816 hardware setup window. Even though there are only two separate headphone outputs on the MR816, you can technically create four studio sends in Cubase 6 and output the other two headphone mixes through stereo outputs on the MR816 to external headphone amps. The only minor complaint about the MR816 is that there are no MIDI connections. If you're using a non-USB MIDI keyboard, you'll need some sort of MIDI interface.

> **Note:** The MR816 can record at up to 96 kHz. It's nice to have that option, but keep in mind that although pros always strive for the highest quality possible, lower settings have been used for years. If necessary (due to hard drive capabilities), I suggest using lower settings for tracking (to save resources) and using higher settings for mixdowns. Even though the performance won't be captured at the best quality using this method, the processing in Cubase will shine through in the mix. Also, recording with compression/EQ has always been optional. There are many working pros who prefer to record using as little processing as

possible, as well as those who choose to utilize all sorts of processing between the recording signal and the recorder. It's all a matter of preference, and there is no real "standard" method when it comes to this sort of thing. If you don't feel comfortable using compression or EQ, you probably should avoid using it before recording it along with a performance.

Rockin' Out with the VST Amp Rack

We've covered all sorts of areas with drums so far, but we haven't even scratched the surface of guitar. Cubase 6 has taken guitar sounds to new levels with the all new VST Amp Rack.

The VST Amp Rack is not unlike a lot of other guitar amp modeling software that's currently on the market. If you are not familiar with amp modeling software, here's a brief explanation. *Amp modeling* is a virtual representation of what a guitar amplifier does to a guitar. Imagine having a computer connected to popular amps so that it can read and calculate what happens to the sound of the guitar as it makes its way through the amp. Now, take the guitar and the amp out of the equation and replace it with a program that simulates what the amp is doing based on the calculations made by the original computer. Now, add *your* guitar to the program to fill in where the original guitar left off. What you get in the end is a virtual guitar amp by simply plugging your guitar into your computer. Now, instead of having one guitar amp, imagine modeling many different guitar amps with different speaker configurations.

Guitar amp modeling has been around for years. One of the first innovators of this technology was a company called Line 6. Line 6 not only creates amp modeling software, but they also create real guitars and amps that are created to be used along with the amp modeling technology. Since Line 6, other companies such as Waves, IK Multimedia, Native Instruments, and even guitar amp manufactures such as Fender and Peavey have jumped on board, bringing us amp modeling software. Steinberg may be a little late to the party, but good things come to those who wait. The average guitar amp modeling plug-in's list price is anywhere from $100 to $300. Seeing as Cubase retails for $500, they're pretty much just throwing us a bone.

I'm not a guitar player, but I work with guitar players. When it comes to guitar tone, I'm picky. I often record heavy-metal guitar, and the thought of plugging a guitar into a computer and rocking out (without cranking an amp up to 11) sounds more than a little strange to me. The fact is that amp modeling technology is getting better and better all of the time, and when using amp modeling, it's easier to dial up a great tone more quickly than using conventional old-school methods.

Even if you're not a guitar player, you'll be able to *hear* what amp modeling can do to a guitar. Once again, we will be referring to the Live Forever demo that was included with Cubase 6. Refer to the first tutorial in this chapter for an explanation of how to locate and load that project into your system. When the Live Forever project is loaded, locate the Guitar Solo track and solo the track. Although my guess is that all of these guitar parts were recorded using the VST Amp Rack, we know for certain that the Guitar Solo is using the VST Amp Rack, because its processing is happening in real time. Select the "e" on the Guitar Solo track to bring up your Audio Channel Settings, and you'll see that the VST Amp Rack is active as an insert (as shown in Figure 3.10).

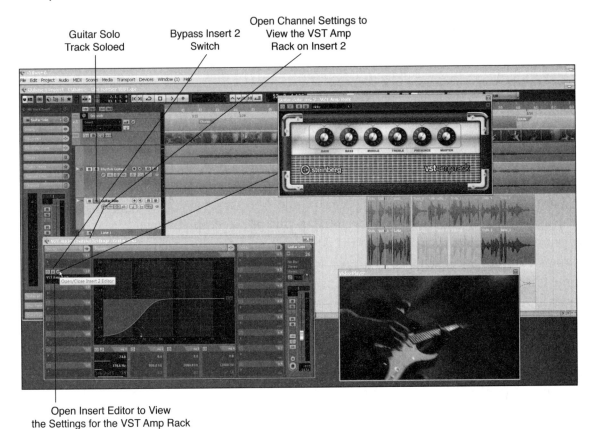

Figure 3.10 Checking out the VST Amp Rack on the Live Forever guitar solo.

Play the track at the point where the solo starts (around Measure 51) and listen to the solo guitar through the VST Amp Rack. Sound good? Now select the Bypass Insert 2 switch (as shown in Figure 3.10) and listen back. What you should be hearing now is the naked guitar without the VST Amp Rack. This guitar was obviously recorded with no processing (except for a little wah pedal action) before going straight into the computer. As you can hear, without the VST Amp Rack, the guitar sound is almost nonexistent! This should be a pretty vivid statement of the power behind the VST Amp Rack.

Note: For the rest of this tutorial, I recommend setting the left locator at Bar 51 and the right locator at Bar 61 and selecting the Cycle control on the Transport panel before playing back the track. When the track is played, this will continuously loop the guitar track so that you can easily audition the sound of the VST Amp Rack.

Next deselect the Bypass Insert 2 switch and select the "e" next to it so that the VST Amp Rack window appears. Notice that this preset (located at the top of the window) is called "Ricky"—a custom preset that was created for this project. You can set the VST Amp Rack to show or hide its controls by clicking on the top of the amp head (as shown in Figure 3.11). Although you can still edit the sound a lot using the minimized version of the VST Amp Rack—and doing so spares you some window screen space—for this tutorial we'll be using the extended view. If the current setting does not look like Figure 3.11, expand the VST Amp Rack to display the extended view.

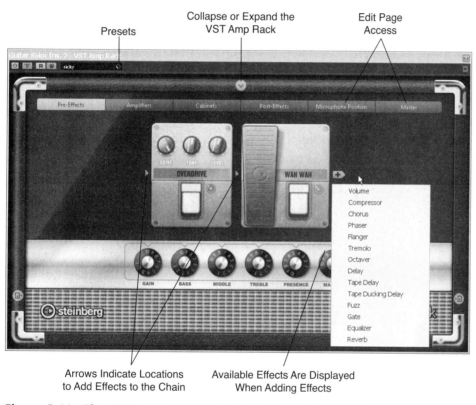

Figure 3.11 The VST Amp Rack displaying the extended view.

There are several different edit pages on the VST Amp Rack, and each represents a different stage of the guitar processing. The edit pages are listed at the top of the amp. The first stage is the Pre-Effects stage. This edit page is used to represent the effect pedals that are used before the guitar sound enters the amp. As you can see in Figure 3.11, this guitar preset includes an Overdrive peddle and a WahWah. The red-light indicator on the Overdrive shows that it is currently active. As you listen back to the track, you'll notice that the WahWah becomes active toward the end of the solo. Most likely, a MIDI pedal was used to program the WahWah as the track was recorded. You can add additional virtual pedal effects before or after the existing effects chain (also shown in Figure 3.11).

The order in which the effect is placed in the chain greatly affects the sound of the guitar. You can't use more than one instance of the same effect in your chain of effects. The effects that are available to choose from include Wah Wah, Volume, Compressor, Chorus, Phaser, Flanger, Tremolo, Octaver, Delay, Tape Delay, Tape Ducking Delay, Overdrive, Fuzz, Gate, Equalizer, and Reverb. Whew! That's a lot of effect pedals. They're all very user friendly and easy to use, though. For more information on them, refer to Help/Documentation/Plug-In Reference/The Included Effect Plug-Ins/ Distortion Plug-Ins/VST Amp Rack.

Next, probably the most critical stage of the amp modeling is the Amplifiers stage (shown in Figure 3.12). The Amplifiers stage offers seven different modeled amp heads to match a fairly diverse variety of guitar tones. These amps include the Plexi, Plexi Lead, Diamond, Blackface, Tweed, Deluxe, and British Custom. All of these amps were modeled after popular amps, such as those made by Fender, Marshall, and Vox. If you're familiar with the look and name of the amp, you'll pretty much be able to guess which is modeled after which. The preset that Live Forever is using is the Deluxe amp. Each amp has its own Gain, Bass, Middle, Treble, Presence, and Master setting. Each of these controls greatly affects the sound of the guitar. If you're a guitar player, chances are you're pretty familiar with these controls already, since they come standard on most amps. You can also choose No Amplifier if you wish to record the guitar as if it were going direct (bypassing the amp processing only).

Figure 3.12 Selecting a modeled amplifier in the VST Amp Rack.

Of course, an amplifier would be nothing without a speaker cabinet, so the next processing stage is the Cabinets stage. You can mix and match the cabinets to fit the amplifiers, or you can simply click the Link Amplifier & Cabinet Choice button to automatically pair the matched cabinet to its appropriate amplifier. You also have a variety of 1×12, 2×12, 4×12, and 4×10 speaker configurations from which to choose.

The next stage is Post Effects. The Post Effects edit page looks very similar to the Pre-Effects edit page. The only difference is that these are effects that are added after the signal is amplified. This would be very similar to using effects loop on a guitar amp as opposed to using pedals before the amp.

Next is a slightly more interesting stage that you don't see on a lot of amp modeling software: the Microphone Position stage (see Figure 3.13). This stage allows you to adjust the microphone position as if you were miking the cabinet yourself. This way, you can alter the location of the microphone (at the center of the speaker cone or at the edge of the speaker cone), the distance the microphone is placed from the speaker, and the type of mic used (between a large-diaphragm condenser mic and one that resembles a Shure SM57). Unfortunately, you can position one or both mics in only one location. To hear more of the large-diaphragm mic, turn the mix position to the left, and to hear the SM57, turn the mix position to the right. If the setting is anywhere in the middle, the sound is a blend of the two microphone types from the same location on the speaker.

Note: If you're looking for a grungy tone, try using the microphone at the edge of the speaker cone. This is where the speaker breaks up the most. When miking real speaker cabinets, it's common to try miking the different speakers in the cabinet as well, because each speaker has slightly different characteristics.

Figure 3.13 Adjusting the microphone position in the VST Amp Rack.

Lastly, in the Master (final) stage, you can apply a final EQ setting, add more volume, or tune your guitar. The volume control is mandatory (when it's inactive, you can't hear your guitar), the EQ can be bypassed, and when using the Tuner, you will only hear your clean non-effected guitar sound.

The VST Amp Rack comes with quite a few presets. I recommend listening to the presets with the Live Forever guitar solo on loop. Between switching presets, pay attention to the configurations (the amps, effects, speakers, and so on) so that you can familiarize yourself with the sound of each amp in the VST Amp Rack.

On a final note, I sat down with a guitar-player friend of mine, and we went through all of the presets. We also played through some other popular amp modeling software. As a pro, I'm still not completely sold that amp modeling is the "end all, be all" for recording guitar. However, I was very impressed not only with Steinberg's VST Amp Rack, but also with the various plug-ins that are currently available. How does the VST Amp Rack stack up with the competition? I'll say that it stacks up pretty darn well. However, I still wouldn't limit yourself to using only the VST Amp Rack if you're serious about guitar. There are other companies that have been doing this a lot longer than Steinberg, and it must be said that you can hear that difference.

Here are a few final tips when recording guitar through the VST Amp Rack.

- Record the guitar straight into the audio interface. Anything in the path will distort the tone of the guitar. Plan on doing all of your processing internally.

- Use a short, high-quality guitar cable into the interface.

- When you record, record the naked, clean guitar sound with the VST Amp Rack as an insert effect on your guitar track's output (so you can monitor and *hear* the effect, as opposed to recording the guitar along with the effect). This will give you the freedom to alter the sound later if necessary. You can always mix down (bounce) your track later so that the effect is recorded on an audio track.

- Check your levels. Never let the guitar peak or "hit the red" on your interface or on the input meter in Cubase while recording. Even though we love distorted guitar, guitar that's distorted on the input is not normally a desirable effect.

- Record with a sound that's at least *close* to what you're going for. Sometimes you play guitar differently based on the setup that you're using, and if you change the setup later, the performance that you have captured may sound as if it is lacking.

Creating the Perfect Take by Comping

As you were playing back the guitar lead in the previous tutorial, you might have noticed that the track *appeared* a little different than the others. That's because the track was built using a collection of guitar takes as opposed to one single "perfect take."

Comping is the "art" of taking the best slices from several "okay" performances and putting them together to create one perfect performance. Comping is something that producers and engineers have been doing since the multitrack recorder was invented, but Cubase 6 takes it to new ultra-easy levels.

The method that you use to capture different takes really depends on what or whom you're recording. One of the easiest methods to create several different takes is to loop (using Cycle mode) the section of the song that you're working with over and over so that the performer can keep laying down multiple passes of the same part. For some performers, this process might be a little uninspiring, but it is very efficient. Before I discuss how to record so that you have several takes, let's take a look at the guitar solo for Live Forever so you can see how comping multiple takes works.

Once again, solo the Guitar Solo track and set the left locator at Bar 51 and the right locator at Bar 61. Zoom in so that you can get a good look at the guitar in this section. The different guitar takes are represented on what Cubase refers to as *lanes*. You'll notice that under the Guitar Solo track, there are five visible lanes. Even though there are five visible lanes, you're only hearing *one* audio track when this section is played.

In this example, each lane has been split in several places. In some places you see Solo_1, and in others you see Solo_4, and so on. Each of these names represents the different guitar takes. The guitar takes have then been edited with the lanes to achieve the final result of the guitar solo that you've probably heard too many times already. Each section of the guitar solo that is in red is a section that is being used to create the final solo. Notice how the waveforms of the sections that are red also match the waveforms of the Guitar Solo audio track. That's because they *are* representing the same audio (see Figure 3.14).

Let's change this solo so that you can see how comping works. First, use the Object Selection tool (the cursor) to select the waveform at Measures 51 through 53 of Lane 4 of the guitar solo. As you select the waveform, notice how it also changes to match in the Guitar Solo audio track. Listening back, you will hear a new intro to the guitar solo (from Guitar Take 4). At this point, the rest of the guitar solo remains the same. Now select the waveform of Solo_3 from Lane 2 (close to Bar 55.2). The ending of this waveform has been cut off. Using the Object Selection tool, you can lengthen the waveform so that the note is not cut off. Notice that when you lengthen the part, the next active part shortens from its start point, as shown in Figure 3.15.

Now let's also split Lane 2 at Measure 57, either by using the Split tool or by pressing Alt/Option while clicking (a shortcut). When the part is split, select the guitar take on Lane 2 between Measures 57 and 58. When the part was split, notice how all of the parts were split in the same place in all of the other lanes. This is normal because you are really working only with one audio track. You can use the cursor keys on your

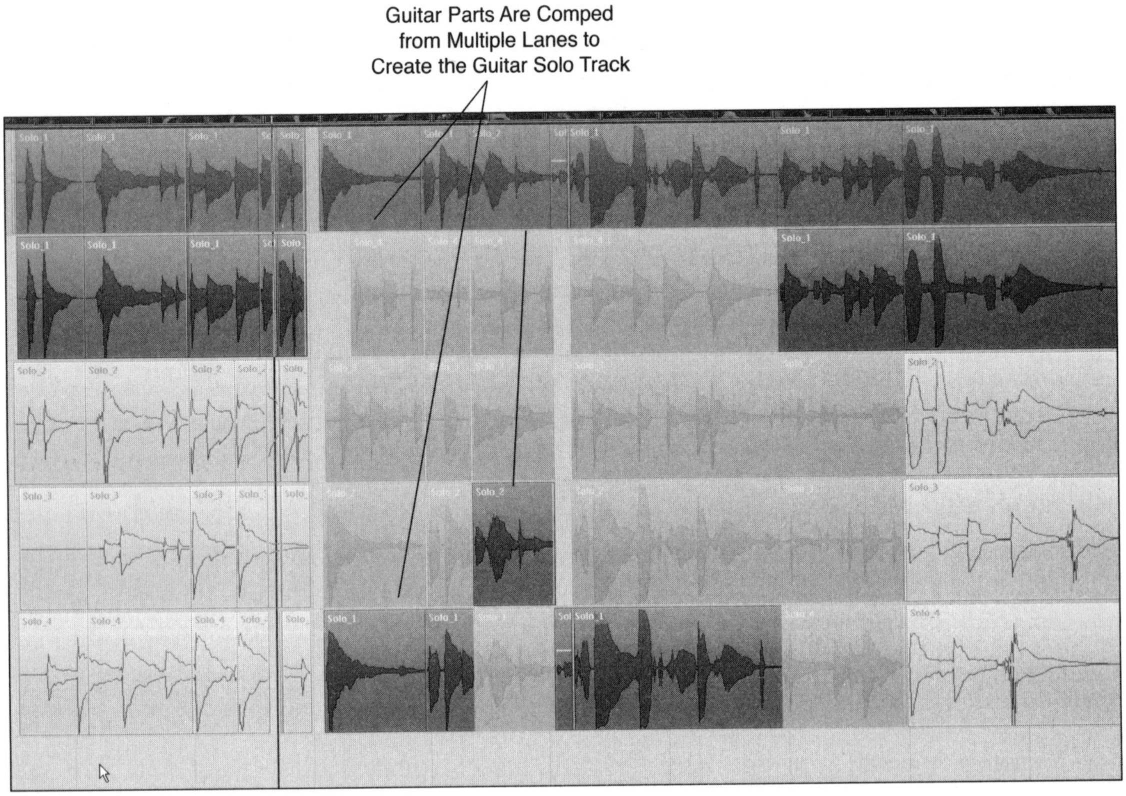

Guitar Parts Are Comped
from Multiple Lanes to
Create the Guitar Solo Track

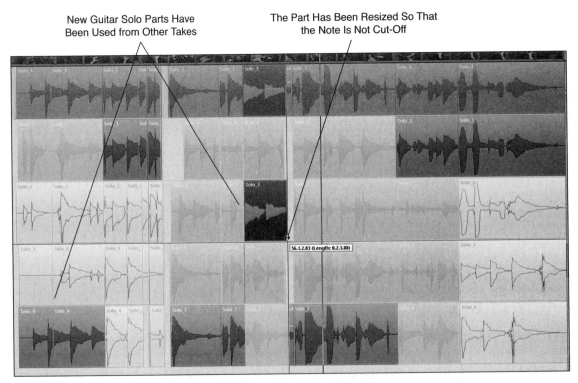

Figure 3.14 A closer look at the comped guitar solo track.

New Guitar Solo Parts Have
Been Used from Other Takes

The Part Has Been Resized So That
the Note Is Not Cut-Off

Figure 3.15 Changing the length of one of the takes on a lane.

keyboard to scroll through the take segments and use the Speaker tool to audition any segment. Soloing one lane at a time will allow you to listen to each lane individually, and you can mute or un-mute sections of the take as necessary. You can glue segments together by selecting them and clicking with the Glue tool. To hide or display the lanes, select the Show Lanes button located on the audio track.

Recording multiple takes via lanes using Cycle mode is a breeze. There are three recording modes you can use (selected via the Transport) when recording audio in Cycle mode: Keep History, Cycle History + Replace, and simply Replace. They're all slightly different, but unless you have a serious problem with deleting bad takes, it's probably easiest and less stressful for all involved to just stick to using the Keep History mode. When recording multiple takes, I recommend always making your lanes visible while recording by selecting the Show Lanes button on the track you're recording.

If you want to record individual takes on a track without looping a section, just select the Show Lanes button and then select Lane 1 and record like normal. When you're finished with your first take, select Lane 2 and continue recording another take. Cubase automatically creates an additional lane every time you record a new lane, so there is no need to create lanes (as you would create tracks) for recording. No matter which method you choose, when recording takes, you will always hear only the last take recorded (and *only* the last take) until you solo each individual lane or comp your takes.

Quick Audio Cleanup

Assuming you already know how to record and edit audio in Cubase, I would like to touch on a few key areas regarding file management and system performance before moving on. Keeping your projects organized and running "clean" will help you get the most out of your system and Cubase. There are a few auto cleanup features in Cubase that I will discuss briefly, but these can be a little scary to use and can sometimes lead to misplaced audio files. Nobody wants that.

As a refresher, allow me to explain how editing audio in Cubase works using my layman's terms. When you make "cuts" on an audio part, you aren't actually slicing the recording. Cubase (and every DAW that I know) utilizes what is referred to as *nondestructive editing.* Your original recording is never harmed unless you physically delete that audio file from your hard drive or your hard drive fails. Even though it appears that you are cutting audio, you are really just setting start- and end-location points with every edit. This means that if you like to cut and paste audio parts, you are not physically copying the audio recording (like copying a sentence using a word processor). You're simply defining that you would like that particular section of audio from your original recording to play from its "cut" start point to its "cut" end point, wherever you paste that recorded section. In other words, the original audio recording is repeating that single section of audio over and over again as it is copied throughout the song. This is a fantastic way to work with audio because you can always modify your edits later by adjusting those virtual start and end points, and you can always undo the edits if you screw up.

The big problem with this sort of editing is that it wreaks havoc on hard drives when there is a lot of start, stop, and repeat action constantly happening on every audio track. Here's an old-school example of how a DAW's audio is handled on a hard drive. Imagine your audio file is playing on a record via a turntable. The turntable is the hard drive mechanism, and the record is your audio file. Now imagine that when you get to the chorus of the song, you'd like to hear that chorus again, so you pick up the needle and replace it farther back on the record. This action is very similar to what is happening every time you cut and paste or edit out sections of any audio track.

Now imagine that you have edits like this across 24 audio tracks in Cubase throughout a three-minute song. Yikes! I'm amazed at what is possible with today's external USB 2.0, eSATA, and FireWire hard drives and the way they work with audio, but every hard drive reaches a point where it just can't perform the impossible, and there's no way to accurately judge when it will reach that point. Before your hard drive crashes, my suggestion is that keeping your system running "clean" will help prevent some unnecessary crashes, protect your original recording, keep projects running smoothly, and help make the projects easier to back up and archive.

The concept behind cleaning up your audio tracks is fairly simple, and I've already touched on it in previous chapters. The key is to bounce edited audio parts into new, easy-to-manage audio recordings. What I will be explaining is a simple method that does not remove your original edits and again is completely nondestructive. (It does not affect the original recording in any way). Here's a simple walkthrough that will explain this concept:

1.   Perform the edits on your audio part as you normally would.

2.   When you're finished making your edits (or at least if you're finished for the time being), select the entire track and duplicate it by choosing Duplicate Tracks from the Project menu.

3.   Now you should have two identical audio tracks. Mute the original track and deactivate any plug-in effects on that track. From now on, you'll be leaving the original track untouched. This has the same effect as deleting the track when it comes to your processor (meaning that it will not create any extra "work" for your system).

4.   Now make sure to select all the audio edits and parts for the duplicated track (as shown in Figure 3.16). When all parts have been selected, choose Bounce Selection from the Audio menu.

5.   Cubase will process the bounce, and a message should appear, giving you the option to replace events. Select Replace, and all of your edits will go away;

Muted Original
Track Edit

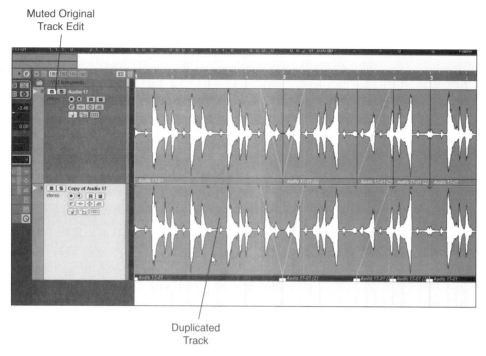

Duplicated
Track

Figure 3.16 Duplicating the edited audio track and preparing to bounce the audio edits.

you'll then be left with a completely new replacement audio track for your original track. This track has one start and one end point (just as your original recording once had). Now when the hard drive accesses this track, it will no longer have to skip around, back and forth, across the original file (see Figure 3.17).

Original Edit
(Untouched)

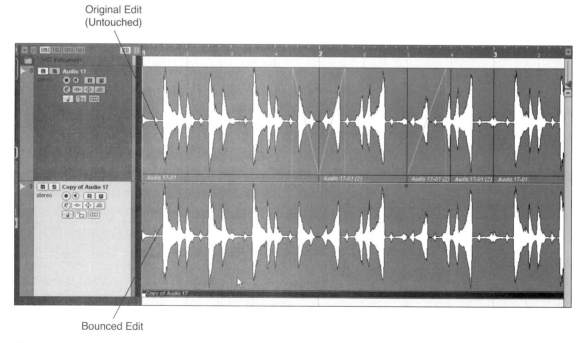

Bounced Edit

Figure 3.17 The newly bounced audio track.

Keep in mind that if you need to re-edit your original part, you can always delete the newly duplicated track and un-mute the original to get back to where you were before you bounced the part. After you've changed your edit and you're satisfied with the result, simply repeat the steps as you did before. If you would like, you can even edit the newly duplicated part and, once it has been edited, create a duplicate for it as you did your original track.

If you get to the point where you're completely satisfied with your edits and you would like to remove all of the pre-bounced tracks, you can resave your project under a new name and then delete the original audio tracks. (Keep in mind that this will *not* remove the original audio recordings from your hard drive.) You can then resave your project once again under a new name. This will not affect the performance of Cubase in any way, but it should at least create a neater-looking workspace.

Note: If you have an audio recording that has several bars of dead space, it will still save your hard drive a little work to keep that dead space within the audio track while working on your project. However, even though the unedited audio track performs better with hard drives, when it comes time to mix, you should probably edit out the dead space to minimize the chances of noise being present in the mix.

In Chapter 23 ("The Pool") of the manual, you can learn more about cleaning up and archiving audio within the Pool window. The Pool window is where all the audio files referenced in your project can be found. If you are used to recording multiple takes, you may not be aware that even if you delete the original parts in the Project window, those original recordings are still on your hard drive and can be located in the Pool. To view the Pool for any project, select Open Pool Window from the Media menu.

When it comes to backing up projects or cleaning them up to use on another system, you'll most likely want to remove all of the unused audio recordings left in the Pool. There are many ways to do this, but the easiest is to utilize the Prepare Archive and Remove Unused Media automated features, also found under the Media menu. If you're working on multiple hard drives and multiple projects, sometimes your file management can get messy. By messy, I mean that half of your audio recordings might be in your main project folder, a few others in another project folder, and even a few others on a whole different hard drive. If you were to simply copy that project's folder and open it on another system, you would be missing half of your original audio files.

The Prepare Archive feature actually creates copies of any audio file that is *not* already located within the project folder and pastes the copies into the project's folder where they belong. When you have all of your files in one location, you should be able to determine easily which files can be removed by using the Remove Unused Media feature.

After you select Remove Unused Media, Cubase will automatically prompt you to remove the files permanently or move them to the trash. I recommend first moving the files to the trash and then playing back your project to ensure that nothing has been removed by accident. (Maybe I'm paranoid, but it's usually for good reason.) When you've determined that everything is working as it should, then right-click the Trash icon in the Pool and select Empty Trash. Once that's selected, you will be prompted to remove media from the Pool or remove media from the hard drive. This is completely optional. If you decide to remove it from the hard drive, keep in mind that it will be gone forever.

Because hard drive space is getting cheaper and cheaper, my thoughts are usually to just remove the media from the Pool. By doing it this way, your project will never access those files again. (They will never become "missing files," either.) If you need to remove the original unused audio recordings to save space (perhaps so the entire project can fit onto a DVD-R or CD-R), so be it.

Note: If you want to create a space-saving project folder (for a CD-R or DVD-R archive) by removing the unused media, I recommend first copying the archived project folder to another location before removing the unused audio recordings from disk. This is just a safety measure that will prevent you from wiping those recordings out of your system forever.

When it comes to making the final archive copy, it's simply a matter of copying the folder (as you would any folder located on your Windows or Mac computer) to the destination media or hard drive. Once copied, the project should open from its new location without any sort of hitch.

A General Overview of Audio Editing in Cubase

Editing audio can be achieved in similar ways from within the Project window, the Audio Part Editor, or the Sample Editor. You should use the Project window when you want to work with multiple tracks and parts at the same time (which is usually the norm). By adjusting your zoom level within the Project window, you can easily achieve advanced cuts and splices, fade-ins/-outs, and processing, and you can access almost every editing feature located under the Edit menu. For working on audio in context with the rest of your audio tracks, the Project window can't be beat (see Figure 3.18).

You only start to run into problems when trying to create seamless edits between two audio parts on the same track. I'm referring to a more detailed edit, such as editing a single syllable in a vocal lyric. In this case, you might want to compile two completely separate takes (or copy a single word from another section of the track) and paste it where the original recording wasn't working. In this case, you need to work on the same audio track, but with separate audio edits (at least two, but possibly several).

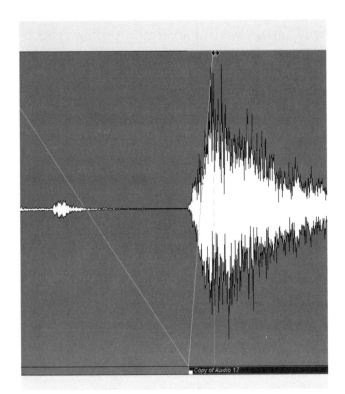

Figure 3.18 Advanced editing from within the Project window.

The best place to view and make these edits is from within the Audio Part Editor. By default, when you double-click on any audio event (a part containing one audio file), the Sample Editor will open. The Audio Part Editor opens only when clicking where there are multiple audio file references (events) contained within one audio part. I find that the easiest way to get to this level of editing is to simply do a "rough edit" from within the Project window (to get the edit close to where it needs to be) and then utilize the Glue tool to glue these rough edits together into a single part (as shown in Figure 3.19).

When the events have been glued together into a single part, you can double-click on the part to view multiple edited audio events inside the Audio Part Editor (as shown in Figure 3.20). Within the Audio Part Editor, you can remove the snap, change the start and end locations of the audio events, and possibly create a crossfade between the two events (if, for instance, the edit is in the middle of a held note).

Of course, you can accomplish crossfades in the Project window as well, but when you're working with such small parts in detail (such as a certain word, note, or sylla- ble), you'll find it much easier to make the edit from within the Audio Part Editor.

To make a crossfade, simply drag one side of one event at the location where you'd like the crossfade and press the X key on the QWERTY keyboard. You can then adjust the length of the fade by adjusting the length of the event. This is a fairly simple yet effec- tive solution when it comes to smoothing out rough patches between edits. To get an

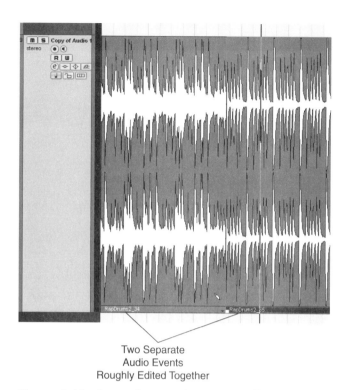

Two Separate
Audio Events
Roughly Edited Together

Figure 3.19 Preparing to glue two audio events together to form a single part.

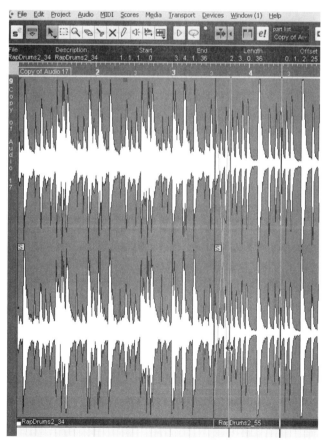

Figure 3.20 Blending multiple parts together by using crossfades in the Audio Part Editor.

even more detailed view of your crossfades, you can utilize the Fade Editor located under the Audio menu after selecting the two events being edited together.

Note: Here's a quick tip regarding crossfades. If you can't create a crossfade back into another section of the same event (and audio file), simply create a duplicate event and bounce it so that it creates a completely new audio file. Then use this as a way of crossfading the event back into itself. Most of the time, Cubase will prompt a warning and offer to create a copy of the file when necessary, but sometimes you may find that manually creating another file is the only option.

You can go as far as working with multiple lanes of audio in the Audio Part Editor, as I described earlier when comping takes and working with multiple lanes in an audio track. It's simply a matter of your personal visual working preference. Remember that you can monitor only one lane at a time.

The Sample Editor is the most detailed audio editor in Cubase. That being said, you will probably find that you can achieve most of your general editing (cuts) in the Project window. I think of the Sample Editor as a zoomed-in look at what you're already working on in the Project window (similar to looking through a microscope) when making precise cuts.

Besides getting a zoomed-in view of your audio waveform, the Sample Editor is also the main access path to the Audio Warp and VariAudio features in Cubase. These features are very important to working with the timing and pitch of audio, and I will continue to go over them in more detail later in the chapter.

When editing in the Sample Editor, you'll be focusing on only one individual audio file at a time, as opposed to multiple audio parts. I find that the Sample Editor is great for getting rid of breath noises, pops, or any other sort of noise that can happen in a short period of time in between critical parts. It's also great for getting into detail with your processing or audio analyzing tools. This editor really lets you zoom in close for a good look at what's going on. The Sample Editor can handle almost any detailed edit.

Note: If you ever run into problems with audio pops or clicks between edits, you might want to consider using the Snap to Zero Crossing feature (located on the toolbar in the Sample Editor). This feature snaps two separate parts together at locations where there is no audio signal in danger of clipping. It's particularly useful when you're editing parts that have some dead space to play with.

Besides your basic cutting, pasting, and crossfade edits, the last main ingredient is the actual audio processing. You can access all the processing tools from the Audio menu.

Even though processing is something you don't need to do for every edit, there are some very useful tools in this menu. Here's a quick breakdown of the audio processing features and their descriptions.

- **Gain.** Simply put, you can use this process to boost or reduce the overall volume level of your audio event. Keep in mind that boosting a signal past 0 dB will result in clipping and possible audible distortion.

- **Merge Clipboard.** This is a quick way to bounce events together, but it also allows you to mix the level between the two audio files. (One file is determined by copying it to the virtual clipboard from the Sample Editor, and the other is the selected file.) Although this is a quick way to mix, you can also do a quick export of multiple audio tracks (mixed the normal way) and then import the bounced audio file back into Cubase. This method might take a couple more steps, but I believe it to be more accurate in the long run.

- **Noise Gate.** This process works similarly to any noise gate effect, but it's not a real-time effect. Instead, it physically changes the audio event by replacing quiet sections (dead space) with complete silence. This can be a very useful cleanup tool; however, it could take a few processes to get the settings right. Keep in mind that you can always undo processes that go wrong.

- **Normalize.** This could be one of the most used and abused processes available. It's mainly utilized to raise a signal to its highest volume without peaking. Keep in mind that this does not compress the audio in the process, and if you have an audio event that has audio peaks and valleys, it will raise the entire audio event's level only to where the peak reaches zero; the valley will still remain at its relative lower level. You can also use the feature to lower the signal peaks to any level below 0 dB.

- **Phase Reverse.** This is a quick way to flip the phase on a recording. Keep in mind that this is not the same thing as recording with the phase reversed on your mics, but it could help with phasing issues if you are using multiple tracks of audio recorded where the same signal has been recorded in separate places with separate mics.

- **Pitch Shift.** This can be a very complex tool for altering the pitch of any recording, but it also can be a great tool for simply raising the pitch up or down a matter of steps. I find the envelope-based pitch shift particularly useful for creating some very interesting pitch-bend audio effects.

- **Remove DC Offset.** This is a utility process that does not really have an audible effect on the audio signal, but you can use it with the Snap to Zero Crossing feature. Basically, if you're running into issues with pops or glitches when using Snap to Zero Crossing, try processing the file with this feature and then try snapping once more. It's not a guaranteed no-fail operation procedure, but it might help, as it makes a slight binary adjustment.

■ **Resample.** You probably won't use this process very often because it alters the tempo and pitch of the recording. My best guess would be to use this for beat breaks or similar effects where the beat slows down or speeds up momentarily. Alternatively, you can use this method to correct sample rates for files that have been imported at the wrong rate, but I recommend importing those files correctly from the start.

■ **Reverse.** This is like playing your recording backward. It's a great effect to use on cymbals, drums, piano, and even vocals. Don't get any wise ideas about putting subliminal messages in your music, though.

■ **Silence.** Anything that is selected during the process will be muted. This is a great tool when you need to keep the space within the part but remove the actual recorded signal from the audio part.

■ **Stereo Flip.** This is a very simple process that swaps the signal from the left channel with the signal from the right channel. I suppose you could use this to do some creative panning tricks, but it's mostly used as a utility for an entire audio recording.

■ **Time Stretch.** This is another complex process. Since the introduction of Musical Mode and the MediaBay, Time Stretch has become more of a utility-like function used for adapting files recorded at a slower or faster tempo to match the current project. It's also handy for changing the length of an entire mix to fit within certain time restrictions (such as making a song that is 3:23 fit perfectly into a 3:30 time slot).

■ **Spectrum Analyzer.** For those who require an alternative view of your audio waveform, this is a welcome addition. Instead of viewing your audio by volume definition, you can analyze the frequency as well. This is a great tool for helping you maximize your EQ settings in a mixdown session.

■ **Statistics.** This is another audio analysis process that provides a list view of values for both the left and right channels of audio. This is a great tool to use to get a quick, detailed, numerical analysis of the recorded audio.

■ **Detect Silence.** This process is similar to the Silence process, but it also allows you to separate the non-silenced audio into individual regions, or parts (Figure 3.21). This can be useful if you need to make timing adjustments on individual notes, beats, words, or phrases.

You can also directly apply and instantly process any VST plug-in effect to the audio event (as opposed to using the effect in real time). Applying these effects might seem permanent; however, I will discuss in the next section how you can remove effects to a

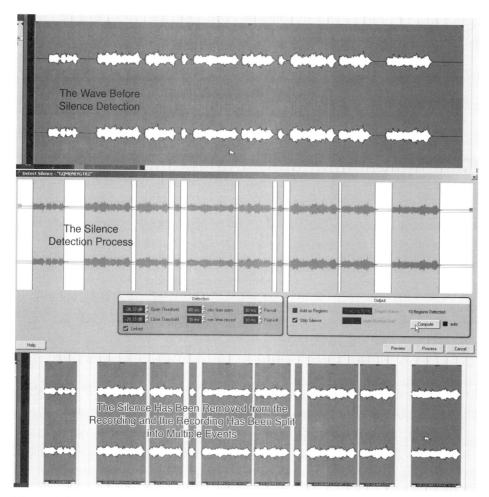

Figure 3.21   Turning one audio event into multiple individual events by silencing the dead-space audio.

certain extent. This process of "marrying" the effect with the audio part is not only a simple solution for enhancing the performance of your system, but it can also make it easier to handle the audio events if you're moving them from one system to another or archiving. To apply these effects, select them from the Audio menu once you select the audio part you wish to process.

> **Note:** The reason I suggest the possibility of applying the effects to audio parts before archiving is because three years down the road, you may need to open this project again, and if your system has changed, some of your plug-ins might not be available. It's better to have the "married" effect and audio track than to not have that original effect as an option. Remember that you can always keep an un-effected copy of the original part archived as well.

Using the Offline Process History

If you haven't learned what the Offline Process History is all about, you're way over-due. As you can probably tell, I'm obsessed with saving, resaving under new names, bouncing and duplicating tracks, and archiving. Maybe it's because there's nothing more frustrating than having to shelve a project after hours of work, only to come back to it later and find that it's not working right for some dumb reason. Re-creating that original magic usually isn't quite as much fun the second time around.

> **Note:** The Offline Process History feature (found under the Audio menu) is not to be confused with the History feature found under the Edit menu. The History feature keeps a working list of everything you've done since last opening and saving the project, and you can undo all of your actions from various locations on that list. The irony is that saving the project actually removes its history (once you reload the project), so if you've made previous changes that you would like to undo, you're stuck with them unless you go back to an earlier version of your project (saved under another name).

Offline Process History works specifically with offline audio processing (any process that has been "bounced" along with the audio) and is more than just a simple Undo feature. Like the History feature, it keeps a list of each process, but it keeps a separate list for the processing that has occurred on each individual audio event, not for the entire project. This means if there was a section of a vocal track where you reversed the audio and added a delay, only the isolated event would display the list containing the reverse and delay processes. If you process an entire part and then edit it into mul-tiple audio event sections, each of those sections will contain the original process in its individual history list. You can modify each individual history list without affecting the history of the other events in the project.

> **Note:** I've previously emphasized that you should create new files as a safety measure while you're working. However, you cannot see the complete history on each individual part when you create new files, because a new file has no history. So if you feel that undoing processes might be something you need to do later on, please disregard my earlier comments about *always* creating new files.

What's particularly handy about the Offline Process History is that you can remove processes from any position in the list without affecting later processes. For instance, let's say you applied compression to a vocal track, then processed some EQ, then added a noise gate and normalized the track. After normalizing, you decided that you really should've had a little more compression on the vocal track. Instead of starting over from scratch, you can go back and modify the compression without losing the later processing. Figure 3.22 displays the Offline Process History for one audio event.

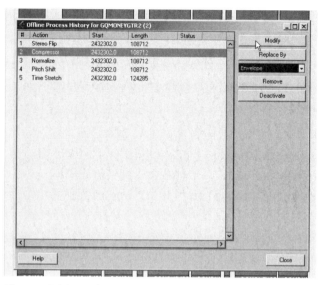

Figure 3.22 Selecting an early process in the Offline Process History.

What actually happens during a modification is this: Once you apply changes to the earlier process stage, Cubase quickly reprocesses (if necessary) the other stages in the order in which they appear. Your choices for modifying each process include removing the effect completely, modifying the settings (of course, the effect has to be modifiable), replacing the effect with a completely different effect, or deactivating (bypassing) the effect (though the effect will still be there to reactivate if needed).

Again, these processes are all associated with their respective event and played back seamlessly. Saving your project does *not* reset the Offline Process History. This means that you can go back and change processes from a project on which you did a "final mix" three months earlier.

All of these features can save you loads of time in the studio, but there is a catch. There are some processes that you cannot modify due to their type and location in the Offline Process History list. Usually, it's because they alter the length of the file. An icon will appear in the Status column, and the modifier buttons will be grayed out to indicate that you're on mission impossible if you attempt the modification. The moral of this story is to do your timing processes (time-stretches) last so that they can be modified, and you won't have to redo a lot of work.

Manually Determining the Tempo of Any Loop

When it comes to manually finding the tempo of an imported audio track, there are several ways to go about it. Everyone has his or her own way. Tapping the tempo along with the track using the Beat Calculator (located under the Project menu) is a useful option. With this option, you tap the spacebar along with the recording (not the project tempo). The tempo will be calculated by your tapping, and then you can apply that setting to the tempo of your project.

Note: When you import an audio loop, Cubase automatically tries to calculate the tempo and sets the loop to Musical Mode. To manually make adjustments to the tempo of a loop, you must deactivate Musical Mode. To learn more about Musical Mode, read the following tutorial.

Personally, I find the Beat Calculator a little clumsy to use to find the *exact* tempo. When I need to determine tempos manually, I like to use the waveform of the audio part and the tempo control on the Transport. First, I edit the audio (most likely without using the Snap feature) so that it's cut just before the downbeat I'd like to use. Next, I position that downbeat (now using the Snap) so that it is locked at the start of a measure (as shown in Figure 3.23). At this point, I haven't even worried about tempo, and

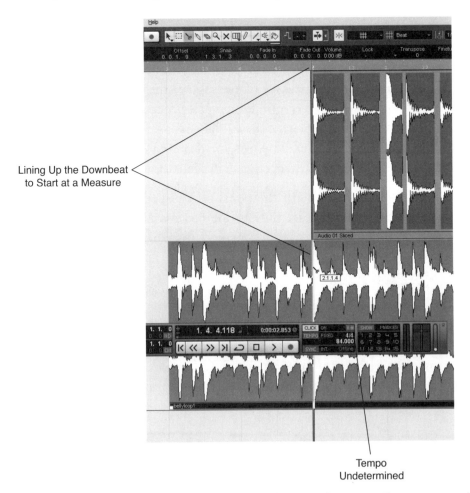

Figure 3.23 Positioning the groove's downbeat at the start of a measure when manually finding the tempo of a groove.

the only part of the file that is going to match the project tempo is the downbeat. Now, I listen to the audio track (without using the metronome) and determine where all my downbeats are. By comparing the audio that I'm hearing while watching the waveform, I can determine the exact location of the downbeats. Now it's just a matter of adjusting the tempo so that those downbeats fall where they're supposed to (Beat 1 of their measures) in comparison to the (grid) ruler. I usually adjust the tempo, then play back using the metronome after the waveform is close enough to compare to the ruler, and then I make more adjustments until the tempo is locked in (as shown in Figure 3.24).

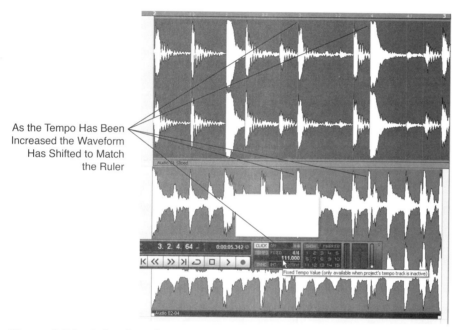

As the Tempo Has Been Increased the Waveform Has Shifted to Match the Ruler

Figure 3.24 Adjusting the tempo on the Transport until the downbeats fall where they're supposed to.

Warping Audio: Musical Mode and Free Warp

Musical Mode is the most basic form of audio time-warping, and it's partially the magic behind importing an audio track into a project at the correct tempo when using the MediaBay. Musical Mode was designed to work with audio that is set at one locked tempo. When importing an audio file, Cubase will attempt to calculate automatically the fixed tempo of that file. This is not always a 100 percent accurate magic calculation. It really helps to have files that have been cut into perfect bar sections (two bars, four bars, and so on, starting with the first beat of the first measure). After importing your audio file, you can view this automatic calculation in the toolbar of the Sample Editor (as shown in Figure 3.25).

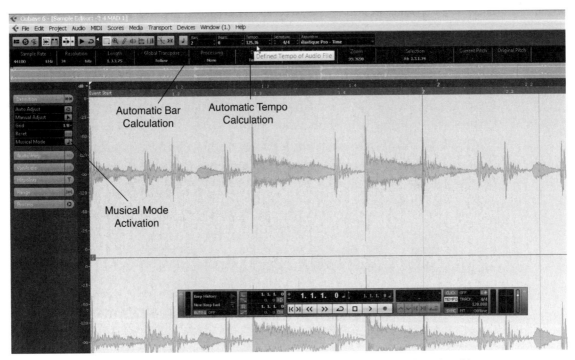

Figure 3.25 Cubase's automatic tempo calculation for an imported audio file.

> **Note:** I'm going to continue this exercise as if that automatic calculation Cubase made for you is correct. To double-check, set the project tempo to match the calculated tempo and play the track back with the click. If you find that your tempo isn't locked to the project, revert to determining the tempo of your audio manually, as I discussed earlier in the previous tutorial. When you've determined the tempo, you can manually change the auto-calculation to the real tempo by typing in the correct info.

You can also see the automatically calculated number of bars that are contained in the imported audio. In some cases, the automatic calculation may double or half the number of bars (for instance, if you are importing a four-bar phrase, Cubase will calculate it as a two-bar phrase). This is understandable, because often this is something that's impossible for software to determine. Manually readjusting the number of bars will automatically recalculate the tempo.

Select the Definition tab and notice that there are two separate rulers located above the waveform. The bottom ruler represents the imported audio file only, whereas the top ruler represents the location where the imported audio file is positioned in the project. If the tempo of your project is not set to the exact tempo of the imported file (as shown in the tempo definition), and if the file you're looking at is not located at the start of the project, then the two rulers will show different values. If you were to set your project tempo to the tempo that was defined automatically, you would be able to hear your audio file in its original un-warped state, and the rulers would align (with the possible exception of the bar numbers).

Selecting Musical Mode means that you will be applying real-time time-stretch processing to the audio file automatically to match the project tempo. Cubase 6 offers many options on real-time time-stretch algorithms. The type of processing you choose determines the quality of the time-stretching. The new élastique Pro algorithms are fantastic. Finding the perfect algorithm, like anything, can be a trial-and-error process and depends on the audio recording you're working with. To change the algorithm, open the dialog from the top of the Sample Editor, as shown in Figure 3.26. To learn more about each of these algorithms, refer to Help/Documentation/Operation Manual/Audio Processing and Functions/About Time Stretch and Pitch Shift Algorithms.

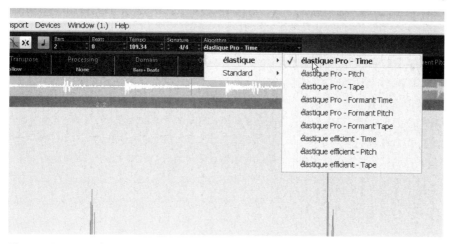

Figure 3.26 Adjusting the real-time pitch-shift algorithm.

When you've selected the algorithm, activate Musical Mode by selecting the button with the musical note. This button is located at the top of the Sample Editor window and within the Definition tab parameters and AudioWarp tab parameters of the Sample Editor's Inspector. Once activated, the tempo of the audio file will automatically adjust to the project's tempo setting. This also means that if you have used a tempo map with tempo changes, the audio groove will automatically alter its tempo to match the tempo changes.

Up until now, I've discussed using Musical Mode for real-time tempo correction, but you can also use Audio Warp to alter/quantize a groove. For large-scale tempo correction (for example, full-length songs), I recommend using the Advanced Tempo Detection and Time Correction techniques as discussed later in this chapter. But to just fix a two- or four-bar phrase, you can use the Definition settings and the Free Warp tools found in the Sample Editor.

Setting the definition is simply fine-tuning Cubase's automatic tempo/beat calculations so that they are more accurate. If you are importing a loop that is already cut to loop perfectly, setting the definition is not really necessary to utilize Musical Mode with real-time tempo changes. As mentioned before, I highly recommend using pre-edited loops when utilizing Musical Mode because it's easier than altering the beat definition.

Using the Definition tab, it doesn't really matter whether the audio track you're using is a perfect fit. The parameters of the Definition tab and the Range tool help Cubase define the tempo and beat calculations. First, use the Range tool to select one measure (from the downbeat transient attack to the downbeat of the next measure) and then select Auto Adjust. Cubase automatically creates a grid for that measure based on its internal calculations. Next, you can activate the Manual Adjust button so that you can adjust the start position of this grid as well as where each beat position falls (using the waveform as a guide). As you define the grid locations, the waveform adjusts (visually only), and the tempo is recalculated based on your adjustments.

The Free Warp tools are what you need to use if you actually want to change the groove you're working with. Perhaps there's a note that falls slightly off beat that you'd like to fix. Or perhaps you would like to adjust a beat so that it is slightly off to match a preexisting groove. After the audio has been defined (with the Auto Adjust grid under the Definition tab), Free Warp is a piece of cake to use. Just select the Audio-Warp tab from the Inspector (while in Musical Mode), and you'll notice that the grid lines now become Warp tabs. Simply use the Object Selection tool to move the Warp tab to the left or right to the corrected position along the ruler, and the attack of the beat will be stretched to the new position (as shown in Figure 3.27). This stretching

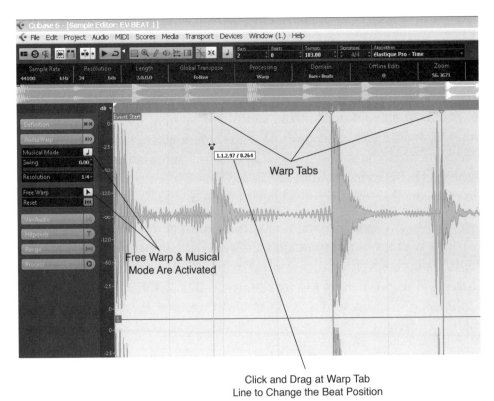

Figure 3.27 Adjusting the groove using Free Warp and Warp tabs.

affects only the surrounding beats in relation to each other, as opposed to affecting the entire audio track, and is the basis for quantizing audio using real-time audio time-stretch processing.

Advanced Tempo Detection and Time Correction

One of the most challenging tasks on any DAW is to work with a free tempo recording. By "free tempo," I'm referring to any recording where the tempo is constantly fluctuating and is not consistent. Any true live performance that is recorded without the use of a metronome is bound to fluctuate in tempo to a certain degree. It's nearly impossible to keep a full band from making slight fluctuations in tempo without some sort of guide to keep them on track. That being said, almost every pop song on the radio today can easily be "locked" to a steady click track.

Cubase has been trying to perfect the art of advanced tempo detection for years. Each version of Cubase has gotten closer and closer to perfection, and the tempo detection in Cubase 6 is no exception. To put the new tempo detection to the test, I decided to dust off my Freedom Rock collection and pull up a track that I love but that is obviously recorded without a click track due to its fluctuating tempo: "Reach Out of the Darkness" (by Friend and Lover). In this example, I'm going to analyze the fluctuating tempo of "Reach Out of the Darkness" and then make it into a fixed tempo, just like today's pop songs.

> **Note:** There are plenty of audio tracks available that have been recorded without fixed tempos. I selected this one because it's a primary candidate for this process, and if you can find the track, you can follow along. If this track were recorded in a perfect world, it would have had a fixed tempo. It has a discernable beat that we can sort of snap our fingers along with. Any free tempo track that doesn't have a discernable beat will not really work with Advanced Tempo Detection, and you will have to manually insert tempo changes in a tempo map. Also, this tempo detection process will work only with tracks that are at least seven seconds long. If a track is shorter than seven seconds, refer to the previous tutorial.

To follow along, start with a completely empty project, create an audio track, and import the recording of "Reach Out of the Darkness" to the audio track. Edit the lead-in of the track so that it starts right at the three-note bass pickup to the downbeat. Next, place the downbeat on Beat 1 of a measure. There's no need to set the project tempo, but if you tried, you would discover that the tempo is impossible to set at a fixed tempo. From the Project menu, select Tempo Detection. The new Tempo Detection panel should appear, as shown in Figure 3.28.

All you really need to do is select the track and then select Analyze. Cubase will automatically generate a tempo map (located just under the audio track). During this

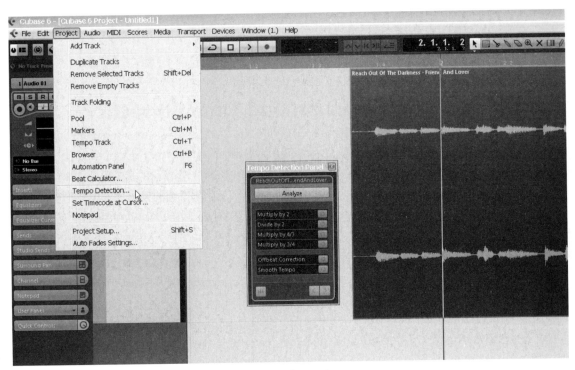

Figure 3.28 The Tempo Detection panel in Cubase 6.

process, a few things have happened that are critical to the way that the automatic tempo detection works. The audio track has been set automatically to linear time base, and the time signature has been changed automatically to 1/4 time (because every song can be counted in 1/4 time no matter what the actual time signature is). Also, the cursor has been changed automatically into the Time Warp tool, which is also represented by the ruler turning red and displaying the various tempo changes (see Figure 3.29).

Select the tempo track and examine the tempo fluctuations from within the Inspector. Except for a couple of obvious miscalculations, the tempo of the Reach Out of the Darkness track seems to fluctuate from 110 bpm to 120 bpm. Select the (audio) click and listen back to the track with the click. If the click sounds off beat at times, this is due to a miscalculation on the part of Cubase. However, most of the clicks are pretty darn right-on, considering how much the tempo fluctuates.

For this particular track, I didn't have many problems with tempo detection until around Bar 250, where the beat drops out. When the beat came back in, for some reason the click track started back up on the offbeats. This is understandable because often the offbeats can have a stronger attack than the downbeats. To fix this minor problem, I changed tools to the Split tool and split the track close to where the change occurred.

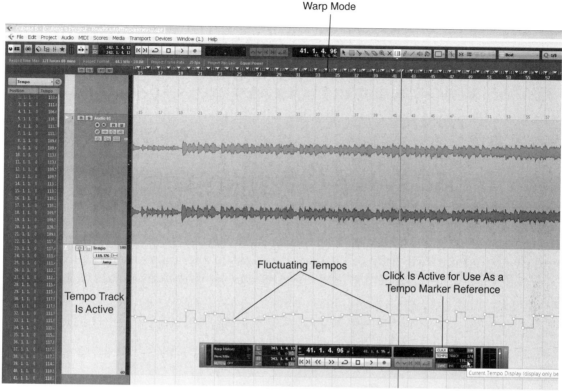

Figure 3.29 A new tempo map has been created for the free tempo recording.

> **Note:** I actually started this entire exercise over when I was finished, and the second time I did not get an offbeat miscalculation. I believe this has to do with how you position the start of the audio track in Cubase. You might not have this issue if you're following along, but in case you do, I will continue writing as if this issue exists. When changing from the Time Warp tool, Cubase may give a warning that the tempo detection session will end. Ignore this warning, because you can always go back and edit the tempo once you've made your edit, and you can reanalyze the tempo if necessary.

Now that you have split the audio file, you will need to reanalyze the second half of the track. If the click is once again detected on the offbeats, selecting Offbeat Correction on the Tempo Detection panel will switch the beat from the offbeat to the downbeat. There are a couple of other options on the Tempo Detection panel that weren't necessary for me for this particular track, but they could come in handy if you run into problems with the automatic calculations. The Multiply by 2 and Divide by 2 options either double or half the time, therefore increasing or decreasing the tempo references. The Multiply by 3/4 or Multiply by 4/3 options are sometimes necessary when working with dotted or swung beat recordings, as opposed to straight beat recordings like in this example. In some cases, you may get a warning from Cubase that it has detected irregular tempo changes. If this happens, you might need to use the Smooth Tempo function and/or manually create the tempo map.

To manually correct the tempo map, you use the Time Warp tool. The name *Time Warp* is not to be confused with *Audio Warp*. The Time Warp tool is a simple tool to adjust the location of the grid lines on a tempo map. It has nothing to do with the Audio Warp process. The Time Warp process is much more similar to setting the definition of an audio loop within the Sample Editor, as discussed in the previous tutorial. Using the Time Warp tool, in this particular case, is just to better align individual clicks that don't match the audio track.

I find that it helps to listen with the click track and then zoom in on the area of the audio track that you're working with. Next, locate the transient of the waveform that is offbeat by listening back with the metronome active. Decide whether the transient was ahead or behind the beat of the metronome. Click on the audio track with the Time Warp and align the transient with the tempo map (as shown in Figure 3.30). Listen back and see whether the click sounds on-beat. If so, move on to the next location; if not, make minor adjustments with the Time Warp tool until it sounds as if the click is aligned with the audio track.

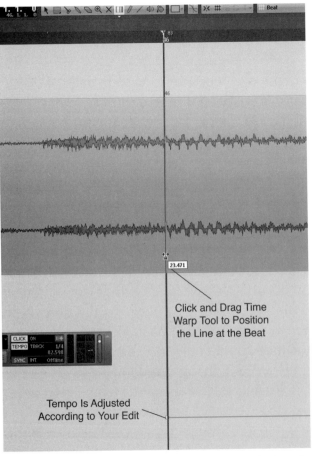

Figure 3.30 Correcting miscalculations with the Time Warp tool.

When your click is completely aligned to the audio track, your tempo map is finished, and you can now do anything with your free tempo audio track that you can do with a fixed-tempo audio track. I've decided I want to get rid of this fluctuating tempo and give this track a fixed tempo of 120 bpm. Just for fun, I'm going to load an instance of Groove Agent ONE with Beat Designer active as an insert and use a preset drum loop to enhance the original groove.

Before we move on, though, we need to set the definition of the audio track. This will make it a perfect candidate for the Audio Warp process, which we will need to utilize to make it into a fixed tempo. To set the definition, select the audio track and then open Set Definition from Tempo, which you can find in the Audio menu under the Advanced sub-menu (see Figure 3.31).

Figure 3.31 Using the new tempo map to set the definition for the free-tempo audio track.

There are only a few options with the Set Definition from Tempo dialog. You have a choice of saving the definition in the project only or saving it in the audio file. You also have the option of switching to musical time base (instead of linear time base) upon closing. In most cases when you are working with music, you will always want to leave the switch to Musical Time Base option checked. With regard to saving the definition data in the project only or in the audio file, I recommend using the Project Only setting unless you are planning to use the track in other Cubase projects. If you decide to save it in the audio file, you are imprinting data that Cubase can understand, but other sources (most likely) may not recognize the data and could (although not likely) create problems with the audio file. If you plan to save with the file, make a backup of the original file before you start this process, and you should never have any problems. When you've made your settings, click OK, and Cubase will process the track.

Once processed, the track will not appear any different in the Project window. The hidden process can be viewed within the Definition tab of the Sample Editor's Inspector. However, the track should now be in Musical Mode, which means all you need to do to get it to a fixed tempo is to deactivate the tempo track and set the desired fixed tempo (which in my case is 120 bpm). Listen back to the perfectly timed Freedom Rock track! Now it's just a matter of adding a Groove Agent ONE track, loading in the Big Beat drum kit, inserting Beat Designer on the Groove Agent ONE track, and then loading the Big Beat preset within Beat Designer. Isn't it extra groovy now (how people are finally gettin' together)?

I could end this tutorial here, but I'd like to add that this isn't just a feature to make bad rhythm sections sound like robots. This is really also a feature to help you enhance tracks that are already perfect *because* of their free tempo. It's very difficult to overdub to a track with a free tempo. Once the tempo has been fixed, you can add MIDI or audio parts and then reset the tempo to its original free tempo, and everything will lock as it's supposed to. Now you don't have to rely on music recorded with a click track to sync to the other tracks. Although it's always been an option to record without using a click, this feature makes it much easier to open up free-tempo creative possibilities in production.

Shortcuts When Working with Hitpoints and Slices

Throughout this chapter I've briefly discussed using hitpoints, slicing audio, and using the free Warp tools. I've taken the time to show you how to modify hitpoints and slices. Now I'd like to take a brief moment to show you how you can utilize these options using Cubase's automatic calculations so you can skip the details and get right into warping and slicing your audio.

Cubase's hitpoint detection has come a long way since the early days of audio editing. Here's a fast way to calculate hitpoints and slice a loop without even opening the Sample Editor. When you have imported your audio loop into a track, select the audio track and then, under the Audio menu, select Calculate Hitpoints from the Hitpoints submenu. Your hitpoints have now been created. If you wish to slice, you can do so immediately after creating hitpoints by selecting Create Audio Slices from Hitpoints, located just below Calculate Hitpoints in the Hitpoints submenu. You can always remove the hitpoints by selecting Remove Hitpoints from the same submenu.

> **Note:** If Musical Mode is active before you create slices, you will need to deactivate it. The Divide Events at Hitpoints function will split the audio part into multiple parts where the hitpoints are created. This is a useful tool for extracting a certain hit from a sample. The Create Markers from Hitpoints option might be good for creating cue points from a long audio track.

After an audio loop is sliced and the tempo is decreased, it can contain gaps. To fix this, you can create crossfades between the gaps. You also can use Cubase's real-time warping to fill the gaps. (Keep in mind that warping is processing.) To instantly fill in those gaps between slices, select either Close Gaps (Crossfade) or Close Gaps (Time Stretch), which are both located under the Advanced submenu under the Audio menu.

Vocal Pitch Correction Using VariAudio

The Auto-Tune effect (real-time vocal pitch correction) has been used and abused on vocal tracks for well over 10 years. Even though Auto-Tune is popular, the actual software is far from perfect. Anyone can tell that there's "something strange" about the way a vocal recording sounds when using it. The Auto-Tune effect can almost sound like a vocoder (the classic "robot voice") at times, especially when it's over-compensating for horrible singers! It doesn't really matter, because people seem to enjoy the sound enough. When it all boils down, it's no different from hearing any other effect (such as reverb or echo) on a vocal, and often it's used on great singers just to get that "sound." More and more great singers are shunning the use of the effect because they don't want people to think they use it because they can't sing!

Note: Cubase's real-time Pitch Correct plug-in works very similarly to the way that Auto-Tune works. For more information on using Pitch Correct, refer to Chapter 4 or to the Plug-In Reference PDF available with the Cubase documentation.

Because the Auto-Tune "sound" has become such a staple, it will always be around (just like the reverb and echo classics). The real question is, how do you achieve pitch correction without it becoming labeled as Auto-Tune? What about those who simply use it as an editing tool to get the most out of a captured performance? After all, pitch correction shouldn't be looked at any differently from altering the timing or cutting and pasting a chorus or verse in a project. In fact, what's the difference if a singer has to sing multiple tracks where each word is edited together to form a pitch-corrected melody? Even some producers of well-respected popular singers use pitch correction. The bottom line is that you need pitch correction, and you also need the effect of it to be discreet.

If you've done your homework, you've probably already heard of Melodyne by Celemony. Melodyne has been available for several years now and offers a slightly different approach to pitch correction. The key ingredient to Melodyne is that the audio is analyzed to extract pitch, length, and timing information. The notes and timing are displayed as if they are on a MIDI-like grid (like the Key Editor in Cubase). The basic principle sounds simple, but it's a very innovative technology. In fact, Melodyne has developed a new technology called Direct Note Access (DNA) that will allow users to analyze recordings of chord structures (up until now, it's only been available for vocals and mono instruments) and break each individual pitch away from its chord to change the harmonic structure of the chord. These guys are definitely on to something, and they've won multiple industry awards to prove it.

Now Cubase introduces VariAudio (which you can find in the Sample Editor by selecting the VariAudio tab). VariAudio is Steinberg's solution to pitch correction. It bears more resemblance to Celemony's Melodyne than it does to Antares' Auto-Tune. The biggest problem with Melodyne is that it's not easily integrated into another DAW. This alone has caused users to choose Auto-Tune over Melodyne in the past. Of course, VariAudio is built into Cubase, so integration is not an issue. Like the original version of Melodyne, VariAudio was designed specifically for vocals and monophonic instruments (with a slight disclaimer toward monophonic instruments).

VariAudio utilizes yet another somewhat generically named "warp" effect called Pitch and Warp. When using Pitch and Warp, a single audio wave is analyzed and broken into so-called *segments*, which represent the various notes (pitches) within the recording. The pitches, of course, are also shown with their actual note length and in the appropriate locations on the grid. When notes are slightly out of tune, VariAudio assumes that you were aiming for a certain pitch and categorizes it with one of the 12 tones in the chromatic scales, as opposed to breaking it down into detail. Intonations and voice inflections that fall within the general area of each of the 12 tones can be important and shouldn't always be raised or lowered to the exact pitch. Intonations and inflections are made up of small pitch increments, or micro pitches. The more the micro pitch is altered, the more of the robot voice effect you're going to hear. Micro pitches are very important to human vocal inflections and are particularly important when a singer uses vibrato. Unfortunately, micro pitches are also the same things that cause flat- or sharp-sounding notes.

In essence, pitch correction should be viewed similarly to time correction or quantization. You want it to sound "on," but you don't want it to sound as if there are robots making the music. There are plenty of hit records that exist with vocal pitch problems, and if you were to take away those pitch "problems" using today's technology, the recording would most likely lose something that most of us didn't notice to begin with. The performance is always the most important element of the recording, regardless of pitch.

Because we are lucky that Cubase 6 has included a great human vocal track demo with their program, I will once again refer to the Live Forever project that we have used and abused throughout this chapter. Hopefully, by now you're a pro at opening up that project, but if you're not sure what to do, refer to my instructions in the first tutorial of this chapter.

There are several vocal tracks included in the Live Forever project. Select and solo the Lead Voice track, which has also been grouped with a Doubled Voice track. On the Lead Vocals Group track, disable the Compressor on Insert 1, disable the RoomWorks reverb on Send 1, and last but not least, disable the two parametric EQ settings. Now, upon listening back to the Lead Voice track, you should hear nothing but an unprocessed female vocal track. There are some minor pitch problems with her performance, but overall her performance is great for today's pop/rock music.

For this example, I want to concentrate on the first chorus. Split the Lead Voice track from Measure 20 to Measure 29. Double-click on the part after it's split. This will open the Sample Editor. When you're in the Sample Editor, select the VariAudio tab and then select the button next to Pitch and Warp. The vocal melody will then be displayed, as shown in Figure 3.32.

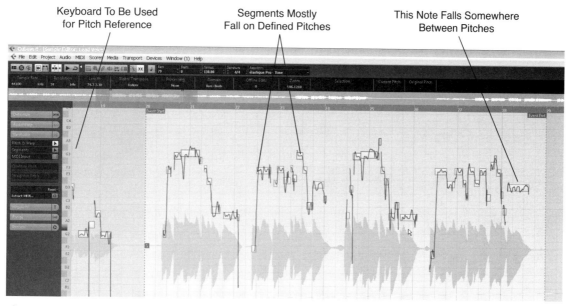

Figure 3.32 The Live Forever vocal chorus, as shown in VariAudio's Pitch and Warp Editor.

If you examine Figure 3.32, you'll see that there is a keyboard on the left, which represents the pitches that have been captured. The pitches have been analyzed and converted into the so-called *segments*, which are displayed as little boxes over the actual waveform. By using the keyboard as a reference, you'll also see that most of the pitches fall pretty much in line with their relative piano key. This means that for the most part, the vocal is in tune. If you position the mouse cursor over one of the notes (zoomed in close-up), it will reveal the general pitch as well as the + or − amount that the micro pitch varies from the exact pitch frequency for the duration of that note (see Figure 3.33).

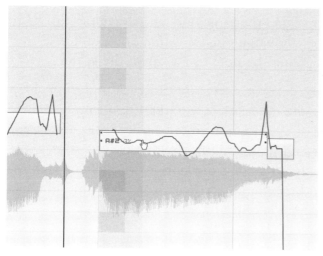

Figure 3.33 A close-up of the lyric (life) "time" in VariAudio's Pitch and Warp Editor.

There are several options when it comes to editing a pitch of a note in the Pitch and Warp Editor. The most basic option is to hone in on the problem note and then move it to the correct position with the cursor. In this particular chorus, there is one note that falls a little farther outside the lines. This is the last note of the chorus. The Pitch and Warp Editor has determined that the note is somewhere between D and D♯3, when in actuality the note should be D♯3. Simply select the note and move it up to the D♯3 position to correct the out-of-tune note. What's great about this form of editing is that the micro pitches are transposed the same. This keeps the natural vocal sound that you're looking for (see Figure 3.34).

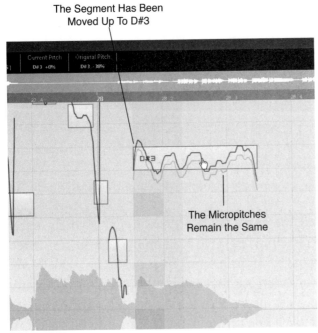

Figure 3.34 The pitchy last note of the chorus has been corrected.

Because the pitch shifting is so natural, you can completely change the melody by transposing individual notes if you'd like. Try taking the same note and dragging it to F3 to change the melody. The great thing about changing pitches is that you don't lose your original timing when you're manually moving the note up or down the scale.

If you *do* need to change the position of a lyric or note, you can click and drag either side of the note to the left or right using the mouse. Keep in mind that this "moving" process is more of an Audio Warp process (as I demonstrated earlier when discussing Free Warp), as opposed to simple cut-and-move editing (with no time-stretching). When you move the note, you're actually stretching the note to the left or right as well as affecting the note just before or after the note you're working with. You can select several notes to move at once, but this is also utilizing Free Warp.

To hear what this sounds like, try stretching the end of the last note so that it shortens the note and ends at Beat 3 of Measure 28 (28.3 on the ruler) and also stretch the start of the note to the left so that it reaches the note before it (as shown in Figure 3.35). Notice how the audio is stretched, just like you're using Free Warp.

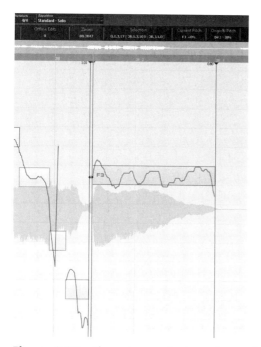

Figure 3.35 Changing note lengths and positions from within the Pitch and Warp Editor.

You can also quantize the pitches to move closer to the pitches that VariAudio has determined automatically. This is a very nice feature for some basic "tightening" of a vocal performance (regarding pitch). Select all of the notes in Measure 27 and move the virtual slider (just like the one you use to calculate hitpoints) under the Quantize Pitch control on the Inspector slowly to the right. Notice how all of the selected segments move closer to the center of the pitch the farther the slider is moved to the right (see Figure 3.36). To undo your changes, you can simply move the slider back to the left.

Another pitch-correcting feature is the Straighten Pitch control, which gives you the ability to quantize or "compress" the micro pitches for each individual segment. I use the word "compress" because with regard to pitches, it acts similar to the way a compressor works with dynamics. It actually limits the range of the micro pitches. The more you adjust the Straighten Pitch slider in the Inspector (just like the Pitch Quantize control), the more the micro pitch variations are reduced and brought to the center of the pitch.

Move the Straighten Pitch slider all of the way to the right to remove all of the micro pitches from the last note of the chorus (see Figure 3.37). Listen back to the result and notice how it sounds more synthetic. The sound of her voice without the micro pitches makes her sound almost robotic and much more as if it has been affected

Figure 3.36 Quantizing pitches from within the Pitch and Warp Editor.

with Auto-Tune. If I'm going for a somewhat more synthetic sound, I've got one! Otherwise, I can lessen the straightening of the pitch for a more natural-sounding vocal by adjusting the slider back toward the left.

The micro pitches of a note can also be "tilted" to create somewhat of an overall pitch-bend effect on a note. To tilt the micro pitches, select the box on the top-left corner of a note (to shift the start of the note) or select the box on the top-right corner of a note (to shift the end of the note). When the box is selected, drag it up to raise the pitch or down to lower the pitch, as shown in Figure 3.38.

During a vocal performance recording, there can be a lot of non-pitched audio recorded. This can be anything from dead silence to breath noises and paper rustling. VariAudio is pretty good at determining what should and should not be considered a pitch, but sometimes the process of creating these pitch segments can result in an undesirable effect. If you need to, you can manually adjust the start and end locations of the segment itself, as well as cut or glue segments (in a case where two notes might have been confused as one or vice versa), or even delete the segment altogether.

To make these types of edits, select Segments under the VariAudio tab in the Inspector. When using the Segments tab, Cubase automatically generates multiple copies of your audio track, which can increase the size or your project and the performance of your system. If you're going to use this mode, I highly recommend starting with a small

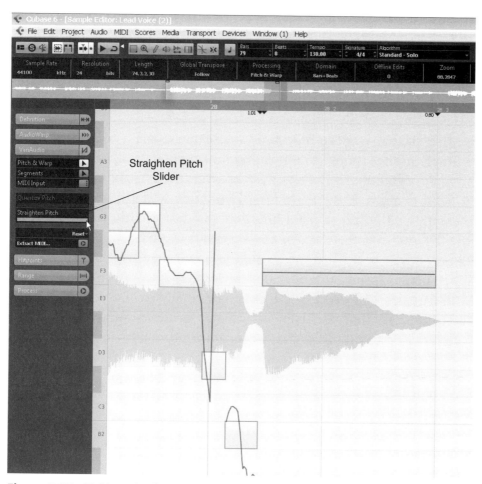

Figure 3.37 Taking the human micro pitches out of the performance.

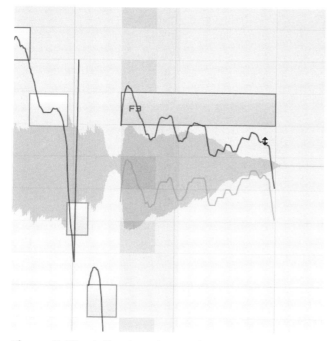

Figure 3.38 Adjusting the pitch curve on a note.

section of audio that has been bounced (as I demonstrated at the start) to keep your system running "clean." Technically, you should change the segment before using the Pitch and Warp feature, but it generally isn't used because the automated calculations of the Pitch and Warp feature are usually pretty accurate. Altering segments is like setting up a new grid for your melody.

You can also use MIDI so that you can reposition the segments via a MIDI keyboard. As easy as it is to simply use the mouse to reposition notes on the grid, this feature is a little bit of overkill unless you're just the crazy keyboard type. The Extract MIDI feature, on the other hand is much more interesting. Extracting MIDI from the segment data is similar to creating MIDI notes from hitpoints (as discussed in the tutorial on drum replacement). By utilizing the data of the segments, Cubase can extract your vocal melody to a new MIDI part. This means that you can then trigger that melody from any MIDI instrument or print out your vocal melody as a score using the scoring tools that come with Cubase. This process is a little more complex than creating notes from hitpoints due to the fact that the segments can be located somewhere *between* pitches. If you're considering using this feature, I recommend quantizing your pitches 100 percent so that they all fall on exact notes.

Last but not least, any processing that is happening when using Pitch and Warp is a real-time process. This means that Pitch and Warp is creating an extra load on your CPU. To reduce this load, you can always flatten (bounce) the processing. To do so, first select the audio part and then, from the Audio menu's Realtime Processing submenu, select Flatten. (Or you can also select Flatten from the Sample Editor's Inspector under the Process tab.) Select the algorithm option and click OK. The original audio track will be saved in its original state in the Pool for safekeeping. You can undo the process later if you decide you want to change it down the road.

4 Mastering the Art of Mixing in Cubase 6

When most of us think of mixing, the first thing we gravitate toward is using a mixing console. In Cubase, however, you can achieve a professional mix without using a mixer. In fact, you rarely need to utilize the VST mixer from within Cubase. Although it's true that certain external gear is irreplaceable in terms of its particular sound, Cubase has made it possible for you to get a similar sound with greater flexibility, and sometimes that flexibility can outweigh the irreplaceable hardware's capabilities.

Another thing many think of when mixing is *automation*. This can range from simple volume changes to panning, muting tracks, EQ, and special effects. Like digital recording, the term "automation" is relatively new to audio and mixing; however, the simple idea of achieving a perfect mix has been around since the beginning of the recording studio, when automation meant an engineer sitting behind a recording console, making adjustments to certain controls as the mix was being created in real time. Later on, engineers used the bouncing of audio tracks as a form of automation (by actually recording effects or volume changes on other tracks). Next came the "Cadillac years" of automation, which involved motorized controls and faders that physically moved during a mixdown session to match the engineer's maneuvers. Although these mechanical faders saved engineers from the signal loss that occurs during the bouncing process (when using analog tape machines), the clunkiness of programming the mechanical faders was tedious and not always 100 percent accurate, and the equipment was ridiculously expensive to own and maintain.

I wanted to spend a little time on the history of automation and mixing to make sure you're aware that automation, like everything else, is a process that is still evolving. The automation features in Cubase are much more advanced than any automated features ever were in the days of analog recording. I've embraced some of the changes in music and technology, but I've tossed aside other changes that I found to be a little clunky and that got in the way of achieving the perfect mix—sometimes the new ways are not always better than the old ways.

In addition to discussing the automation elements in Cubase, this chapter will briefly touch on the other mixing tools and show that, even though they exist, they're not always necessary to use. There are easier and (in my opinion) better ways within the program to achieve the best results possible. I'll also discuss some of the new features in Cubase 6, interfacing Cubase 6 with other hardware outboard gear, the included plug-ins, and some basic tips and settings to use when creating the final output mixdown file. I will also include a special section on mixing using the new Steinberg CC121 controller, for those who would like to physically get their hands on the mix and work with a motorized flying fader.

Making the Most of Cubase's Mixing Tools

As I've discussed, Cubase offers multiple tools that ultimately provide the same end result. The reason the program has so many options is because there is no single perfect tool. I'm devoting this section to sorting through all the technical nonsense to show you why each tool is important and how you can achieve better results with each tool than you might already know.

First off, let's take a look at the VST mixer. This is where most people seem to go when starting a mix. After all, the VST mixer appears to be the centralized point at which all the audio signals come together in Cubase. It's a great way to work with multiple tracks at once, but because there can be so much going on in the VST mixer, most of the time you're going to end up seeing more than you need, which can be annoying or over-whelming at times. The VST mixer is designed so that you can hide elements when you don't need them, but the working environment can still appear to be cluttered with controls, and continuously changing views can become tedious.

The process of mixing is usually thought of as the last production stage of a project. I believe that mixing starts before the recording even starts and is a continuous process. By the time it comes down to a final mix, you should be concentrating on the overall balance of your audio in detail, but the basic balancing of the elements is always a factor. By keeping everything "mixed as you go," you'll find that the final stage of mixing is not as overwhelming and is actually quite simple.

My advice is to work only with audio tracks if possible. Back in the early days, we used to keep MIDI tracks separate from audio tracks. This way, we could save our audio tracks for instruments that couldn't be recorded via MIDI, and we could preserve the recording quality of the synths by not recording them to analog tape. These days, there's no real point to keeping the audio and MIDI separated because Cubase 6 has virtually *unlimited* audio tracks, and the digital recording quality sounds identical to that of the unrecorded synth. If you're using VST instruments or any sort of MIDI instrument, I feel that it's better to create an audio track for that instrument before mixing, as opposed to trying to blend in "live" audio from MIDI instruments with prerecorded tracks.

I'm aware that sometimes recording live audio is the only option, but in most cases where you're creating a final mix, there's no need to utilize MIDI or VST Instrument tracks. By having your synth's actual sound recorded as an audio track (as opposed to just the MIDI data), your synths will be easier to archive for future remixes as well.

Of course, you can use the VST mixer to help you get the right recording levels when creating these synth audio tracks, but this should all happen before the actual mixing session. During the final mix, you'll be able to concentrate on making volume changes to the synth's audio track as opposed to its VST Instrument track or MIDI track. So, once again, before the final mixdown session, all your synths (as well as other instruments) should be on audio tracks, your MIDI tracks can be muted, and your synths should be disabled (to save you processing power). You can even go as far as to delete the MIDI tracks and instruments and resave the project under another name to clean up your mixing environment ahead of time.

The same way that creating audio tracks for your synths can help in making the final mix simple, you can also bounce other multiple audio tracks (such as the individual components of a drum kit or background vocal tracks) and effects (such as delays or reverb) to stereo audio tracks to simplify your mixing environment. By reducing your mix to fewer audio tracks before the final stage, you'll simplify the mixing process, eliminate the audio "mess" that the mixer can present, and create parts that are easier to edit—and you'll be able to mix the majority of your project within the Project window. Keep in mind that by bouncing tracks in this manner, you'll also be sacrificing the ability to alter the individual tracks later on during the final mix. Just use your best judgment to decide whether this is a step you can afford to take.

Even though the VST mixer can be used to display EQ/effects and volume/pan settings during a mix, I find that it's simply easier to see and make adjustments to that channel by using the Audio Channel Settings display. You can access this by selecting the "e" from any audio track in the Project window (as shown in Figure 4.1).

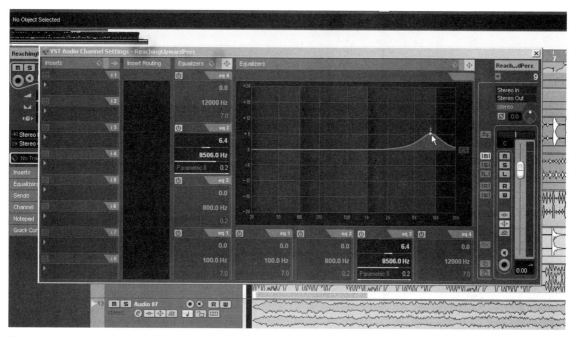

Figure 4.1 The Audio Channel Settings display.

Using the Audio Channel Settings display (instead of the VST mixer) makes sense when you're mixing in linear form from within the Project window, as opposed to trying to record your faders with automation in the VST mixer, where it's not humanly possible to see what's happening because you can't visualize where your mix is going to or coming from.

Here's an example of what I mean by mixing in *linear form*. Compare Figures 4.2 and 4.3. Figure 4.2 shows a mix in linear form within the Project window. You can see what has happened in the mix, what is happening right now, and where the mix is going. The same mix is shown in Figure 4.3. Even though you can see multiple channels at once, you can't visualize where the mix is headed to or coming from.

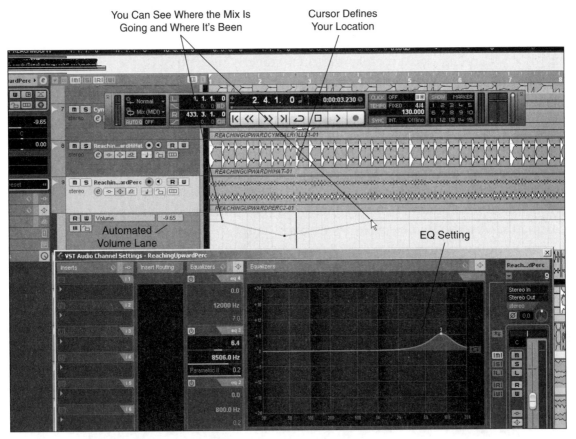

Figure 4.2 Mixing within the Project window.

Even though you can't see EQ or effects settings using the Project window alone, each channel's Audio Channel Settings display shows everything else that you really need to see, and you can access it at any time.

Automation Techniques in the Project Window

As I discussed before, there are multiple ways to automate a mix in Cubase. When most people think of automation, they think about flying faders and knobs. Some people

Figure 4.3 The same mix shown in the VST mixer.

also think that the ideal way to program automation is by turning a knob on a console and then having it repeat that maneuver for them automatically. Although the hands-on approach might seem appealing, it comes with a catch: It has to do with what happens when you want to change or correct the automation maneuver you performed. Because of the nature of hands-on automation programming, sometimes it can get messy when it's altered, and then you find yourself spending extra time correcting and repairing the automation data. Automation can be an indispensible tool when it comes to mixing. The key is in the *method* by which you program the automation.

Previously, I demonstrated how mixing in the Project window makes more sense than mixing using the VST mixer due to the way the Project window works in a linear fashion. This mainly concerns the automation. Technically, automation involves the Read and Write automation buttons in Cubase. The Write buttons, however, only need to be used when you are *physically* maneuvering a button, knob, or fader within Cubase in real time as the project is playing back.

Getting back to the basic idea that automation is strictly programming a mix, examine Figures 4.4 and 4.5.

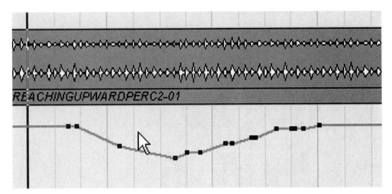

Figure 4.4 An automation performance from physically manipulating a fader using the VST mixer.

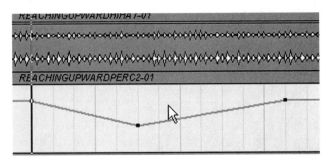

Figure 4.5 An automation performance "programmed" manually from within the Project window.

For this example, I simply wanted to fade out a track at one point and then bring it back up in the mix. I decided to perform this maneuver in several ways so that I could demonstrate the minor differences in the end result. In Figure 4.4, I used the Write automation button and moved the fader using the mouse in real time as I listened to the part. Notice how the movement created a lot of automation events; although it was a simple move, it appears to be complex and a bit messy (visually).

In Figure 4.5, I created an automation lane for volume in the Project window and then simply drew in the mix I needed (using the Pencil and Line tools) for the track I needed it on. Notice how it looks pretty straightforward and not so messy. After I finished automating using both methods, I listened to each track, and they sounded pretty much the same.

Note: Cubase offers a variety of Line tools for helping you create natural-sounding fades (adjustable from the toolbar). The important thing to know is that the more uniform (less messy) the automation line is, the less work the automation will create for your system.

When you factor in that 1) you can see the entire project in linear form within the Project window without having to use the VST mixer, 2) you can easily create automation without the need to perform a maneuver perfectly, and 3) it sounds no different, then it makes more sense to use automation by drawing it in an automation lane in the Project window than it does to accomplish this by moving a virtual fader while writing automation. It also saves you from having to flip back and forth between various windows. If you absolutely need to move a fader during automation, you can always use the fader in the Audio Channel Settings display and save yourself from having to utilize the VST mixer.

Keep in mind that even when you draw automation in an automation lane, your fader will still move on playback as if it were physically moved during the writing process. Figure 4.6 shows even more examples of panning and effect automation that have been drawn in the Project window.

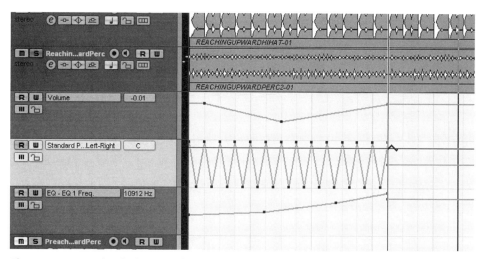

Figure 4.6 Multiple lanes of automation drawn in the Project window.

When it comes to creating automation lanes, simply select the type of lane you need by changing the parameter in the Type field of the newly added lane. By selecting More (in the default list of parameters located in the Type field), you can view the entire list of available parameters for that channel (see Figure 4.7). If you have difficulty finding the particular lane you'd like to create, you can click the red Write button located on the control that you would like to automate (manually adjusting the virtual control that you're automating), and a lane will be created for it automatically under the audio track you are working with.

Not all automation events work as well as others. In fact, I find that basic volume and muting automations can be achieved more easily with some basic part editing in the Project window. Here's how it works. Let's say you're creating a mix, and there's one lyric on a vocal track that's just a little softer than the other words on the same track. Using an automation lane for such a quick volume change is possible, but it's not the

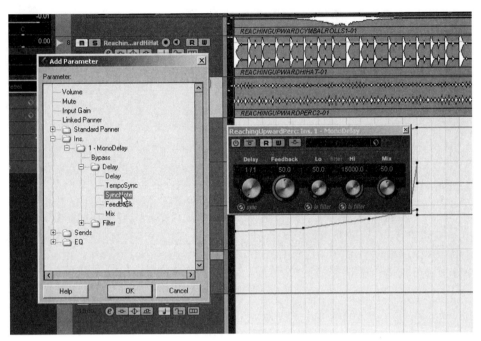

Figure 4.7 Creating a specific automation lane using the list of available parameters.

easiest or most focused method. The easiest way is to cut the audio event so the word that needs to be louder becomes its own isolated audio event (using the Split tool or another method); then, adjust the volume of the isolated audio event by increasing the gain level of the event's envelope, as shown in Figure 4.8.

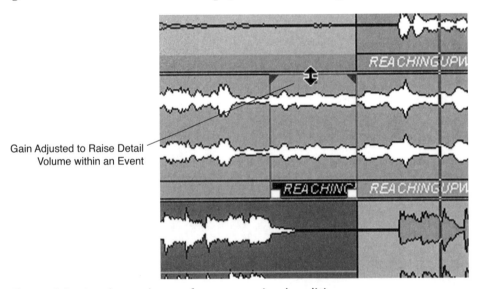

Gain Adjusted to Raise Detail
Volume within an Event

Figure 4.8 A volume change from some simple editing.

You can apply this same type of mixing on a broader scale as well, and it works even better when muting individual parts and sections in a mix. It's much easier to mute an audio event using the Mute tool than to record mute automation. You can also fade in and out from audio event to audio event using the control located at the top-right or -left corner of the event. Figure 4.9 shows how I've created a mix similar to the one in Figure 4.5 using audio editing as opposed to automation lanes.

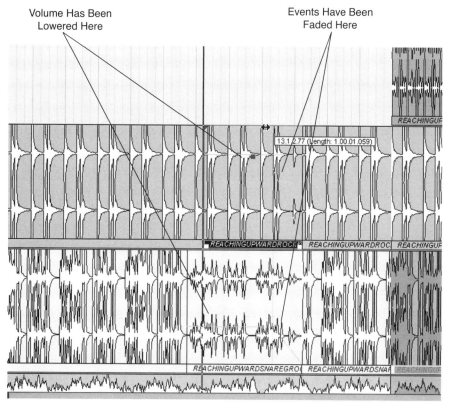

Figure 4.9 Broad volume changes using some simple events editing.

If you find yourself juggling a lot of automation lanes and working with real-time automation programming, the Automation panel (shown in Figure 4.10) could become a helpful tool. Access this panel from the Project window's toolbar; it allows you to quickly adjust the type of automation mode you want to work with: touch, auto-latch, or cross-over. To expand the panel and access more features, select the arrow to the right of the mode from the toolbar.

Figure 4.10 The Automation panel.

Once the panel is displayed, you can easily access buttons that will allow you to quickly enable or disable automation, bypass certain automation types (suspend automation), display selected automation lane types, remove unwanted automation, and more. To make a long story short, this panel is Cubase's answer to the problem of messy real-time automation. If you absolutely find that you need to program automation in real time, then you will find this to be an indispensable tool. To learn more about the features of the Automation panel, refer to Help > Documentation > Automation > The Automation Panel.

Note: Remember that when it comes to mixing, not everything needs to be automated. In fact, your standard mix usually requires that the settings on several tracks remain the same throughout the final mix. This means that once you have your volumes, EQ, and effects set for some tracks, there's no need to automate them.

Using Cubase's Effect Inserts and Sends

Before I discuss the VST plug-ins in Cubase, I believe there are still some working professionals who don't understand the difference between using a send and an insert on a track. An *insert* effect is inserted directly into the signal path of the track on which it is activated. This effect's sole purpose is to process that one particular audio track. When several insert effects are used on one individual track, the order in which they are inserted will make a big difference to the final result of the sound.

A good comparison of an insert effect is sort of like using a stompbox with a guitar and amp. The guitar signal enters the stompbox before passing through to the amp. If you're using several pedals at once, the order of the pedals will affect your sound. It can be as subtle as, "Would you like *delay* on your distorted guitar or *distortion* on your delayed guitar?" But there is an audible difference.

Because insert effects are dedicated to each particular track, using a lot of insert effects creates multiple instances of that effect, and each of these instances creates more of a burden on your computer's processor. When you're utilizing an insert effect, you control the mix of that effect (compared to the original direct signal) from the instance of the effect itself.

Using a *send* is the standard method of handling an effect when you need to use it on several tracks simultaneously. For instance, you might want to use the same reverb sound on several different drum or vocal tracks at once. The mix level of the effect on each track is determined by controlling how much signal (from each individual track utilizing the send) is sent to the effect. To utilize a send effect on a track in Cubase, you must first create an FX channel track from within VST Connections or from the Project menu.

You can use effect sends pre-fader or post-fader. Because each effect send acts like its own fader (by defining the level of signal sent), a pre-fader send means that the level of the fader on the audio channel of the audio track will not affect the level that's sent to a send destination (because the signal from the send is being sent from the audio channel *before* it reaches the channel fader in the path of the signal flow). A post-fader send means that the level of the signal from the channel's fader *will* affect the level of the signal sent to the effect send destination (because the signal is directed to the send *after* going through the channel fader).

When using an effect via a send, you need to determine whether you would like to use your effect's send as a pre-fader or post-fader send. The default method is to use the send in post-fader mode, but occasionally you might like to bypass the channel fader to send the signal directly to the effect. This type of routing is possible by selecting the Pre Fader button on the effect send (see Figure 4.11). Normally, when using multiple post-fader sends, since the signal is split, the order of each send effect on a track makes no difference in the final sound (as it does when using effects via inserts). When using a pre-fader send, you're going to end up hearing more of the affected sound than the original unaffected sound if the channel fader is at a lower level than your send's level.

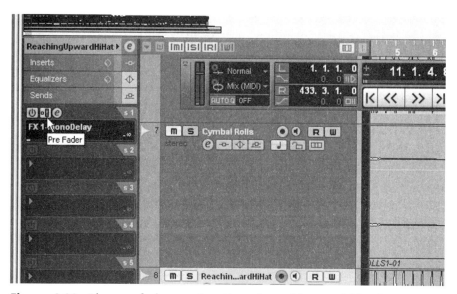

Figure 4.11 The pre-fader send option viewed from within the Inspector.

Note: You can get very creative just by changing your effect's signal routing. Remember that sends primarily are used when working with multiple channels and utilizing the same effect. Although EQ and dynamic plug-ins are commonly used as insert effects, any effect can be used with an insert, but the order of your effects as they're inserted will affect the sound of the overall combined effect on that track.

An Overview of Available Plug-In Effects

Cubase comes with a lot of plug-ins. In case you didn't know already, there's a full Cubase manual dedicated to the included effects. You can find this under the Help menu by selecting Documentations and then selecting Plug-In Reference. My aim in this section is to walk you through the massive group of effects and give you a "quick and dirty" reference guide from an outside perspective so you can jump in and start using them right away.

Delay Effects

When it comes to delays, Cubase 6 offers a variety of choices: MonoDelay, StereoDelay, ModMachine, and PingPongDelay. Although some delay types aren't included (multi-tap delay, sampling delay, tape delay, and so on), most of the time you should be able to get by with these four basic digital delays because they cover a wide range.

MonoDelay is probably the most useful and can provide whatever standard echo effect or slap-back effect is necessary. StereoDelay is like two linked mono delays and is primarily used on stereo recordings where you need slightly different delays on the left and right channels. PingPongDelay is similar to MonoDelay but is designed to feature only delays that are linked to a stereo panning effect. The main difference is the *spatial* control, which helps define the width of the panning. The ModMachine delay allows you to filter the feedback of the delay. This effect is normally used when you want something to sound weird or spacey, but it can also be used subtly.

The most important detail in all of these plug-in delays is the ability to sync to your project's tempo. Years ago, engineers had to break out their calculators to compute the tempo speed in milliseconds to get their delays to fall on the beat. Today, using Cubase, you just have to select the Sync button (as shown in Figure 4.12) and define the beat where you'd like the delay (1/4 notes, 1/2 notes, 1/8 notes, and so forth). All of the delays are VST3 effects.

Figure 4.12 Syncing the delay to match the tempo of the project.

Distortion Effects

As I demonstrated the new VST Amp Rack in Chapter 3, you're already aware that Cubase 6 has some incredible guitar signal processing. However, distortion isn't just for guitars; it's often used on other instruments and vocals. If you don't feel like your vocal or organ is mean enough, try running it through the VST Amp Rack just as you would a guitar. You might be pleasantly surprised by the results.

If for some reason the VST Amp Rack doesn't cut it for you, and you're looking for a grungy distortion, your next best bet would be to try the AmpSimulator or the Distortion plug-in. The AmpSimulator effect offers the most control over the distortion and provides a speaker cabinet emulator (similar to the VST Amp Rack). DaTube is a software simulation of basic classic tube distortion (similar to that found on vintage mic pres) and is mostly used to give vocal tracks some extra warmth. The SoftClipper is similar to DaTube in that it's a subtle effect and isn't really meant to be noticed. It gives you the sound of clipping without actually clipping the signal (which is definitely something you don't want in your mix).

The Grungelizer is quite different from the other distortion effects. It simply adds noises that are commonly found in older recordings (such as AC hum, vinyl, and tape hiss) to give the processed signal more of a vintage sound.

Last but not least, the Bitcrusher is designed to distort the signal by simulating a lower bit rate and is used primarily to achieve a low-fi sound.

Dynamic Effects

When it comes to processing dynamics (loud/soft audio levels), Cubase has got it all. The following dynamic effects work in similar ways, but each has its own defined characteristics. With this much variety, possibly the only reason to use third-party plug-ins of this type would be to have an alternative.

Out of all of these, the Compressor and the Limiter cover the most basic features in their respective categories. Because they work so well together, I usually prefer to use VST Dynamics, which covers all the bases and also includes a noise gate (similar to the Gate effect mentioned little later).

The Expander is another type of processor specially designed to maximize loudness when working with audio that covers a wide dynamic range (very loud to very soft). The MultibandCompressor is slightly different and enables you to compress a certain frequency range as opposed to the full range. This can help greatly in controlling the dynamics of certain frequencies without losing some of the frequency range. Multiband compression comes in very handy with audio tracks that contain a wide range of frequencies (such as a full mix used as a sample). VintageCompressor is simply an alternative to using the Compressor plug-in and simulates a more classic-sounding compression.

The Gate plug-in is simply a complex noise gate without any sort of compression or limiting. It is an automated muting type of effect, which responds according to the level of the audio signal of the track. MidiGate allows you to program the open and close of the gate via a MIDI track (as opposed to using the signal level) and acts independently from the signal (more like a programmable on/off switch). Both of these types of gate plug-ins could be used to create some interesting choppy effects to an audio track or simply to remove unwanted noise.

The DeEsser was really designed with one purpose: to remove the sizzling sound that the letter "s" can sometimes bring to a vocal track. The EnvelopeShaper works similarly to a noise gate, except it can also boost the signal (as opposed to only cutting the signal). It also gives you more control over the attack and release of the affected signal.

The Maximizer is a simple compressor/limiter specifically designed for getting a louder signal without running the risk of clipping. Be careful, though, because distortion can be added during this process. Overuse could lead to less clarity and definitely to a reduced dynamic range, which is not always a good solution for making a signal louder.

EQ Effects

The standard four-band parametric EQ that you get on every audio channel in Cubase is a lot better than the EQ you're going to get from most other hardware mixing consoles, but Cubase offers several alternatives if that's not enough.

If you're already familiar with the standard parametric EQ, you will find that the StudioEQ is very similar. One slight difference is that you can control the overall output level of the EQ. Keep in mind that by having the option of using the EQ as a plug-in, you can alter the sound of your effects chain within a group of inserts, which is something that you can't use with just the standard four-band channel EQ alone.

The GEQ10 and GEQ30 are both graphic EQs. (The number following GEQ reflects the number of EQ bands available.) Graphic EQs allow you to get into more detail with multiple specific frequencies, as opposed to concentrating on only four frequencies when using the parametric EQ. Because of their nature, graphic EQs are often used on audio that covers a wide range of frequencies (such as a full music mix). All three EQ plug-ins are VST3.

> **Note:** Even though effects can sometimes appear to be very similar, they often offer subtle differences in sound. You will discover that certain types of effects work better when working with certain types of audio. If one particular type isn't cutting it for you, try another.

Filter Effects

Filter effects generally consist of an automated EQ-based effect and are often used to create sweeping sounds in dance music. Cubase offers five filter effects, and they are all VST3. All of these filters can be a lot of fun to play around with, and they come with a variety of presets to give you a better idea of their capabilities. Out of these effects, DualFilter and ToneBooster are not automated, but they can be automated manually using an automation lane under the audio track.

DualFilter is a unique high-pass/low-pass filter effect with a band booster to give it an extra kick if necessary. Using ToneBooster is a way to add a little harmonic distortion to a certain frequency range without clipping the signal (similar to an overdrive pedal for guitar).

StepFilter, Tonic, and WahWah are sweeping filter effects that can be synced to match the tempo of the project. Out of the three, Tonic offers the most control for creating some interesting filtered textures. WahWah is similar to the guitar effect and can be controlled via a MIDI foot pedal, but it can also be used like an envelope filter without using a foot pedal at all. The Chopper sounds more like a noise gate or tremolo that syncs with the project tempo and "chops" up the signal in time. You also can use it like the AutoPan to create a harsh panning-type effect.

Modulation Effects

The modulation effects in Cubase cover a lot of ground. All of these modulation effects are VST3 plug-ins except for the RingModulator, Tranceformer, and Metalizer.

AutoPan works best on mono recordings to create an automated left/right panning effect. The Rotary effect is a similar panning effect but simulates the Doppler effect, such as a Leslie Cabinet on a Hammond B3 organ (which consisted of an amplified speaker spinning around at various speeds inside a cabinet).

Tremolo is another classic effect where the amplitude of the signal increases and decreases quickly. The Doors used a similar effect on some famous recordings.

Vibrato can sometimes be confused with Tremolo, but Vibrato actually modulates pitch up and down quickly, as opposed to volume, creating a slightly different effect (similar to the vocal tremolo effect).

Chorus, StudioChorus, and Flanger are classic effects as well and are basically created by using varying degrees of delay with a little extra modulation. The main difference between Chorus and StudioChorus is that the StudioChorus effect is like using two choruses in one.

Even though the Cloner might sound like a chorus, its effect actually works like a harmonizer by creating a double of the original pitch and slightly detuning the doubled pitches.

The RingModulator is another classic effect that also duplicates the original signal, but then blends it with a sine wave to create yet another unique (almost metallic) quality. Both the Metalizer and the Tranceformer effects are variations of the RingModulator, each with its own characteristics.

Last but not least, the Phaser is another classic effect that can sometimes be confused with a Flanger. The Phaser actually utilizes an LFO (*low-frequency oscillator*), as opposed to using a delay, to alter the frequency spectrum that in turn gives you sort of a swooshing sound.

> **Note:** When using some of the VST3 modulation, dynamic, filter, or delay plug-ins, it's possible to use side-chain inputs on the effects. A side-chain input lets you specify another signal to trigger the effect, in turn creating yet a different effect for the signal that's being processed. This can be a very useful mixing technique when blending or matching multiple tracks. For more information on side-chaining these effects, refer to Help > Documentation > Operation Manual > Audio Effects > Using the Side-Chain Input.

Pitch-Shift Effects

Pitch Correct is a real-time plug-in effect that allows you to specify a scale and a degree to which the note should be "pulled" to the correct pitch. It is very easy to use, but it offers a different result from that of VariAudio. Whereas VariAudio is a pitch editor that utilizes the Audio Warp technology to correct pitches, the Pitch Correct plug-in uses a technology similar to that of Antares' Auto-Tune.

Although I prefer the more "natural" result of pitch correction using VariAudio over Pitch Correct as a plug-in, I can say that all of the pitch "bases" are pretty well covered between these two pitch-correction tools in Cubase. Now that we have Pitch Correct, there's not as much need to use Auto-Tune when working with Cubase as there was in the past.

The Octaver works similarly to an octave foot pedal and simply creates a duplicate pitch two octaves below the original pitch. It also gives you control over the volume of each of the two octaves.

Reverb Effects

Cubase 6 comes with some big guns in the basic reverb department. With these combined reverb processors, you're going to find that there are fewer reasons to use a third-party reverb plug-in. My only complaint is that it would be nice to have some simulated "spring reverb" effects, as well as some other classic reverb sounds. Sometimes the new technology sounds *too* good!

REVerence is a high-quality convolution reverb effect that truly delivers incredible results. Convolution reverbs are the latest and greatest in reverb technology (using impulse-response modeling). RoomWorks is another fantastic digital reverb. (Room-Works SE is similar but with fewer parameters and is less CPU-consuming.)

Spatial + Panner and Surround Effects

The spatial effects included in Cubase offer a fairly basic way to modify the general field of sound of a particular audio track. The MonoToStereo effect uses a delay to spread a mono signal across the stereo field. StereoEnhancer is a basic stereo widener you can use to spread out the image of the sound across the stereo field. Although popular, this effect shouldn't be overused on parts that are prominent in the mix (due to the coloration effect on the sound).

The surround plug-ins include the Mix6To2 mixer (which is simply a submixer that converts surround mixes back into a stereo mix) and MixerDelay (which is a necessity when it comes to creating a mix outside of your normal L/R stereo field). MixerDelay replaces SurroundPan from Cubase 5 with more options for control.

Tools and Mastering Effects

The last group of VST plug-ins aren't effects at all; rather, they're extra tools that can help you analyze audio as well as work with other equipment. The MultiScope tool covers three basic audio analysis tools, including an oscilloscope, a phase correlator, and a frequency spectrum analyzer; they can all come in very handy and enable you to take a closer look at your audio in real time.

The SMPTEGenerator and TestGenerator are great, particularly if you're working with some analog tape recorders in addition to Cubase. The SMPTEGenerator can output timecode to a tape track, which can then be redirected to Cubase for Cubase to "chase" and lock to the tape machine. The TestGenerator can create test tones that can help calibrate recording meters (basic alignment), as well as serve other testing purposes.

The Tuner is just like a guitar tuner. It's simply a tool that analyzes the tuning of an instrument and is best used on an input channel as an insert. It has no real effect on the instrument. Last but not least, you can use the UV22HR (by Apogee, included in Cubase 6) to dither from a higher bit depth to a lower bit depth to best preserve the recording quality. For more on dithering, please refer to my tutorial on "Creating the Final Output: Exporting Audio" a little later in this chapter.

To summarize, the bang for the buck that you get with Cubase 6 in terms of plug-ins is phenomenal, especially when you consider that most third-party plug-ins can cost as much as or more than Cubase. Even with all the third-party plug-ins available, I still find myself using the Cubase plug-ins because, most of the time, they're as good as the rest—and sometimes they're even better.

Interfacing External Hardware Effects Processors

As just discussed, Cubase is chock-full of plug-ins that can meet the demands of most users. However, as wonderful as it would be to have *everything* in one box, it's simply impossible. If there's a sound you're looking for that's "outside the box" (or not available as a plug-in), you're going to have to approach routing the effect a little differently. I don't think there's a single new processor that can't be duplicated by a plug-in. But on the other hand, there are a lot of vintage processors for which people often have a soft spot. This section will discuss how to interface an older analog external classic processor with Cubase.

> **Note:** Most of the time, the only reason to use an external digital processor (such as that included with the MR816) would be to reserve some of your processing power (because most digital processors can be better simulated with similar plug-ins).

Interfacing with an external processor is similar to setting up to record an external instrument. You must first create an interface point under VST Connections. This time, however, you'll need to designate at least one specific output from your audio interface as the effects send and at least one specific input from your audio interface as the effects return.

> **Note:** Even though a lot of vintage processors have stereo outputs, they often are not *true* stereo (dual-channel) effects. So instead of using two outputs on your audio interface, you can probably run only a single output from your interface into the mono input of the external processor, and then run the stereo signal from the effect processor back into two separate inputs on your audio interface. This way, you can still capture the pseudo-stereo effect from the processor.

For this example, I'm going to run a mono signal out to a classic Roland delay's input and then return the processed signal from the Roland's output to Cubase. First, open the VST Connections window. Select the External FX tab and then select Add External FX. Next, enter the info as needed into the Add External FX dialog (as shown in Figure 4.13).

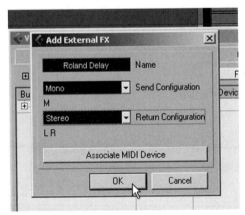

Figure 4.13 Setting up a connection to an external processor.

You can take the time to create a MIDI device (if your vintage gear actually responds to MIDI) by using the Associate MIDI Device button, but it is not necessary if you're simply looking to process the signal and manually make adjustments on the processor itself. Once you have entered the required info, you just need to designate the ins and outs of your audio interface, as shown in Figure 4.14.

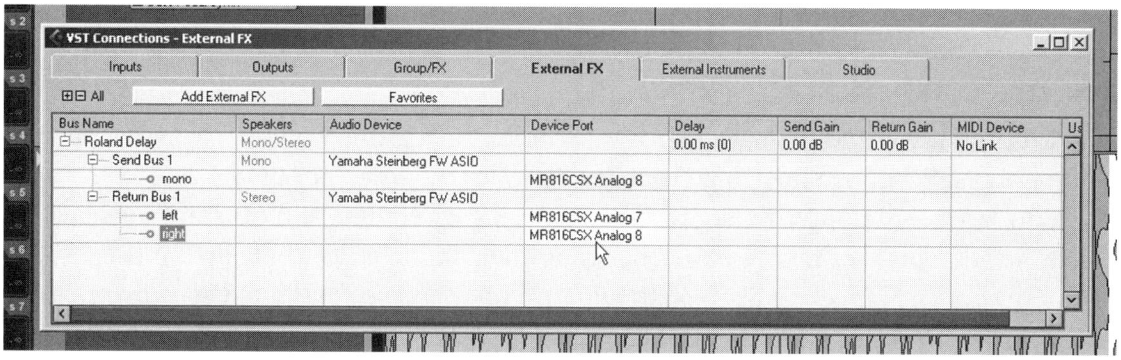

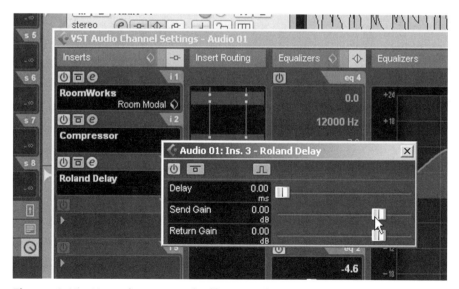

Figure 4.14 Designating the effects send and return ins and outs.

In this example, I have specified Output 8 on my MR816 as the mono send for my Roland delay and specified Inputs 7 and 8 on the MR816 as the stereo returns. There are other options in this same window for adjusting the input and output gain. Adjusting the delay compensation here may be necessary, too, depending on the gear you're using and the way you're monitoring in Cubase (so that you aren't hearing more delay than you intend).

When you're finished making your settings, you should be able to open the effect as an insert or create a send for the effect, and it will appear under the External Effects heading in your list of plug-ins. Once your effect is active on an audio track, you will be able to select the input/output level and delay compensation controls as well by selecting "e" from the active effect (as shown in Figure 4.15).

Figure 4.15 Now the external effect can be treated similarly to an internal effect plug-in.

Of course, when you're using any external hardware, you still have to deal with ground loops and noise along with all the other regular issues, as if you were recording the old-school analog way, but that's a small price to pay to get "the sound." You also need to utilize Real-Time Export when creating a final mix with external hardware, because the processing must occur in real time. I discuss Real-Time Export more later on in this chapter.

Mixing with the CC121

If you absolutely *have* to get your hands on a fader during the mixing process in Cubase, there's no easier way than using the CC121. What's great about the CC121 is that there's no reason to assign faders to certain tracks or channels. You start by selecting an audio track that you want to mix (by using the channel select buttons on the CC121 to quickly change from channel to channel), and then you select the red W button on the track by using the same buttons located on the CC121 before performing your mix (see Figure 4.16). You can go back and add moves (such as muting, EQ, or panning), and the automation will be created without affecting the other automation type. Keep in mind that to hear (and see) the automation that you performed previously, you also need to have the green R button (read automation) selected.

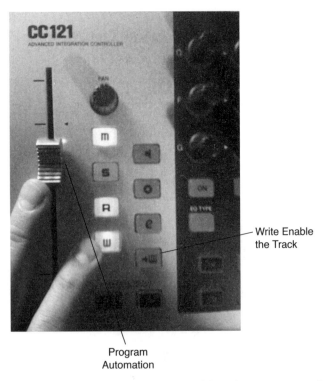

Write Enable
the Track

Program
Automation

Figure 4.16 Preparing to record hands-on automation with the CC121.

The fader itself is motorized and should move exactly as you programmed it during the write automation process. The Mute buttons will light up as a channel is muted, but the knobs (pan, EQ) remain stationary. You repeat this process for each individual track, making adjustments to only one track at a time (which is recommended when it comes to writing automation anyway). Your single flying fader will display the motions of whichever track is selected during the playback of your project.

Even though I own the CC121 and I *still* prefer to program automation by drawing it in, I think that there is something appealing about having the flashy lights and moving fader in the studio. It makes working a little more fun, it's quick to program, and it's a great conversation piece for other artists or producers who might be working with you.

Creating the Final Output: Exporting Audio

If you've gotten this far, chances are you've already exported an audio mix in Cubase. I'd like to discuss a few details concerning available features that you might not be aware of, as well as some recommended settings for getting the best possible results during an export. You start every audio mixdown export by selecting Export Audio Mixdown from the Export menu located in the File menu. Upon selection, the Export Audio Mixdown dialog will appear, as shown in Figure 4.17.

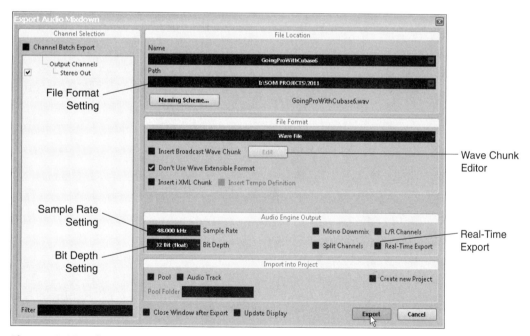

Figure 4.17 The Export Audio Mixdown dialog box.

There are multiple ways to export using Cubase 6. The most common is a standard stereo mix export. By default, the format that most Mac users will mix down to is AIFF, and the format that Windows users will default to is WAV. Although Cubase *does* offer other formats, if you're creating a stereo mix for broadcast, I highly recommend that you stick with either an AIFF or a WAV file. The reason is that most of the other file formats are compressed. The difference in file type can greatly affect the quality of the recording.

There are folks who will debate me, but for the best quality with the least amount of loss, you should export at 48 kHz (or as high as 192 kHz) and utilize 32-bit (float). This is the best way to go even if, for instance, your project was recorded in 16-bit and at 44.1 kHz. The file size for the mix will be larger, but when it's your final mix, you should always use the best possible settings. You can always dither down and change the resolution after you have created a file using a wave editor, such as WaveLab, or even in Cubase.

Here's why it's important to use those settings (in my layman's terms): Cubase uses 32-bit (float) internally in its processing. This means that any signal processing that occurs (VST plug-ins) will be crammed into a smaller bit depth if the output settings are less. When extra data is crammed into a tighter space, some of that data gets either lost or distorted.

Dithering down is an important step that will affect the final sound. To *dither* is to add "noise" to the process while stepping down to the next smaller bit depth. Adding noise might sound like a bad thing, but in theory, this noise ends up getting (mostly) lost, and the important audio (which might normally be affected by the bit conversion) is kept. Even if your soundcard is 24-bit, this export process will make no difference, because it is an *internal* process. You can hear the difference between an export that's done at 16-bit and an export that's done in 32-bit. It's more difficult to distinguish the difference from a 24-bit mix and a 32-bit (float) mix. Remember that you can dither down to a lower bit depth without much loss, but dithering up to a higher bit depth later will not make your mix sound any better—so opt for the higher bit depth when exporting.

Without getting too technical, 32-bit (float) is 24-bit with an 8-bit "cushion" for processing. A 32-bit (float) has been the standard in processing for some time, but now that operating systems are capable of running at 64-bit, we might be seeing changes within the next couple of years. It can be very taxing to stay current with the changes, but in the future you should know that if your internal processing is handled at 64-bit (Cubase 6 currently utilizes 32-bit floating-point for its internal processing on both 32-bit and 64-bit versions), then you'd want to export in 64-bit as well. Cubase 6 is capable of exporting in Waves64 format (64-bit), but because most processing is handled in 32-bit (float), there's no real benefit to using this format in Cubase at this time (except that you can export a file as large as 4 GB as opposed to the 2-GB limit for WAV files).

Broadcast Wave files allow you to record data as well as audio. This is similar to tagging MP3s, except there isn't much room for data. The catch is that the data can be accessed only from programs or CD players that can read Broadcast Wave files—and even though there are many people who use them, there are many who have no idea how to access the data. What this boils down to is that the info you can put into a Broadcast Wave file is good only if it's accessible. For general mixing and file handling, just keeping your file name correct is good enough, without having to worry about tagging a Broadcast Wave. For cases where it's necessary, you can add up to three lines, include a timecode reference, and include the date and time (as shown in Figure 4.18).

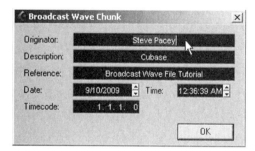

Figure 4.18 Creating a Broadcast Wave Chunk for your export.

Creating a Broadcast Wave file is as easy as exporting a WAV file; just check the box that is labeled Insert Broadcast Wave Chunk and select the Edit button to enter the appropriate data. After you have exported the file, the data can be viewed in other programs, such as WaveLab from within its Wave Attributes dialog box (shown in Figure 4.19).

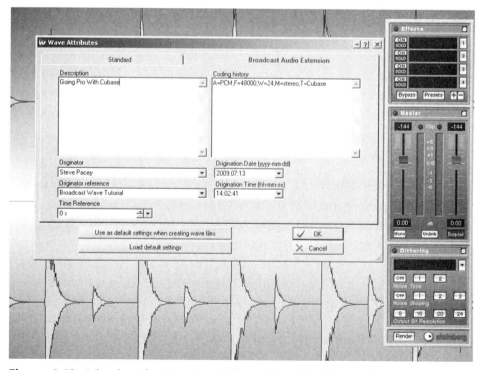

Figure 4.19 Viewing the Broadcast Wave Chunk in WaveLab.

There are a few other check boxes in the Export Audio Mixdown dialog box that need to be addressed: Don't Use Wave Extensible Format, Insert iXML Chunk, and Insert Tempo Definition. For the most part, unless you're creating surround-sound mixes, there's no good reason to use Wave Extensible Format, and you're better off leaving its box checked for a standard stereo mix. Wave Extensible Format was created by Microsoft for managing multichannel files, such as 5.1 surround sound.

In regard to Insert iXML Chunk, Cubase will export the data from your Project Setup (including Author, Company) along with the audio file you're exporting. Also, if you select Insert Tempo Definition, the project tempo will be saved along with the file.

Both of these features seem like nice additions, but they can create problems if the audio file is being opened on a system that does not recognize the data. Because of this, these two check boxes are better left unchecked when exporting audio, but at least you have the opportunity to experiment, and you can always export another version with a slightly different name to identify which one includes the data and which one does not.

Using Real-Time Export versus Standard Export

Despite what several believe, there usually is no significant benefit to exporting via real time as opposed to doing a standard export. Sometimes, though, a real-time export is a *must* due to CPU clipping that can occur during a standard export when using certain plug-ins or when using external processing. Unfortunately, when you're listening in real time, you can't hear whether your CPU will clip during export. However, if you're using a lot of processor plug-ins (and particularly third-party plug-ins), you run a greater risk of clipping during a standard export.

I normally utilize the standard export. I also *always* listen to the export from beginning to end to make sure there aren't any problems with the final output. If there is noticeable clipping, I redo the export using a real-time export, and when I'm finished, I check my work again to make sure there isn't any audible clipping during the processing. It might sound redundant, but double-checking is the only way to guarantee accurate results.

It's pretty standard for me to use Import into Project after exporting audio so that I can listen to the finished result. I usually do that by selecting Audio Track at the bottom of the Export Audio Mixdown dialog so that the export is brought right back into the project that it came from. The important thing to remember when importing a final mix back into the project is that you need to solo the export on its track (so that you aren't monitoring files from the original mix); you also have to make sure to bypass any effects that you might have on your master bus.

After you have played back your mix and determined that you need to do a real-time export, you can check the Real-Time Export box from the Export Audio Mixdown dialog (refer to Figure 4.17). When you export your audio using the Real-Time Export option (as opposed to the standard export), Cubase will play the project in real time from the left locator to the right locator and create a file during the entire process. While this real-time export is happening, you can't make any changes, and you shouldn't even touch your computer until the process is complete. If you would like to watch your meters for clipping during the process, you need to select Update Display from the Export Audio Mixdown dialog and then position all of the meters that you intend to watch before actually clicking the Export button. Be careful, though—sometimes the extra effort of updating your display can push your CPU right into the "clip zone," which is exactly what you're trying to avoid.

If you still run into problems with your processing, I suggest going back into your mix and applying the processing directly to the track (bouncing) to save on processing power before attempting the mix again. After your track has been bounced, deactivate the original "problem" plug-in before attempting another mixdown export.

5 Interfacing Cubase 6 with the Rest of the World

E ven though you really *can* do almost everything in Steinberg's little world, there are times when you just can't avoid working with other platforms. Cubase covers almost every angle, but Steinberg has always left the door open for outside possibilities. In this chapter, I'll go over interfacing Cubase with some other popular platforms (such as Pro Tools, Nuendo, and Reason), as well as working with video.

Working with a Cubase Project in Nuendo

For those who aren't familiar, Nuendo is Steinberg's top-of-the-line DAW and is used in professional studios all over the world. Nuendo and Cubase are very similar. In fact, if you know Cubase, you can easily go from working in Cubase to working in Nuendo and hardly realize the differences. Nuendo has become slightly more common in professional studios, mostly due to its design for working in a post-production (motion picture– and video-related) environment. Does this make it a DAW that's more pro? Not really. The tools used to create music in Cubase slightly outshine the latest standard version of Nuendo, which could possibly make Cubase a better DAW for anyone specifically working with music production. As a pro, there may be times in your career when you need to take your project to another studio. If that studio has Nuendo (or Cubase), transferring your project into their system will be much easier than if their system were any other DAW (such as Digidesign's Pro Tools or MOTU's Digital Performer).

As I mentioned in the introduction, Cubase 6 and Cubase Artist 6 are now fully compatible with each other. That means you can open a Cubase 6 project in Cubase Artist 6 and vice versa (keeping in mind that the extra features in Cubase 6 will not be available in Cubase Artist 6). Nuendo *also* recognizes and opens Cubase project files. Because of this, all you need to bring to the other studio is the folder that contains all of your Cubase project and audio files. If you've followed the backup procedures as I discussed in Chapter 1, and your files are organized properly within the project folder, you shouldn't have an issue loading your project into Nuendo.

However, there are a few catches to making this transfer. The first is that, most of the time, in order to make a smooth transition from Cubase to Nuendo, the software version of Nuendo you're transferring to should be as current as (or newer than) the version of Cubase you're using in your project. So if your own software version is newer than the studio you're going to, there could be compatibility issues. Check with the other studio first to make sure that this is not the case. Steinberg provides a compatibility chart on its site (www.steinberg.net) in case you have questions. If there appears to be a version-compatibility issue, I recommend following the instructions in the next section regarding using Cubase with any other DAWs to ensure compatibility.

There's also an issue regarding plug-in compatibility. If you're taking a Cubase 6 project into a studio with Nuendo (or Cubase), and they don't have, for example, a certain distortion, VST instrument, or reverb that you've used in your project, then that plug-in will show as missing on the other studio's system. So you will not be able to use that plug-in on their system. If you can make certain that the studio to which you're transferring your project has the same plug-ins that you've used in your project, you should be okay. If for some reason they have some but not all of your plug-ins, you should bounce the effect(s) that they don't have to an audio track in your project so that you can still re-create the effect on their system. Once you've bounced the effect, remove the plug-in from your project and resave the project under a new name so that the plug-in doesn't appear as missing on the other system during the transfer.

As with plug-in compatibility, you also have to make sure that you're not using any ReWire instruments or video players (such as QuickTime) in your project if that software will not be available on the system to which you're transferring. If the programs *are* available, the software versions of those programs on the other system should also be the same versions or newer than the ones on your own system. As I discussed the start of the book, moving from a 32-bit system to a 64-bit system could also affect the ability of ReWire instruments, video players, and plug-ins.

There's one more slight catch that has to do with some data that is only available in Cubase and that Nuendo isn't capable of editing. This issue is not a big deal, but if you're regularly working between the two platforms, you should consider downloading and installing (in the Nuendo system) the Nuendo Expansion Kit (NEK) from Steinberg's website. It provides a few more editing tools and VST instruments that are missing in Nuendo. This expansion is for Nuendo 4 and 5. (At this time it has not been determined whether it will be necessary for Nuendo 6, which is not yet on the market.) However, if you're converting your Instrument tracks to audio tracks before moving to the Nuendo system, you're less likely to need this upgrade. With regard to compatibility issues between different versions of Cubase and Nuendo, you can always check Steinberg's website (www.steinberg.net) for status updates if you're unsure.

Note: There shouldn't be any issues when transferring Cubase or Nuendo projects between Windows or Mac platforms because Cubase and Nuendo run on both platforms. Just keep in mind that you will need to bounce plug-ins that are not cross-platform before you go to the other studio.

When it comes to transferring files from your system to the media (another hard drive, CD-R, DVD-R, and so forth) that will be used to load the project into the other studio's system, remember that you need to transfer the entire project folder, which contains not only the project files, but *all* of the files associated with the project. To do this, I recommend using the Back Up Project feature (located under the File menu) to duplicate to a new folder everything that's necessary to run your Cubase project. When the new folder is created, label it something like "Nuendo Project" and then copy it to your new disk. I recommend testing (by loading) the transferred project in your own Cubase system from the same media before trusting that everything was transferred successfully and heading out to the other studio.

To open the transferred Cubase project in the Nuendo system, select Open from the File menu and then select the project (.cpr or .bak file) you would like to open from the project folder located on your transferred media.

Transferring to Pro Tools or Another DAW

Working between two different studios has always come with compatibility issues. But even though you can run into problems when working between multiple DAWs, it's a lot easier than it used to be. For example, in the "old" days, we had to think about whether the project was on 16-track 1/2″ or 24-track 2″, whether the studio was using ADAT or DA-88, Dolby or DBX, and so on. You actually used to have to *log* everything! Yuck!

Even though there are many different types of DAWs out there (Pro Tools, Digital Performer, SONAR, Logic, and so on), they all do pretty much the same thing. If you need to work in another program, transferring your Cubase project to it isn't very difficult if you follow the instructions in this tutorial.

Using OMF Files between DAWs

Utilizing OMFI files during a transfer can be a useful way to work between two different DAW programs. OMFI stands for *Open Media Framework Interchange*, and this file format has been developed as sort of a basic "translator" when working between multiple DAW platforms. There are currently two versions of OMFI files. (The extension is abbreviated as .omf.) If you'll be transferring your project to new versions of DAW software, you'll want to use the OMF 2.0 format. You should verify with the studio which format their system needs, as some older software versions may recognize only OMF 1.0 files.

OMF 2.0 utilizes only very limited data from your Cubase project. When you create an OMF file, it does *not* translate the project tempo, pan settings, EQ settings, or effects settings. It covers only the volume settings made within the parts of the mix (not automation), and it ignores muted tracks, treating them as though they are part of the mix. This means that any real mixing prior to the transfer will be lost in the standard creation of an OMF file. Of course, the usual reason a project is transferred is for mixing or remixing, so in some circumstances this might be a reasonable loss.

Another thing that you should know when transferring your project via OMF is that its standards require that every audio file be in stereo format and at 16-bit or 24-bit. If you're working with mono files, they will be converted to stereo files in the process of exporting the OMF. Also, if you're working in 32-bit (float), your project will have to be truncated to 24-bit (or 16-bit) resolution before creating the OMF, or else the file will be truncated automatically to the output settings during the OMF export.

So, depending on what you need out of the mix, there are multiple steps you can take to make sure that your Cubase project opens correctly on another DAW. If you would like to preserve your EQ and automation settings (your mix), the easy way would be to export new audio files with those particular EQ settings within the audio file itself (in other words, bounce the mix). If you're unsure whether you want to keep those EQ/automation settings, you can always make a duplicate of the track in Cubase and remove the EQ, effects, and automation from the duplicated track. This way, you will have both an unmixed and a mixed track to A/B when you're at the other studio (as shown in Figure 5.1). Do *not* mute the duplicate track, as it will need to be unmuted during the Export Audio Mixdown process.

Using Channel Batch Export in Cubase

A surefire way to ensure that all of your tracks stay in time is to set your left locator to the very start of the project (even if your audio starts a few measures from the first bar) and set your right locator a few bars after the last audio track ends. By doing so, you'll be creating new audio parts (disregarding all of your previous edits) that all start at absolute zero. When all the audio files start at the exact same point, there's no chance of sync issues between the tracks after import, which will eliminate any confusion. You should make notes regarding the project sample rate and tempo so that you can make the appropriate settings on import into the new DAW.

Note: If you haven't named your tracks yet, there's no better time than now (before the export). Naming your tracks will make it much easier to set up your mix on the new DAW system.

As I mentioned before, OMF files can be exported only in 24-bit or 16-bit. If you're working in 32-bit (float) and you want to use the OMF format, you'll need to export

All EQ, Automation, and Effects Have Been
Deactivated on the Duplicated Bass Track

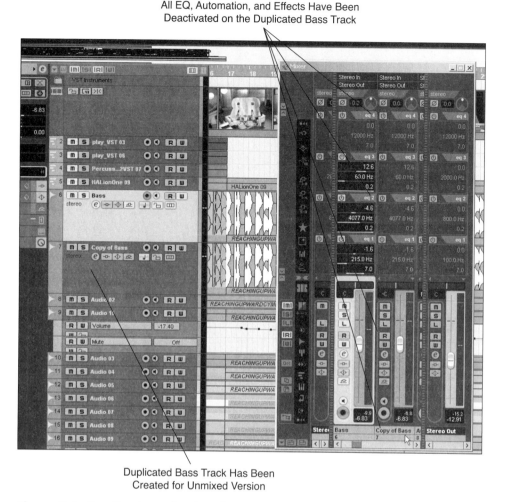

Duplicated Bass Track Has Been
Created for Unmixed Version

Figure 5.1 Duplicating mixed and unmixed tracks before export.

your mix in 24-bit. In this truncating process, some debate that it's best *not* to dither—stating that it's better to save the dithering process for later, when you're creating a final stereo mix (or even later, if you're having your final track professionally mastered). During the export process, you will be creating duplicate files that will all be the same sample rate and bit depth, which is something you can verify again after the export process.

After your mixed and unmixed tracks are set up and your left and right locators are set, the last settings are to be made within the Export Audio Mixdown dialog (accessed from the File menu). Before moving to this step, it's always a good idea to save your project under a new name (such as Joe's Mix Export to Pro Tools-1). In the Export Audio Mixdown dialog, adjust your Bit Depth setting to either 16-bit or 24-bit and set Sample Rate to the desired setting (this can be up to 192 kHz) from within the Audio Engine Output section. Because you're going to be creating duplicate audio files for every track in this Cubase project, check the Channel Batch Export box in the upper-left corner; then select Audio Channels in the panel below it (as shown in Figure 5.2).

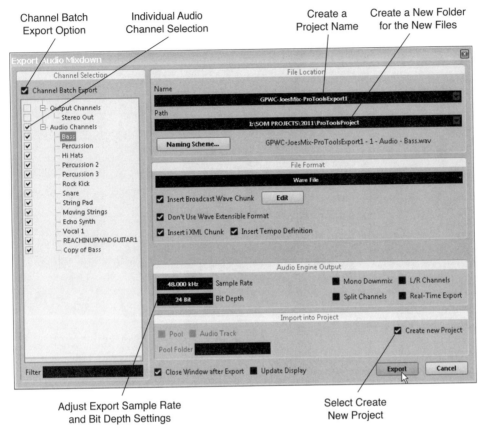

Figure 5.2 Settings for the Channel Batch Export option.

It's possible that you can also export your audio from VST instruments or effects as an audio track (if you haven't yet taken the steps to do so) by selecting them for export along with the audio channels. Now create a name (usually the project name) that will be associated with all the tracks, a location to store these new audio files (path), and the file type (either Wave or AIFF).

Cubase 6 has a new feature for defining the name on tracks during batch export. If you select Naming Scheme (see Figure 5.3), a dialog box will open to display the way that your tracks will be named on export. With this feature, you have the option to choose from up to five (the default is four) individual fields to create specific track names. When you have determined the fields, you can verify the format from within the dialog window.

Regardless of whether you choose to use this new naming feature, check the Create New Project box under the Import into Project section and the Close Dialog after Export box. When you're finished, click Export, and Cubase will begin exporting the audio channels.

After exporting, a new project will be created with all new audio files (tracks). The original tracks have been bounced, and the bounced files (represented in the new project) now contain all the processing that was active in the original project. Because this is a new project, there are no active plug-ins or EQ, and there is no automation being

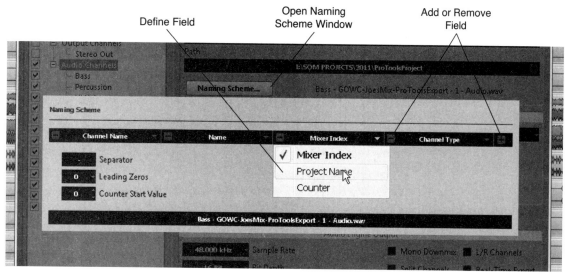

Figure 5.3 Making the final export settings.

used. Also, all of these new tracks should appear as one "block" of audio tracks (as opposed to many various lengths) because the left and right locators were set and all the tracks were exported at once. Lastly, you'll notice that all the track names are similar, with the addition of the name that you created during export (see Figure 5.4).

Figure 5.4 The newly created "transfer" project.

At this point, your tempo is also reset to the standard 120 bpm, but you should be able to reset the tempo to your old settings to get things somewhat back to normal. If you were working with a tempo map (with tempo changes), unfortunately you will have to re-create that tempo map on the new system. You could export a tempo map from Cubase in the form of a .smt file (from the File menu), but this format is only recognized by Steinberg software.

With this new project, you should listen to your mix to verify that all the data has transferred without problems. During this listening process, you'll need to temporarily mute any duplicated unmixed tracks that you also created during the export process. If there are any problems with your mix at this point, you'll need to go back into the original project, adjust your settings, and redo the export until you get back to this point again and everything sounds the way it should.

Creating an OMF

When your mix has been verified, you're ready to create an OMF file for export. If you've muted tracks or changed volumes, you should un-mute the tracks once again before proceeding. There are a couple of different ways to create an OMF 2.0 file. Because it's not difficult to make the OMFs at this point, I recommend creating both of them to take with you in the transfer process. The first way is to include the audio within the OMF itself, and the next is to create an OMF that references audio files within a folder. To create the OMF files for your newly bounced project, select Export from the File menu, and then select OMF. The OMF Export Options dialog will appear, as shown in Figure 5.5.

Use the Select All button to check all the tracks that are to be converted to the OMF file. If necessary, you can deselect certain tracks on the left. Check the boxes From Left to Right Locator and Copy Media. It's important that the left and right locators are set as they were when you originally bounced the material. Duplicate audio files will once again be created during this process. Select the OMF 2.0 File option (or OMF 1.0 File, if necessary), as well as Export All to One File. Check the Export Clip Names box and set Export Sample Size to Same as Project. (Because you've already converted to 24-bit or 16-bit, your project should be ready.)

Note: If you want to include the event's volume envelope and fades, you can do so by checking the Export Clip Based Volume and Use Fade Curves options. Note that these options will work only if you are exporting an OMF 2.0 file. Keep in mind that this only relates to mixing that might be included from editing within the event and doesn't include automation-lane data. These options would be more beneficial if you had bypassed bouncing the mix, as was done in the previous step (which, again, is *not* recommended if you need to retain EQ and effects settings).

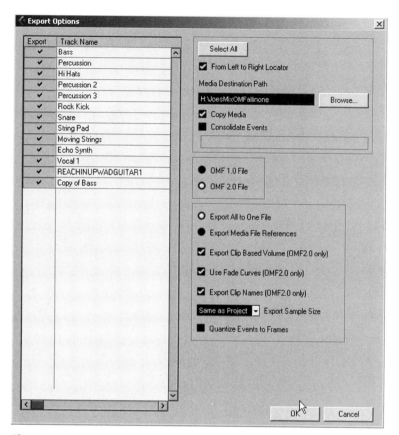

Figure 5.5 The OMF Export Options dialog box.

The final step in creating the OMF is to define a destination folder for the OMF files and then name the OMF file itself. When setting the Media Destination Path in the Export Options dialog, I recommend creating a new folder with the project's name and with OMF in the title somewhere. After you've created the folder, click OK and then create a name for the OMF. Again, I recommend using the project name, though this time with something that specifies that this is the all-in-one file (as you will be creating two types). When you have your name in place, save the OMF. You will see the export process occur as it normally does when exporting batch files.

When the process is complete, repeat all the steps again, but this time select the Export Media File References option. Create a new destination folder and name the OMF something to signify that it's the "reference" OMF. When this process is complete, you should have two separate folders containing two separate batches of files for your Cubase project (as shown in Figure 5.6). You can copy these folders to any hard drive, CD, or DVD and then transfer them to the new DAW by using that DAW's Import OMF option.

For testing purposes, I recommend attempting to reload the OMF files into Cubase from scratch before you leave your studio. To do so, simply select Import from the File menu and then select the OMF file from your newly created OMF folder. Then

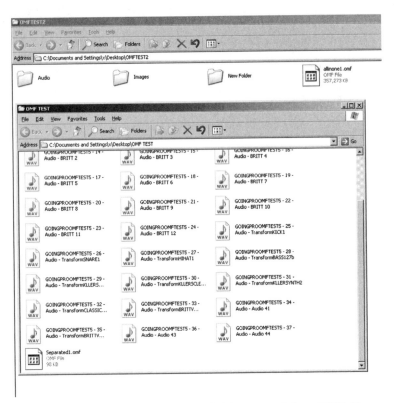

Figure 5.6 A close-up look at a folder containing OMF files.

click the Select All button again and create a new project on import. You should see something very similar to your original bounced Cubase project. On listening, it should sound identical to your original bounced Cubase project, as well. Remember that when you load the OMF, you'll need to mute either duplicate mixed or unmixed tracks before listening and mixing if they were originally created before bouncing.

> **Note:** Keep in mind that you can also create an OMF without bouncing to add to your collection of OMFs. My thought when transferring to another DAW is that the more options you can provide, the better off you're going to be. In a worst-case scenario, if necessary, you should also be able to import each track (audio file) individually from the OMF file and then manually sync them by setting them all at absolute 0 and adjusting the tempo of the new DAW.

Index

COURSE TECHNOLOGY
CENGAGE Learning
Professional • Technical • Reference

Course Technology PTR
COURSE CLIPS

Course Clips are interactive DVD-ROM training products for those who prefer learning on the computer as opposed to learning through a book. *Course Clips Starters* are for beginners and *Course Clips Masters* are for more advanced users.

Digital Performer 7
Course Clips Master
Don Barrett ■ $49.99

Pro Tools 9
Course Clips Master
Steve Wall ■ $49.99

Pro Tools 8
Course Clips Starter
Steve Wall ■ $29.99

Ableton Live 8
Course Clips Master
Brian Jackson ■ $49.99

Individual movie clips are available for purchase online at **www.courseclips.com**

COURSE TECHNOLOGY
CENGAGE Learning
Professional • Technical • Reference

Like the Book?

Let us know on Facebook or Twitter!

facebook.com/courseptr

twitter.com/courseptr

Fan us on Facebook or Follow us on Twitter to learn about upcoming books, promotions, contests, events and more!

COURSE TECHNOLOGY
CENGAGE Learning
Professional • Technical • Reference

SERIOUS RESOURCES FOR SERIOUS MUSICIANS

From interactive DVD-ROMs on the latest music software offerings to comprehensive books on music production, recording, engineering, and the music industry, Course Technology PTR has a solution for every musician.

Becoming a Synthesizer Wizard
Simon Cann ■ $34.99

Provides the first book that explains what a modular synthesizer is, how it works, and how to use software synthesizers to make music.

Using Reason Onstage
G.W. Childs ■ $29.99

The book starts out by providing valuable key commands that are helpful to know during live performance, and then moves quickly on to controller setups, song layout suggestions, and Combinator 2 tips and tricks that will dramatically improve any musician's onstage performance.

Getting Great Sounds
The Microphone Book
Tom Lubin ■ $39.99

This book explains all aspects of all kinds of microphones, how they work, and how to use them in session recording.

 **COURSE CLIPS**

Introducing *Course Clips*!

Course Clips are interactive DVD-ROM training products for those who prefer learning on the computer as opposed to learning through a book. *Course Clips Starters* are for beginners and *Course Clips Masters* are for more advanced users. Individual movie clips are available for purchase online at www.courseclips.com.

Pro Tools 8
Course Clips Master
Steve Wall ■ $49.99

Pro Tools 8
Course Clips Starter
Steve Wall ■ $29.99

Ableton Live 8
Course Clips Master
Brian Jackson ■ $49.99

New Comprehensive Guides from our *Power!* Series

Order now at **1.800.648.7450** or visit **courseptr.com.**

Course Technology PTR products are also available at Borders, Barnes and Noble, Guitar Center, and Amazon.com.

COURSE TECHNOLOGY
CENGAGE Learning

Professional • Technical • Reference

COURSE TECHNOLOGY PTR:
BOOK PUBLISHER FOR THE AUDIO COMMUNITY

Home Recording Studio Build It Like the Pros, Second Edition
Rod Gervais • 1-4354-5717-X
$39.99 • 352 pages

Covers everything including room design, electrical considerations, room treatments, codes, permits, and special needs. The author offers over thirty years of experience and a comprehensive and cost-effective plan that will have even novices building-and recording-in no time.

Mixing and Mastering with IK Multimedia T-RackS: The Official Guide
Bobby Owsinski • 1-4354-5759-5
$29.99 • 192 pages

T-RackS is a popular stand-alone audio mastering application that includes a suite of powerful analog-modeled and digital dynamics and EQ processor modules that also work perfectly as plug-ins during mixing. Learn how to use this tool from the bestselling author of *The Mixing Engineer's Handbook* and *The Mastering Engineer's Handbook.*

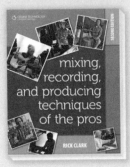

Mixing, Recording, and Producing Techniques of the Pros, Second Edition
Rick Clark • 1-59863-840-8
$39.99 • 400 pages

A truly thorough look at the recording world, this in-depth collection of interviews with recording, mixing, and producing legends covers everything from recording strings and horn sections to using creative production techniques on the latest musical styles.

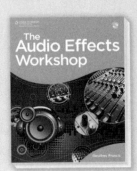

The Audio Effects Workshop
Geoffrey Francis • 1-4354-5614-9
$34.99 • 352 pages

Make sense of the complicated world of audio effects and when to use them with this hands-on book/DVD package. Covers noise gates, EQ, compressors, expanders, limiters, chorus, delay, reverb, modulators, stereo imaging, stereo panning, and more.

Big Studio Secrets for Home Recording and Production
Joe Dochtermann • 1-4354-5505-3
$34.99 • 304 pages

Learn about microphone technique, acoustics, EQ, compression, using effects, how to produce, arrange, and mix, and how to master with this book. The companion CD-ROM illustrates the examples with graphics and audio, providing a hands-on approach to learning all the concepts.

Going Pro with Logic Pro 9
Jay Asher • 1-4354-5563-0
$29.99 • 208 pages

Addresses the needs of the professional Logic user, guiding you from customizing setups of Logic Pro 9 for workflow enhancement, through the recording and editing processes, to preparing final delivery media.

Getting Great Sounds: The Microphone Book
Tom Lubin • 1-59863-570-0
$39.99 • 320 pages

Explains all aspects of all kinds of microphones, how they work, and how to set-up microphones for all types of session recording regardless of the type of studio or the microphones available.

Critical Listening Skills for Audio Professionals
F. Alton Everest • 1-59863-023-7
$49.99 • 216 pages

Through hundreds of illustrations and an accompanying disc containing high-resolution MP3 files with nearly five hours of narration of the entire course, you can acquire the audio discernment skills of a seasoned recording engineer by studying this at your own pace, in your own home.

Find us on Facebook at **facebook.com/courseptr** and Twitter at **twitter.com/courseptr**

Order now at **1.800.648.7450** or visit **courseptr.com**

Course Technology PTR products are also available at Barnes and Noble, Guitar Center, Amazon.com, and other fine retailer